Hieroglyphs and History at Dos Pilas

Hieroglyphs and History at Dos Pilas

Dynastic Politics of the Classic Maya

by Stephen D. Houston

UNIVERSITY OF TEXAS PRESS AUSTIN

Printed in the United States of America
First edition, 1993

♾ The paper used in this publication meets the minimum requirements of American National Standard for Information Sciences—Permanence of Paper for Printed Library Materials, ANSI Z39.48-1984.

Library of Congress Cataloging-in-Publication Data

Houston, Stephen D.
Hieroglyphs and history at Dos Pilas : dynastic politics of the Classic Maya / by Stephen D. Houston. — 1st ed.
p. cm.
Includes bibliographical references and index.
ISBN 0-292-73855-2 (alk. paper)
1. Dos Pilas Site (Guatemala) 2. Mayas—Writing. 3. Mayas—Politics and government. 4. Mayas—History. I. Title.
F1435.1.D67H67 1993
972.81'2—dc20 92-6369

*To my grandparents, whose generosity
made this book possible*

Contents

Tables

Preface

IN THE LAST thirty years, and particularly in the last decade, the pace of Maya hieroglyphic decipherment has accelerated rapidly. Some scholars would even argue that 70 percent of the script is now deciphered (Mathews 1988:49). Most Mayanists agree that the progress results from four developments: the growing number of specialists, who tend to be in close communication with one another; the application to decipherment of the complementary disciplines of linguistics, art history, and archaeology; a consensus about how to approach decipherment; and a general agreement about what constitutes a convincing "reading." The result has been not only a burgeoning set of deciphered or near-deciphered signs, but a deepening understanding of Precolumbian America's most elaborate writing system.

Maya decipherment would thus seem to be an unequivocal success story. Yet some archaeologists—the traditional "consumers" of epigraphic knowledge—have expressed a general skepticism of glyphic research. They also voice the suspicion that the advances have taken place perhaps a little *too* quickly, with little time for sober evaluation of decipherments. In the view of some, epigraphers have been naïve in viewing Maya records as reliable historical sources, particularly when such texts are likely to be self-serving at best, and mendacious at worst (Pendergast 1989:69). A few of the more extreme materialist archaeologists go so far as to question the relevance of epigraphy to scientific archaeology. Why, they ask, should the limited information expressed in monuments, the dynastic intrigue and arcane rituals of the elite, have any bearing on broader studies of Maya economy and society? A particular decipherment might be true or convincing, but it is unlikely to have any wider significance.

In some ways such remarks reveal more about archaeologists than about epigraphers. After all, many of the critics possess little knowledge of glyphs, and certainly have not kept abreast of the latest work. At the same time, any reasonable epigrapher would acknowledge the validity of the more serious reservations, since they raise valuable questions about the nature of Maya inscriptions. I am persuaded that specialists in hieroglyphs do need to pay more attention to evaluating their sources and to justifying the inferences they draw from glyphic texts. If there are skeptics about the relevance of epigraphy to broader issues, such as the reconstruction of political organization, then epigraphers must show systematically, logically, rigorously why such critics are wrong. Similarly, archaeologists need to develop some facility with epigraphy, if only to evaluate information of potential relevance to archaeology. It is my firm belief that both parties would benefit from a heightened sensitivity to the limitations and strengths of glyphic evidence.

This book is an attempt to address the historiographical problems and anthropological usefulness of Classic Maya inscriptions. Rather than examine matters of small interest to archaeologists, such as phonetic readings, verbal affixation, and the like, it focuses on relations between dynasties of the Late Classic period (ca. A.D. 550 to 850), when many hundreds of political monuments were erected in the Maya Lowlands. In particular, it concentrates on the Pasión River region, a remote corner of what is now the Republic of Guatemala, and the key Pasión site of Dos Pilas, which has unusual epigraphic potential. Inscriptions at Dos Pilas are relatively plentiful, yet still comparable in quality and number to texts from competing centers. As a result, the prospects are excellent for assessing the completeness and accuracy of Dos Pilas' history against the records of rival dynasties. Perhaps more important, the rulers of Dos Pilas were clearly preoccupied with political matters, choosing to record their relations with family, neighbors, subordinates, friends, and enemies to a degree unusual at other Classic sites. Here, as perhaps nowhere else, excepting possibly the Usumacinta drainage, epigraphers have enough historical data to describe the nature of Maya dynastic interaction and to reconstruct something of Classic political organization.

Of course, Dos Pilas and Pasión texts do have their problems. At all Classic sites the epigrapher must grapple with ambiguous dates, murky syntax, incomplete corpora (and knowledge!), as well as the inherent difficulties of using isolated events, personalities, and elite rhetoric to reconstruct general historical patterns. Dos Pilas is no exception. One of my aims in writing this book has been to help the reader sort through the difficult terminology and lexicon of Classic Maya political organization, as well as the historiographical problems of dealing with political texts. As historians and anthropologists, we also have the temptation to generalize from the Pasión example to other regions of the southern Maya Lowlands. In this book, I make no pretensions to pan-Maya reconstructions, although I do feel that some basic patterns and organizational principles, to be discussed in the final chapter, exist throughout the southern Maya Lowlands.

The future of Dos Pilas and Pasión epigraphy is promising. At least two archaeological projects are working in the region (Kevin Johnston of Yale University at Itzan and Arthur Demarest and Stephen Houston of Vanderbilt University at the Petexbatun sites), and the results from these expeditions should amplify the record presented in this book. For perhaps the first time in the southern Lowlands, archaeological research will build upon a sound basis of historical epigraphy. We shall soon see whether the promise of the "conjunctive approach," of combining historical and prehistorical disciplines, can be fulfilled in an area that is particularly amenable to it.

In its present form the book is a revised and expanded version of a thesis submitted in 1987 to the Yale Department of Anthropology; one chapter (Chapter 4) is in turn a revision of a chapter to be published in the *Epigraphy* volume of the *Supplement to the Handbook of Middle American Indians* (Houston in press). The work reported here is based on two seasons of fieldwork, undertaken in 1984 and 1986, as well as research conducted during subsequent visits to the region under the auspices of the Proyecto Arqueológico Petexbatun, directed by Professor Arthur A. Demarest of Vanderbilt University. This work was made possible by permits graciously awarded by Licenciadas Edna Núñez de Rodas and Beatriz Díaz de Soto, former Directors of the Guatemalan Instituto de Antropología e Historia, and by their successor, Licenciado Leopoldo Colom Molina. Other officials at the Instituto, particularly Profesor Rafael Morales and Señor Miguel Valencia, provided information and material assistance. Licenciada Dora Guerra de González, Director of the Museo de Arqueología y Etnología, kindly gave me access to the bodega of the museum, where several Pasión monuments are stored.

The grants that facilitated my work included support from the Doherty Foundation, of which I was a fellow in 1984, Sigma Xi, and the National Science Foundation, which awarded me a Doctoral Dissertation Improvement Grant. Sources at Yale University filled gaps in this funding, and I am indebted forever to the Albers Foundation for keeping the project afloat when it seemed rather to be sinking. Members of my committee, Drs. Michael D. Coe, Frank Hole, and Mary Ellen Miller, wrote letters of support that were crucial in obtaining funds. Later, in 1988, Dean Russell Hamilton of Vanderbilt University subsidized another visit to the ruins, as did grants from the National Geographic Society, the National Endowment for the Humanities, and the H. F. Guggenheim Foundation. A publication subvention from the Mellon Foundation, administered by the Department of Anthropology, with Thomas Gregor as chair, helped defray some of the costs of this book.

I prepared this book in two countries: Guatemala and the United States. In Guatemala, I counted heavily on the support of the brave and stoic men who guard the Petexbatun ruins, among them Señores Carmen Castellanos, Alejandro Córdoba, Juan Hernández (the current Inspector of Monuments), Eligio Max, Polo Moro, Oswaldo Ordóñez, and Bene Zac (who also taught me a smattering of Itza). Their supervisor at the time, Inspector Francisco Chub A., ensured that my second season ran smoothly by delivering supplies to the trail leaving Paso Caribe.

My very heartfelt thanks go also to those who worked for me under conditions that were less than luxurious. Boyd Dixon assisted greatly in 1984, and in 1986 Kevin Johnston served as my very competent and personable assistant. In 1986 Nikolai Grube stayed longer than he expected, helping both to draw monuments and to map and explore caves at Dos Pilas. My workers in 1986 were no less helpful—indeed, they were wondrously patient with their greenhorn employer. These gentlemen included Alfredo Salazar (foreman), Joaquín Cuc, Tomás Cuc, Israel Cupul, Teo Garrido, Saturnino Juárez, Napo Mariona (best cook on the Pasión!), Ervim Mis, Ricardo Muñoz, Gaspar Requena, Jorge Ríos (surveying assistant), Nolberto Ríos, Carlos Requena, and Salvador Salguero (worst cook on the Pasión!).

In Paso Caribe, Don Luis Madrigal made furniture for the camp and provided mules to transport our supplies. In Sayaxche, Richard Hood and his wife Mirna provided hospitality and good meals. Another resident of Sayaxche, Don Aidelaido, supplied expert and (sometimes) efficient boat service. In the cooler highlands I found warm friends at the Centro de Investigaciones Regionales de Mesoamérica (CIRMA), Antigua Guatemala, where Stephen Elliott and the late William Swezey found me a place to study and write. Other friends in Antigua, Daniel Chauche, Marion Hatch, Mike Love, Jayne Lyons, Jacques and Parney Van Kirk, Ed Shook, Dennis and Louisa Wheeler, and Jean and Peter Wright, have made my visits there memorable. Daniel Chauche also developed many of my photographs, which never quite measured up to his exacting standards as a professional photographer. Arquitecto Federico Fahsen and Larry and Omie Kerr took some of the edge off Guatemala City with their warm hospitality.

In the United States, I thank above all Dr. Michael D. Coe, who supervised my education at Yale. Other members of my dissertation committee, Drs. Frank Hole and Mary Ellen Miller, always made me feel as much a colleague as a student. Perhaps my greatest intellectual debt, however, is to Dr. Floyd Lounsbury, who first inspired me to study Maya hieroglyphs. I have learned much from this kind and gifted teacher. Other friends at Yale, especially Karl Taube, now of the University of California, Riverside, contributed much to my thinking. At Vanderbilt, I have had many stimulating discussions with Drs. Arthur Demarest, William Fowler, and, in particular, John Monaghan, who has commented on portions of this manuscript. Stacey Symonds of Vanderbilt kindly contributed the statistical appendix to Chapter 3.

Some parts of this book were written at Dumbarton Oaks, where I was fortunate to hold a Junior Fellowship in the fall of 1985. Anita Cook, Peter Heather, Margaret Maclean, Rebecca Stone, and Emily Umberger, all fellow Fellows, made life fun and interesting, and Drs. Elizabeth Boone and Gordon McEwan provided a nurturing and intellectually charged atmosphere.

This work would be much impoverished without the advice and information of fellow epigraphers. In particular, Dr. Peter Mathews of the University of Calgary and David Stuart of Vanderbilt University were generous in sharing with me their encyclopedic knowledge of Mayan writing. Parts of Chapters 4 and 5 have the shape they do because of conversations and collaborative work with David, who has been my friend and inspiration for the better part of a decade. In my opinion, no epigrapher living matches David's uncanny facility with glyphs. Finally, Ian Graham helped immeasurably by allowing free access to the archives of the Corpus of Maya Hieroglyphic Inscriptions Project. It is principally through Ian's work that others have recognized the importance of Dos Pilas and other Petexbatun sites.

At the University of Texas Press Theresa J. May, executive editor, and Carolyn C. Wylie, manuscript editor, gave good advice and thoughtful editorial suggestions about various drafts of this book. To them go my warm thanks.

But my greatest debt is to my family. My wife, Nancy Dayton, read parts of the manuscript, suggesting many improvements, and helped with preparation of the final draft. Her love and friendship have sustained me. Nancy's parents, Charles and Connie Dayton, allowed us to occupy their summer home, where I finished my research free from the distractions of New Haven. My thanks go also to my father and mother, Dr. A. C. Houston and Maj-Britt Houston, for their support of my graduate studies. My ultimate debt, however, is to my grandparents, the late Athleen and Sam Houston, who financed much of my education at both the University of Pennsylvania and Yale. I dedicate this work to them.

1. Introduction

ALONG THE RIVERBANKS, hillcrests, and swampy lagoons of the southern Yucatan peninsula lie the ruins of Classic Maya civilization, which flourished between the approximate dates of A.D. 250 and 900. One of the central problems of recent scholarship has been to explain the society that created this civilization. Who were its rulers, and how did they rule? What was the nature of interaction between such lords? Who were their subordinates, and how were they organized? Were the "kingdoms" or polities of small or large size? And how did the polities change over the course of the Classic period?

Among the newest and most exciting approaches toward answering such questions is Maya epigraphy, which, among other things, uses hieroglyphic records to determine how the Classic Maya organized themselves politically. During their heyday, and even slightly beyond it at a few sites, the Classic Maya of the southern Lowlands erected stone monuments with hieroglyphic writing. Until recently, relatively little was understood of these monuments and less still of the writing that embellished them. Early students, such as Ernst Förstemann (1904), had determined the basic calendrical structures of the script, but found the noncalendric hieroglyphs more difficult to decipher. As a result, Maya writing began to be seen as the province of esoteric information, with little bearing on broader studies of ancient society (Thompson 1950:15).

Only with the stunning breakthroughs of the last thirty-odd years did it become clear that monumental writing recorded history, at least as this was expressed in the narrow terms of royal biography and in the accounts of contemporary interactions between Classic lords (Berlin 1958; Proskouriakoff 1960; 1963; 1964). The breakthroughs in turn inspired a large number of studies, ranging from reconstructions of dynastic sequences at important Classic sites (Proskouriakoff 1960; 1963; 1964; Kelley 1962; Berlin 1970; 1973; 1977; 1987; Riese 1971; 1980; Mathews and Schele 1974; C. Jones 1977; Mathews 1980; 1988; Beetz and Satterthwaite 1981; C. Jones and Satterthwaite 1982; Houston and Mathews 1985; Stone, Reents, and Coffman 1985; D. Stuart 1985c; Houston 1987) to more regional treatments of Classic history, focusing on relationships between rather than within dynasties (Marcus 1976; Mathews 1985). Such studies, and particularly those of Joyce Marcus (1973; 1976), showed conclusively that Classic script touched not only on elite history, but also on the ways in which Maya polities interacted with one another and how they organized themselves internally. In short, Maya script had become of immediate relevance to students of political organization.

For epigraphers, glyphs present three major challenges. First, the texts must be deciphered; and, second, general and reliable inferences must be drawn from them. The third challenge will be in some respects the most difficult, for it cuts across disciplinary boundaries: the epigraphic data must be compared with information from archaeology and comparative anthropology. These provide invaluable and complementary perspectives that allow us to conceptualize Maya political organization as a living and dynamic system.

RECONSTRUCTING MAYA POLITICS

Some attempts have already been made to integrate archaeological, epigraphic, and anthropological evidence in the study of Maya political organization. In the case of earlier scholars, such as Sylvanus G. Morley (1946) and J. Eric S. Thompson (1954), research was necessarily incomplete and intuitive, since "history" to them involved either Postclassic documents transcribed into Roman letters (Morley 1911) or spatial and chronological patterns of dates in the Maya Lowlands. Orderings of sites into presumed hierarchies were based in turn on crude estimates of site size or by number of dated monuments. Ironically, the same limited information led Morley to a grand if vaguely defined view of political organization, with large centers holding considerable power over smaller ones, and Thompson to a fragmented landscape of small "city-states" (1950:7). It has only been in the last twenty years, with greater control over archaeological and epigraphic information, that Mayanists have developed new techniques and concepts for understanding Maya polities. These studies are of two kinds: those emphasizing archaeological evidence and those based on epigraphy. Both are necessarily regional in scope and neither excludes the other, although some treatments, such as Olivier de Montmollin's, pay little attention to epigraphy, and others, such as Peter Mathews', give clear priority to glyphic interpretation. A review of such approaches will show that the most satisfying approaches are those incorporating historical data.

Archaeological Approaches

As a concept, political organization has been defined and widely accepted as the "maintenance or establishment of social order, within a territorial framework" (Radcliffe-Brown 1970:xiv). It is perhaps for this very reason that archaeologists studying Classic Maya politics have emphasized spatial arrangements or "territorial frameworks," often by using the techniques of the "New Geography," which seeks to understand human uses of space through methods combining statistical rigor and positivist philosophy (Haggett 1965). In the Maya area, such efforts typically rest on a number of assumptions. One is that lines drawn between sites correspond to possible boundaries between centers—the nodes of so-called Thiessen polygons (Flannery 1972;

Hammond 1974; Flannery 1977; and, with a useful modification pointing to "boundary centers" between rival polities, Dunham 1989). Another is that the more important the site is, the larger its size will be. And, as a third premise, the closer a small city is to a large one, the higher the likelihood that it is politically subordinate to it. By extension, the very largest sites, such as the imposing ruin of Tikal, are thought to have been regional capitals of far-reaching influence. Thus, careful studies of spatial patterns are presumed to reveal both site and political hierarchies.

Several people have tried to deduce political hierarchies from measures of site size, among them Richard E. W. Adams, who has applied geographical methods to the southern Maya Lowlands (Adams 1984; Adams and Jones 1981). Adams began by tabulating Maya sites according to their number of courtyards, Tikal with eighty-five, El Encanto with one, and so on. If grouped together by architectural styles and spatial contiguity, these sites fell not only into a scale from largest to smallest, but also into regional clusters, which, by inference, Adams terms "hierarchical tributary regions" (Adams and Jones 1981:318). In Adams' view, Tikal was the regional capital of an area embracing sites falling into four hierarchical levels—again determined by number of courtyards—with a site such as Naranjo as an immediate subordinate, and, farther down the list, in a position of negligible importance, the center of Ucanal (ibid.: Table 1).

The usefulness of Adams' method is that it is explicit. What is problematic is its application and underlying premises, and here the criticisms are of both an empirical and a methodological nature. In the first place, the tabulation of courtyards is inaccurate; Caracol, for example, is now known to be a vast site (Chase and Chase 1987), and in other cases it is uncertain how Adams and his colleagues used maps to arrive at courtyard estimates. In the second, political importance or autonomy is not on *prima facie* grounds necessarily commensurate with site size; this is an assumption that must be taken on faith, despite the fact that size may just as easily correspond to economic power or length of occupation. Criticisms can also be directed at the delimitation of regions, since the inclusion of Caracol in the Tikal sphere is as arbitrary as the exclusion of Calakmul, which is only slightly more distant from Tikal than Caracol. Finally, Adams' division of sites into hierarchical levels within "tributary regions" is haphazard: for reasons that are unclear, sites with four courtyards have been placed in a different category from those with five.

Adams does support some of his intepretations by referring to Joyce Marcus' ideas of regional capitals (see later discussion), which have an epigraphic basis, and, more recently, by interpreting iconography at the site of Río Azul, which he places under Tikal's sovereignty. Despite Adams' assertions, there is at present not a single explicit epigraphic link between Tikal and Río Azul, so that this connection remains unproved.

More recently de Montmollin has studied Classic political organization along similar lines. His focus is on a Classic Maya "polity" centered on Tenam Rosario in the Mexican state of Chiapas (de Montmollin 1988; 1989). De Montmollin's knowledge of political anthropology is sophisticated, particularly his view that individual polities do not easily fit into "types," but rather vary according to certain features, such as whether they have segmentary structure or unitary structure, or, as is more likely the case, fall somewhere in between (de Montmollin 1989:17). Equally perceptive is his criticism of the way archaeologists "blend demographic, status, political, and spatial variables" in interpreting site size (ibid.:85), as Adams has done. The problem is that the size of a site may result from any number of factors, some of which will be difficult to detect archaeologically.

What is unfortunate, however—and de Montmollin is virtually alone among archaeologists in this—is his eschewal of epigraphic information in favor of an exclusively archaeological and comparative approach (1989:47–48). In de Montmollin's argument, the closest parallels are those from Africa. The result is sometimes unpersuasive, particularly in those cases where terms float free from the archaeology they are intended to describe. For example, de Montmollin has attempted to establish amounts of tribute by "comparing ratios of civic-ceremonial (and elite) architectural components to non-elite residential architectural components" (ibid.:103); the assumption here is that a site with a high ratio of elite to non-elite architecture is likely to have received more "tribute" than a site with a low ratio (the tribute would presumably have been absorbed into the construction of monumental buildings). Yet the argument is unconvincing, for there is no compelling reason why tribute, which by definition involves both goods and services, should correspond proportionally to elite architecture, especially when some authors have suggested that the actual energy involved in such construction was relatively small (Abrams 1987).

But de Montmollin's study has a more fundamental problem. His basic unit of analysis, the Tenam Rosario "polity," apparently exists only because he says it does and because such a unit would fill the valley de Montmollin has chosen to survey (1989:40–42). The irony is that de Montmollin has chosen to examine a Classic Maya polity in an area that is notoriously lean on inscriptions. With epigraphic evidence for such a polity, de Montmollin's study might have been more compelling.

Perhaps the single lesson to be learned from archaeological approaches to Classic Maya politics is that they are in themselves insufficient. They can detect patterns, but very few of these will be clear or easy to interpret. Epigraphy complements archaeology with a historical line of evidence, which often speaks directly to the problem of examining ancient political organization.

Epigraphic Approaches

Of the models making heavy use of Maya epigraphy, Joyce Marcus' is perhaps the most far-reaching in its implications (1973; 1976; 1983). By examining the distribution of Emblem Glyphs (Berlin 1958), Marcus proposed a reconstruction of political relations between Classic centers. She assumed that the pattern of intersite references reflected ancient political relationships, so that subordinate sites would men-

Table 1-1. ***An example of site hierarchies in the southern Maya Lowlands***

Regional Capital	Tikal
(Primary Center)	?
Secondary Centers	Naranjo Aguateca Machaquila
Tertiary Centers	Jimbal Ixlu Uaxactun
Quaternary Centers	El Encanto Xultun Nakum

Source: Marcus 1976: Table 4.

tion the Emblems of superordinate ones, which in turn ignored all but their superiors (if they had any) or their rivals (if they did not; Marcus 1976:46–50). Marcus postulated a four-tier hierarchy from her epigraphic studies, beginning with centers without local Emblems and ascending to "Regional Capitals" or "Primary Centers." In addition, Marcus felt that hierarchies were integrated by marriage alliances. Thus, "small centers were tied to regional capitals by marriage alliances, and . . . non-local women played important political roles at dependencies" (ibid.:170). As a conceptual armature for relationships between regional capitals (and following a suggestion by Thomas Barthel [1968]), Marcus cited evidence from two stelae, Stela A from Copan and Stela 10 from Seibal, which contained references to three foreign "capitals" in addition to a local Emblem. Marcus believed the four Emblems represented a marriage of politics and cosmology: a set of four capitals, which apparently changed through time, presided over quadrants of the Maya political universe (Marcus 1976:17; 1983:464; 1984).

There is much to praise in Marcus' study. It is not only ingenious in its treatment of Classic intersite relationships, but highly influential; to some extent, all subsequent research on Maya society has been shaped by her seminal work. Her insistence that marriage formed an important part of political intrigue is now supported by all epigraphers. Yet subsequent study has also led to modifications of her theory. To illustrate this point, let us examine one of her four-level hierarchies from the perspective of more recent thinking in Maya epigraphy.

Tikal stands alone as a primary capital (Table 1-1). Below it are the supposed dependencies of Naranjo, Aguateca, and Machaquila. In fact, not a single one of these sites possesses inscriptions referring to Tikal (Houston and Mathews 1985:14). The tertiary level is equally tenuous: with the exception of one sculpture, Tikal Stela 11 (C. Jones and Satterthwaite 1982:29), the monuments from Jimbal and Ixlu postdate Tikal's period of stela erection. Thus, they cannot be made to support the notion of Tikal's regional dominance during that time, since this would require coeval records at relevant sites. Similarly, Uaxactun can be shown to move away from Tikal's direct control during and perhaps slightly before the inception of the Late Classic period (ca. A.D. 550 to 850; Mathews 1985:33, 44–46). Finally, the quaternary level violates Marcus' principal criterion for this tier: that they lack Emblem Glyphs of their own (Marcus 1976:47). A local Emblem has been found at Xultun (Houston 1986), and the inscriptions of Nakum, which are badly eroded, can neither support nor refute Marcus' arguments. For now Nakum is simply irrelevant.

In sum, Marcus' hierarchies do not have genuine epigraphic integrity; that is, the conclusions deduced from Emblem Glyphs do not accord with detailed studies of their epigraphic context. Marcus states that her hierarchies, unlike those proposed by Morley (1937–1938: 4:247), derive from glyphic material, with the result that "secondary, tertiary, and quaternary (sites) generally, *but not always*, conformed to site size differences" (Marcus 1983:464; emphasis in original). This remark notwithstanding, she includes twenty-eight sites in a list of hierarchically disposed centers, of which only sixteen have legible Emblems. Thus, Marcus' hierarchies are based as much on relative distance and site size as they are on Emblem Glyph distribution. As a final criticism, we know now that the crucial texts from Copan and Seibal, which supposedly attest to four capitals, refer at Seibal at least to visits by foreign royalty or their proxies (Houston and Stuart 1989a). There is thus little or no *explicit* epigraphic warrant for Marcus' inference of regional capitals.

Marcus' study invites a more general criticism. It tends to use piecemeal evidence from poorly understood inscriptions, and, as a result, consistently underestimates both the complexity of local history and its value in authorizing particular reconstructions of Classic political organization.

More recently, Marcus has revised her model by suggesting that scholars should pay greater attention to Colonial descriptions of native polities in northern Yucatan (Marcus 1990). She argues that far too many Mayanists grope for explanatory parallels in Classical Greece, feudal Europe, and Japan (unmentioned but also relevant to her argument are Africa and Southeast Asia); the more useful material is far closer to home, in Spanish documents. Marcus also suggests that most models to date, including hers, have underestimated changes in political composition; that is, rather than being a set of polities immutable in size and power, Maya "kingdoms" may occasionally have fissioned into smaller units, or, conversely, fused into larger units of confederated states subordinate to sites such as Tikal or Copan. She likens the overall pattern to waves of "peaks" and "troughs," and the specific pattern of fusion to the *mul tepal*, "joint rule," documented for Postclassic Yucatan (Roys 1957).

In its main thrust, her revision cannot be faulted, as is shown in Chapter 5. Nonetheless, there are specific problems with this new presentation, ranging from ones of method to ones of substance. For example, Marcus is critical of colleagues looking elsewhere for structural and comparative analogues to Classic Maya political organization; yet her essay also refers to ancient Mesopotamia and Egypt for analogous patterns of union and dissolution. Much more debatable is her contention that Postclassic Yucatan, and the closely related polities of Postclassic Peten, operated on political principles similar to those of the Classic period, especially of the southern Lowlands. By implication, there existed broad similarities across the Maya region in the units of political oganization, the terms that might be applied to them, and the particular offices that populated the political landscape.

In my opinion, the assertion of structural uniformity and continuity across the Maya Lowlands is still far from being proved. Research on diverse topics has convinced many Mayanists that regional variation, especially when viewed through the prism of time, played a large role in the development of the Maya. Moreover, it is inconsistent for Marcus to insist on the methodological priority of the direct-historical method (Steward 1942), in this case principally involving documents from Yucatan, while neglecting the hieroglyphic texts and archaeological remains of Classic era Chichen Itza and the Puuc sites, which would seem most relevant to that approach. On present evidence these texts do indeed appear to record institutions of collective, possibly fraternal rulership (Krochock 1989; Freidel and Schele 1989), but, ironically, they are in stark contrast to those of the southern Lowlands, where there is far less emphasis on certain family names (Grube and Stuart 1987) and far more concern for genealogical documentation (Schele, Mathews, and Lounsbury 1977).

Where Marcus does use ethnohistoric evidence from the southern Lowlands, it is from Peten Itza, in the lake district of northern Guatemala. In my judgment, the connection between the groups occupying this region during early Colonial times and the dynasties of the Classic period is highly tenuous. Not only did the former speak a Yucatecan language, the latter probably a Cholan, but the two are separated by close to a thousand years of tumultuous change in the Peten (G. D. Jones 1986:75). Equally doubtful is Marcus' contention that the Itza polity located near the lakes was centralized and hierarchically organized and therefore constitutes a parallel to similar polities of the Classic period. The "kingdom" of the Itza was in fact a congeries of factionalized groups, many on exceedingly poor terms with one another (G. D. Jones 1989:9). To accept them as a single, well-integrated polity is to absorb uncritically the statements of the purported rulers of the kingdom.

Perhaps the most striking feature of Marcus' revised model is that she has changed relatively little of the substance of her arguments. For example, she assigns great significance to several different accession glyphs, suggesting that they connote elevation to different statuses; in fact, the differences are merely ones of phonetic substitution, with virtually no change in meaning (Mathews and Justeson 1984). Moreover, she does not recognize that many of her historical conclusions—the assignment of women to certain sites, the reconstruction of confederacies or regional groupings, the supposed absence or presence of references to "subordinate" sites at "superordinate" ones—have been rejected by subsequent epigraphic work (e.g., Houston and Mathews 1985). Marcus is surely correct in stressing the importance of native documents. But these documents should not be those written a thousand years later, but rather the hieroglyphic texts of the Classic Maya themselves. If the Classic period is the focus of our study, then the titles, political concepts, and modes of elite interaction recorded in contemporary inscriptions must take precedence over those of a different time and place.

A model based on more up-to-date epigraphic information has been proposed by Peter Mathews (1985; 1988). Mathews has devoted several years to the study of Emblem Glyphs, which are described in more detail in Chapter 4. These are the titles of the highest rank, *ch'ul ahaw,* and usually designate a lord as a *ch'ul ahaw* of such-and-such a place or, as Mathews argues, of such-and-such a polity. Mathews believes, first, that these lords exercised dominion over polities that were largely autonomous and, second, that they exerted control from certain primary centers. By drawing Thiessen polygons between and around these centers, Mathews sketches the approximate boundaries of ancient Maya polities during the Classic period. The result is that Maya states do not appear to have been as large as Adams or Marcus supposed, but correspond rather to the densely packed "peer polities" of the Old World (Renfrew 1986).

Marcus (1990) has criticized Mathews' study on three counts. First, it does not conform to her definition of "archaic states," to which she assigns Maya polities. Second, his data contradict hers. And, third, Mathews' reconstruction of the Classic political landscape gives only as much importance to Tikal as to much smaller centers, for the sole reason that their rulers held the same rank.

Of these three criticisms, two can be readily dismissed. Marcus should not provide a rigid and arguable definition of Maya polities and then fault Mathews for failing to confirm it. Nor is it an inherent weakness of Mathews' findings that they contradict those of Marcus; rather, Marcus should look to the quality of her own empirical evidence, which, though valuable for the time, has been modified or replaced by Mathews' detailed historical research. But Marcus' third criticism is valid. The fact that two rulers held the same title and therefore (presumably) the same rank, does not mean that they wielded the same political or economic influence, or that they were fully autonomous, particularly if one ruled over an immense site, the other a small one. It is also possible to criticize the use of Thiessen polygons. As conceptual devices, they do not take account of buffer zones, where the power of the overlord varied, or areas where political organization was at a much reduced level (Houston 1987). Mathews has since acknowledged some of these problems (Mathews 1988:361–362).

Of recent work, Mathews' demonstrates the greatest fidelity to epigraphy, in that it builds upon a deep historical understanding of Maya inscriptions. Yet, at the same time, it displays a degree of historical literalism, as well as overconfidence in the use of Thiessen polygons, which do not live up to their promise of delimiting territory. On a more abstract level, Mathews' reconstruction is almost entirely a historical description. I believe this is a weakness, since a description of where and when a polity existed cannot replace an understanding of how it operated. It is at this point that the epigrapher has to draw on anthropological models, since without such concepts we can never effectively understand the dynamism of Classic Maya political organization.

CONCLUSIONS

From the above, three points follow. First, Classic Maya politics cannot be understood by archaeological methods alone, but should also draw on epigraphy. Second, general impressions of those hieroglyphs, outdated readings, or superficial studies of glyphic distribution can have little role to play when decipherments have rendered them obsolete. Third and last, even a sophisticated epigraphic treatment of political organization should conceptualize Classic Maya politics according a broader, anthropological framework.

This book builds on all three conclusions. Its approach is fundamentally epigraphic and historical, although it also supplies the archaeological background of the inscriptions. It not only draws on recent readings but also presents an evaluation of its conclusions according to comparisons with evidence from other societies. Perhaps most important, it explores an alternative approach to Adams' and Marcus', and rather akin to de Montmollin's, in that it stresses a regional rather than pan-regional point of view.

A strong argument can be made that a regional emphasis to epigraphic study is not only desirable but necessary. The complexity and variability of Classic history militates, at least at present, against a pan-Maya perspective. Similarly, a study that is too narrow, namely one focusing on a single, isolated site, is less relevant to reconstructions of political organization, which by definition involves interaction between polities and between sites; this had been made clear by David Stuart's groundbreaking work on provincial lords (Stuart 1984a). Perhaps the real difficulty is simply that of finding an area in which both large- and small-scale problems can be addressed.

I believe one area meets all our requirements: the Pasión region of Guatemala and its key site of Dos Pilas. For one, hieroglyphic inscriptions in the Pasión drainage are numerous and widespread. This is an important condition, in that Classic inscriptions are statements of propaganda, subject to revisionist manipulation and often of suspect truthfulness (Mathews 1985:52–53). The comparison of records from neighboring and often competing centers improves the chances of reconstructing reliable history. An additional feature of Pasión and Dos Pilas texts is that the inscriptions are approximately coeval, but not so narrowly spaced in time as to preclude studies of political change. In consequence, they offer both a synchronic and a diachronic view on Late Classic political organization.

This book presents a detailed study of Dos Pilas and Pasión history and its implications for Classic politics. Chapter 2 introduces the archaeological setting of Dos Pilas inscriptions. Chapter 3 continues with a physical description of the monuments and a brief discussion of their iconography. Chapter 4 synthesizes Dos Pilas history in its Pasión setting, and Chapter 5 uses such evidence to examine overall patterns in Late Classic political organization.

2. Dos Pilas and Its Archaeological Setting

THE HISTORICAL MONUMENTS of Dos Pilas existed in a regional setting—the Pasión River drainage—and in a particular site—Dos Pilas and its environs (Fig. 2-1). To understand these texts we must take a closer look at the places where they were found; their location in various sectors of the Dos Pilas site; their proximity to monuments at other sites, such as Arroyo de Piedra and Tamarindito; and their immediate architectural context, whether palace, plaza, or pyramid. One of the most useful ways of organizing such information is according to a "nested box" model (Hammond 1975 : 6), in which the region contains a subregion, and the subregion a site. This chapter applies the model by presenting the Pasión drainage as the region and the Petexbatun area as the subregion, before focusing on the ruins of Dos Pilas.

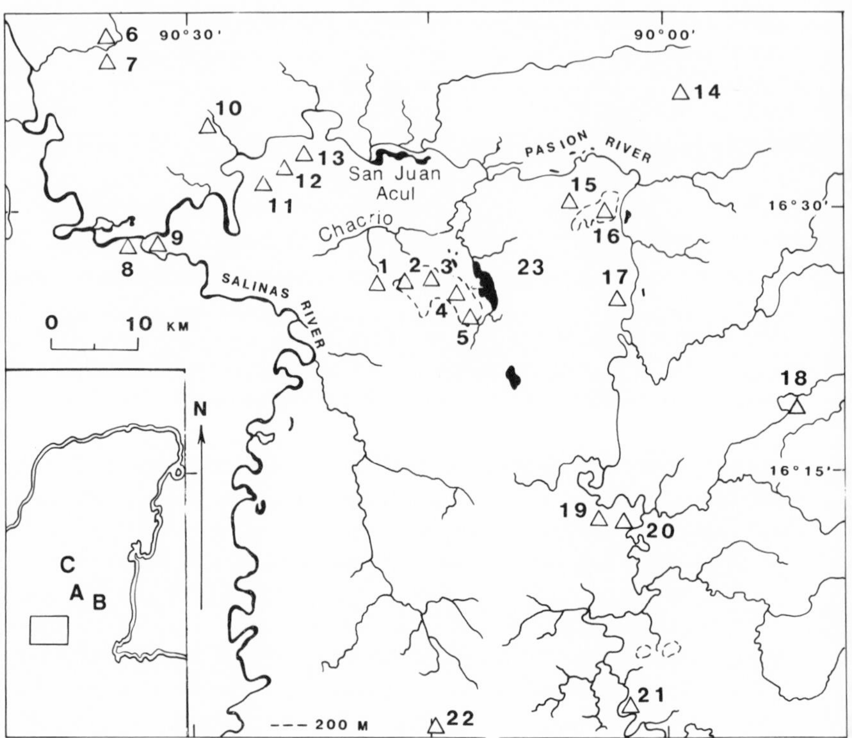

Figure 2-1. Archaeological sites in the Pasión drainage: 1, Dos Pilas; 2, Arroyo de Piedra; 3, Tamarindito; 4, El Excavado; 5, Aguateca; 6, El Pato; 7, El Chorro; 8, El Pabellón; 9, Altar de Sacrificios; 10, Itzan; 11, La Amelia; 12, El Caribe; 13, Aguas Calientes; 14, El Chapayal; 15, Anonal; 16, Seibal; 17, El Cedral; 18, Machaquila; 19, La Reforma III; 20, Tres Islas; 21, Cancuen; 22, Chinaha; 23, Punta de Chimino. Inset: A, Tikal; B, Naranjo; C, Calakmul.

A common theme in recent archaeology is the importance of regional variation within the Maya area, based not only on environmental factors but also on details of material culture (Hammond and Ashmore 1981:27–28). A tangible result of this thinking has been a series of zonated maps, presented in refined form in successive volumes of the School of American Research Maya seminars (Culbert 1973; R. E. W. Adams 1977a; Ashmore 1981a; Sabloff and Andrews 1985). However, as gross measures of regional affinity, the maps are only marginally useful. The "central zone," for example, is probably far more homogeneous than neighboring zones, which are more weakly defined. Also, the seminar maps are ahistorical presentations that conceal variation through time.

A useful counterpoint to such zonations is a consideration of regionalisms in Maya writing, touched on briefly by J. Eric S. Thompson (1950:58). Viewed in this way, the zone embracing the southern Peten, in hieroglyphic style as disparate as can be imagined, subdivides into at least three regions: one centered on the Pasión drainage; another embracing the Naj Tunich cave, Sacul, and Ixlu; and another, more heterogeneous area including the sites of Lubaantun and Nim Li Punit, in what is now Belize (Mathews and Willey 1991). Although the meaning of such regions is not entirely clear, they may represent areas of intense interaction during the Classic, as is indeed suggested by glyphic evidence (see Chapter 4; Caldwell 1964).

The zone centered on the Pasión drainage is better defined than most (Fig. 2-1). The drainage itself consists of a large riverine system extending from the hills of the Alta Verapaz northward to the confluence of the Pasión and Salinas rivers. Together with the Lacantun, these rivers join to form the Usumacinta, which eventually empties into the Gulf of Mexico. The main drainage, along with that of tributaries such as the Machaquila, comprises an area of more than 5,000 square kilometers, a good portion of the present-day Department of Peten, Guatemala. This area corresponds roughly to the eastern half of the "Chapayal Lowlands" (Vinson 1962:429). In geological terms the drainage consists of two formations of Lower Eocene date and another of Upper Oligocene date, as well as more recent fluvial and eolian deposits (Vinson 1962:455; see Willey and Smith 1969:39–47 and Willey et al. 1975:9–23 for physiogeographic summaries). Fault lines run along the western side of Lake Petexbatun (Fig. 2-2), a body of water that is, depending on water level, variously an affluent and effluent of the Pasión; the fault lines continue north to intersect with the Pasión near San Juan Acul and the Arroyo Pucte (Mapa Geológico de Guatemala n.d.). Near Lake Petexbatun, the faults engendered a prominent escarpment that is close to 13.5 kilometers in length.

The soils of the Pasión drainage range from poor to good in their agricultural potential, at least as this concept is defined by modern agronomists (Proyecto de evaluación forestal FAO-FYDEP 1968). A major soil class is the Sarstun Series (Group II), which is suitable for nonintensive agriculture without the addition of substantial quantities of fertilizer. Contiguous soils belong to the less fertile Yaxha Series

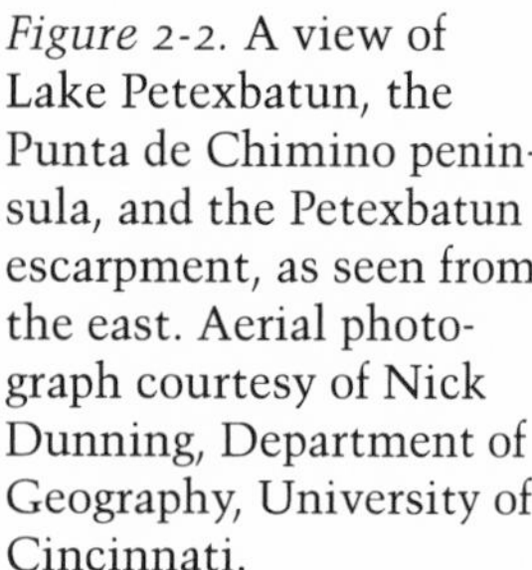

Figure 2-2. A view of Lake Petexbatun, the Punta de Chimino peninsula, and the Petexbatun escarpment, as seen from the east. Aerial photograph courtesy of Nick Dunning, Department of Geography, University of Cincinnati.

(Group IIIB). A striking feature of soil distribution in the Pasión is that virtually all ancient settlements of great size lie astride the boundary between the Sarstun and Yaxha series (Fig. 2-3; cf. Green 1973:287). In part this may result from the marked preference of the ancient Maya to settle on high ground, where the Yaxha soils lie, but with an eye to remaining close to major bodies of water, the province of Sarstun soils. There may be another factor influencing settlement: R. E. W. Adams proposed that many of the low-lying areas near the Pasión contain remnants of raised fields, which are visible today by radar (Adams 1980:209; Adams, Brown, and Culbert 1981:Fig. 1; Adams 1983:Fig. 13.2). Thus, the location of major Pasión sites may have been conditioned by proximity to zones of intensive agriculture, although there are grounds for skepticism about the supposed "ground confirmation" of these features (Adams 1983:320; Nicholas Dunning, personal communication, 1990).

In archaeological terms the Pasión drainage is a region displaying substantial archaeological homogeneity during the Classic. This is expressed in several ways: by a shared inventory of ceramics, by an apparent paucity of masonry vaults (with implications for the visibility of lightly covered subsurface remains; see Pollock 1965:423), and by the presence of a characteristic ensemble of outset stairways with flanking panels. Many of the stairways exhibit hieroglyphic texts, which are particularly common in the ruins atop the Petexbatun escarpment.

Figure 2-1 notes the location of the Pasión sites discussed in this report. Dos Pilas (Site 1) is one of a series of ruins located within kilometers of one another on the edge of the Petexbatun escarpment; the proximity is especially pronounced in the case of Arroyo de Piedra (Site 2), which lies within 3 kilometers of outliers at Dos Pilas. The other Pa-

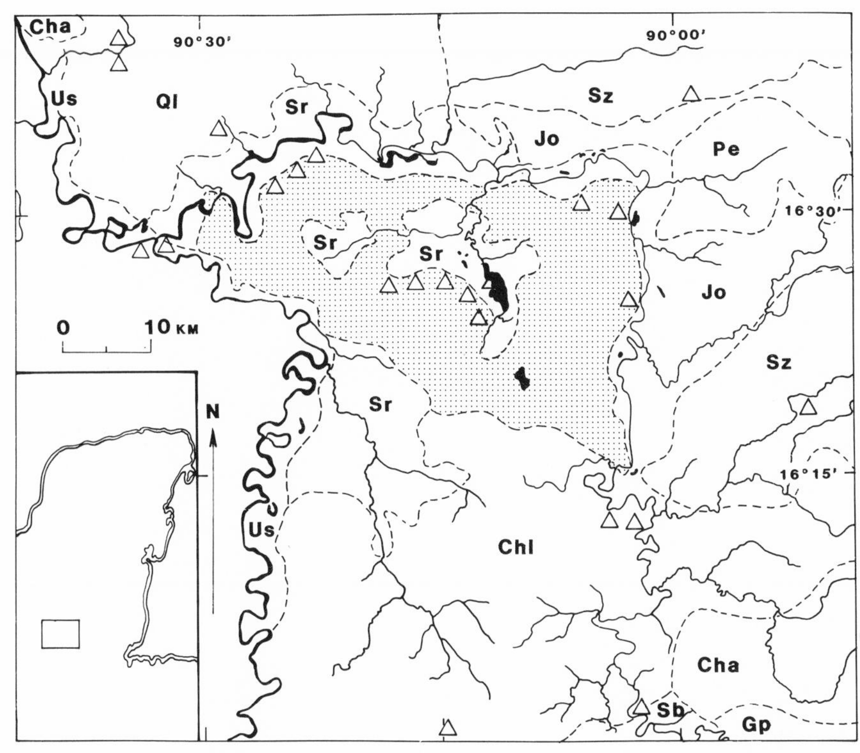

Figure 2-3. Sites and soil classes in the Pasión drainage: Cha, Chacalte; Chl, Chapayal; Gp, Guapaca; Jo, Jolja; Pe, Petexbatun; Ql, Quinil; Sb, Sebol; Sr, Sarstun; Sz, Sotz; Us, Usumacinta. After Instituto Geográfico Nacional, Suelos de Guatemala, Peten Sheet.

sión sites also occur on high ground, especially on plateaux above the course of the Pasión River.

The Pasión drainage is probably of a piece archaeologically with the western half of the Chapayal Lowlands, an area that is still poorly known (Bullard 1965). Local informants insist that this region contains mound groups built not of stone rubble and masonry, but rather of mud and sand ballast covered by small veneer stones (*ladrillos*). It is difficult to evaluate these descriptions without visiting the ruins, which are of difficult access and now heavily looted. What is clear is the striking similarity between the structures described by local residents and some of the constructions excavated at Altar de Sacrificios (A. L. Smith 1972: Fig. 75*c, d*). Most likely the composition of the ballast depends on relative proximity to the river and its supply of river cobbles and sand (Willey and Smith 1969: 35). It is not, then, a significant criterion of regional difference.

The salient feature of the Pasión sites is their great quantity of carved monuments, many with glyphic texts. Peter Mathews and Gordon Willey (1991: Fig. 2) list a total of 211 carved monuments out of a total of 354 monuments; the figure is in fact even higher, with a total of more than 220 carved monuments out of a sample of 364 monuments. This number compares favorably with most other regions in the southern Maya Lowlands. Of greater importance is the fact that these carved monuments and the political information they contain are not limited to a few massive centers; rather, they come from a much larger set of sites, including several of unprepossessing size. This monumental record affords an unusual opportunity to examine relationships between centers at the elite level during the Late Classic. The relative accessibility and close spacing of these sites further encourages a regional perspective that is less easily obtained in other parts of the southern Lowlands.

Of the Pasión centers, the best known are probably Altar de Sacrificios and Seibal. Certainly they are the most thoroughly excavated (Willey and Smith 1969; Willey et al. 1975). Despite such renown, Altar and Seibal do not appear to have been very important during the Late Classic, when certain centers between them served as the seats of prominent dynasties (Houston and Mathews 1985; Johnston 1985). The most important of these is Dos Pilas, both for its rich inventory of monuments and because of its apparent political dynamism. Ironically, for its size and apparent significance Dos Pilas has been among the least studied sites in the Pasión River drainage, although this is now changing with the intensive efforts of the Vanderbilt project. Relatively few of its sculptures have been reported in more than a summary fashion, and of the two published maps, one is impressionistic (Navarrete and Luján 1963: Fig. 1), and the other the result of a hand-compass survey (Houston and Mathews 1985: Fig. 2).

PREVIOUS WORK IN THE PASIÓN DRAINAGE

Previous archaeological work at the sites of Altar de Sacrificios and Seibal is ably summarized in publications of the Peabody Museum, which is itself responsible for most major work in the region (Willey and Smith 1969: 3–6, passim; Willey et al. 1975: 6–7; Tourtellot 1983a: 3–4, 19; 1988). Additional reports have appeared on the sites of Cancuen (Maler 1908; Morley 1915; 1937–1938; Tourtellot, Sabloff, and Sharick 1978) and Itzan (Tourtellot, Hammond, and Rose 1978; Johnston 1989), both explored under the auspices of the Peabody, as well as Aguateca (I. Graham 1961; 1967; Orrego 1981), La Amelia, El Caribe, Aguas Calientes, La Reforma III (Morley 1937–1938), Tamarindito (Vinson 1960: 6), Tres Islas (Forsyth 1980), and Machaquila (I. Graham 1963, 1967). All these sites contain carved monuments, which have been reproduced in various sources (e.g., Istituto Italo-latinoamericano 1969; Greene, Rands, and Graham 1972). Several reconnaissances by Ian Graham will soon be published, possibly by the Middle American Research Institute at Tulane University (I. Graham, personal communication, 1985).

THE LOOTING OF THE PASIÓN

Time is now running out for the archaeology of the Pasión, which is among the most heavily looted areas in Central America. Most of the thieves are native to the area, often tilling fields next to sites. Agents in the *municipio* capital of Sayaxche usually receive and ship the goods to the departmental capital of Flores and beyond. The damage of such depredation has been enormous. The site of Tamarindito now lacks the better part of two of its three hieroglyphic stairways, and two of the largest mounds at the site, Structures 1 and 44, contain deep trenches.

Other Pasión sites have been damaged to the same degree or worse. More than half of the structures at the small center of El Excavado have been trenched, some as recently as 1984. Aguateca has been robbed of one of its stelae (now in a public collection in Chile, Museo Chileno de Arte Precolombino 1983); its mounds still bear evidence of desultory digging. Several large mounds at El Caribe, particularly those near the looted hieroglyphic stairway, contain deep pits, apparently driven to bedrock. Looters have also sacked all but one piece of the hieroglyphic stairway at La Amelia (although the two figural panels are now on public display in Sayaxche and Guatemala City, respectively, and another is reported on the banks of the Pasión, to which it had been dragged). Comparatively few monuments remain at the important site of Itzan (Johnston 1989:Chart 1), although most pieces still appear to be in Guatemalan collections, some in Guatemala City and a smaller number in Antigua. There are persistent rumors that Altar has been despoiled of some of its monuments. As at Itzan, farmers continue to damage its structures and stelae by slash-and-burn agriculture (see I. Graham 1970:430). Gordon Willey and Ledyard Smith are prophetic in this regard: ". . . if a sizable resident population develops along the river, then guard or caretaker maintenance at [Altar] would be highly advisable" (1969:38). Ironically, political unrest in Guatemala may be reducing the traffic in antiquities. Looting in the Pasión has diminished in recent years because of the presence of guerillas, who have not looked favorably on such activities, possibly for the reason that looters might observe and report their patrols.

The only major sites to escape substantial damage are Arroyo de Piedra, Seibal, and Dos Pilas. All three are now protected by employees of the Guatemalan Instituto de Antropología e Historia. Only two small mounds at Dos Pilas have been trenched, and most of the monuments taken from the site are in the custody of Guatemalan authorities, or have been traced to particular collections (e.g., J. Jones 1969: Item 108; a fragment until recently in the Peter Wray collection, Emmerich 1984:Figs. 32-33; I. Graham 1971:61). The pristine quality of these sites makes them attractive for further investigation.

PREVIOUS WORK AT DOS PILAS

The site of Dos Pilas was reportedly discovered in 1953 or 1954 by José María and Lisandro Flores of Sayaxche (Vinson 1960:4; Berlin 1960:26; Navarrete and Luján 1963:5). Very likely the ruins were already known to local residents. Miles Rock recorded a small hamlet near Lake Petexbatun as early as 1887 (Rock 1895). The hamlet apparently contained Spanish-speaking people (Sapper 1897:Karte V; Tourtellot 1983a:441–442), who perhaps petitioned that Capuchin friars be brought to the area in 1870 (Soza 1957:187). Juan Galindo mentioned a road passing by Lake Petexbatun on its way from Flores to Guatemala City (Galindo 1833:59; Tourtellot 1983a:442), a route designed, perhaps, to accommodate the lakeside settlement (or possibly it was the trail or *camino real* itself that attracted settlers to Petexbatun in the first place). It seems inconceivable that the Petexbatun villagers would have been unfamiliar with the ruins, although the significance of the sites probably escaped them.

Since 1954 the attention of visitors has focused on sculpture. Within months of the "discovery," José and Lisandro Flores guided Jorge Ibarra and José Alberto Funes to Dos Pilas; these visitors later published a brief account of Dos Pilas in a Guatemalan City newspaper, with poor photographs of several monuments (*El Imparcial*, April 14, 1954). The next visitor of note was the French adventurer Pierre Ivanoff (Navarrete and Luján 1963:5), who traveled to Dos Pilas in 1960 and subsequently published a grandiose account claiming discovery of the ruins (termed "Dos Pozos" after two of the many springs at the site; Ivanoff 1968). Inexplicably, Ivanoff also felled most of the trees in the Dos Pilas plaza, producing a clearing that is visible in aerial photographs taken less than two years later (Ian Graham, personal communication, 1984; IGN Photograph 116; Navarrete and Luján 1963:5). Later visitors include G. L. Vinson (1960), who changed the site name to the no less inaccurate "Dos Pilas," Joya Hairs and Terence Grieder (1960), Merle Greene (Greene, Rands, and Graham 1972:194–203), John Graham (1973:208–209), Ian Graham (1967:9), and, in the last fifteen years, hundreds of tourists. Ian Graham in particular has done much to investigate the site. His unpublished sketch map is highly accurate, as are his renderings of selected Dos Pilas monuments.

Until recently, archaeological information on Dos Pilas has been scant. Pre-Vanderbilt excavations consisted of little more than random test pits, of doubtful benefit in a site of this size and complexity. Ivanoff claims to have made many "sondages," but states that nothing came of them (Ivanoff 1968). Carlos Navarrete and Luis Luján were more conscientious in their records of excavations at Dos Pilas (1963:9, Figs. 2 and 5). However, for reasons of limited time, they made only a few superficial pits and removed rubble around some sculptures. Around 1970 someone placed a sondage—a 2-meter-by-2-meter pit backfilled by Vanderbilt in 1989—to the west of Structure L5-33 (Forsyth 1980:59). The purpose of this pit is as unclear as the identity of the person(s) who made it, and in any case the enterprise was soon frustrated by the heavy rubble core that might be expected in such a location. Marco Antonio Bailey, who died before issuing a report, was the last to excavate at Dos Pilas before the arrival of the Vanderbilt project. Some of the pits in and around the Dos Pilas plaza are likely to be his work; he also turned at least one monument (Stela 14) near Structure P5-7 (Juan Hernández, personal communication, 1984).

The Yale project began field study at Dos Pilas in January 1984. The first season concentrated on reconnaissance, and included mapping and exploration at Dos Pilas as well as other Pasión centers with monuments. Throughout, the emphasis was on finding additional inscriptions and recording something of the architectural context of these monuments. The Yale project explored at Aguateca, Arroyo de Piedra, Dos Pilas (and its outlier, La Paciencia), El Caribe, El Excavado, Itzan, La Amelia, Tamarindito, and a number of smaller sites rumored to have texts, such as Punta de Chimino, which lies on a peninsula jutting into Lake Petexbatun. We assumed, correctly as it turned out, that the search for inscriptions necessitated close study of site settlement and architecture. Discoveries of monuments at Tamarindito and Dos Pilas fully justified this assumption, for several important finds were made during the course of systematic mapping.

The 1986 field season concentrated exclusively on Dos Pilas. Between May and September of that year the project mapped 750,000 square meters of the site (Site Maps 1–3).[1] Concurrently, members of the crew documented Dos Pilas' monuments. Both tasks reflected our desire for an exhaustive survey of surface features at the ruins, with the ultimate aim of providing a base for future excavations at Dos Pilas (see Freidel 1986b). Since then, the Vanderbilt investigations have relied heavily on the Yale maps, although some parts of them have been replaced by more detailed plans by Takeshi Inomata and Joel Palka. Placement of additional datum markers by Inomata also shows a cumulative error (ca. 1.5 to 2 meters) in elevations on the Yale maps, especially toward the Duende outlier. Future researchers should use the more precise elevations determined by Inomata.

LOCATION AND DESCRIPTION OF DOS PILAS

Aerial photographs and tape measurements permit the exact identification of Dos Pilas' location: 16°26′45″N, 90°17′45″W, at the site plaza. The ruins lie at an approximate elevation of 150 meters above sea level and at the western end of the Petexbatun escarpment, which drops precipitously to swamplands 750 meters north of the Structure P5-7 outlier. In total, elevations at the site vary over 60.22 meters. The vegetation of low-lying tracts contrasts strikingly with that of Dos Pilas proper. There is a superabundance of *corozo* (*Orbignya cohune*) and *kantutz* palm (*Scheelea lundelii*) alongside hardwood trees. Ancient settlement in such areas is slight, although it tends to cluster toward the lip of the escarpment.

The soil and flora of Dos Pilas correspond to the Tropical Moist Forest Life Zone, an area of multistratal deciduous or evergreen forest (Holdrige 1947:367; Hartshorn 1983:121–122). The underlying rock is a bedded limestone thoroughly riddled with caves, which can flood—sometimes with alarming rapidity and noise—during the rainy season. Many caves appear to have been used by the ancient inhabitants of Dos

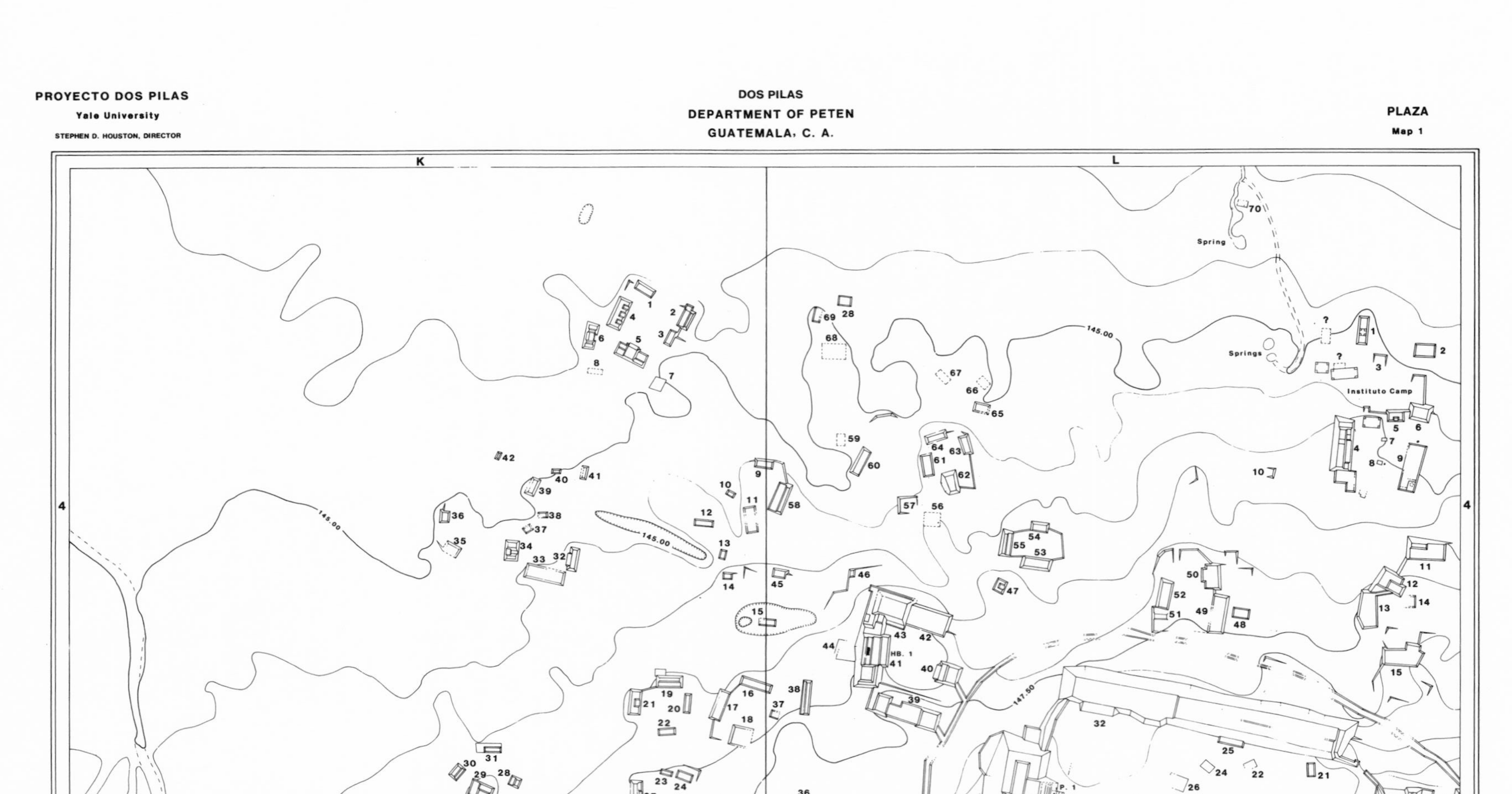
PROYECTO DOS PILAS
Yale University
STEPHEN D. HOUSTON, DIRECTOR
DOS PILAS
DEPARTMENT OF PETEN
GUATEMALA, C. A.
PLAZA
Map 1
K
L
4
Spring
Springs
Instituto Camp
145.00
147.50
HB. 1
P. 1

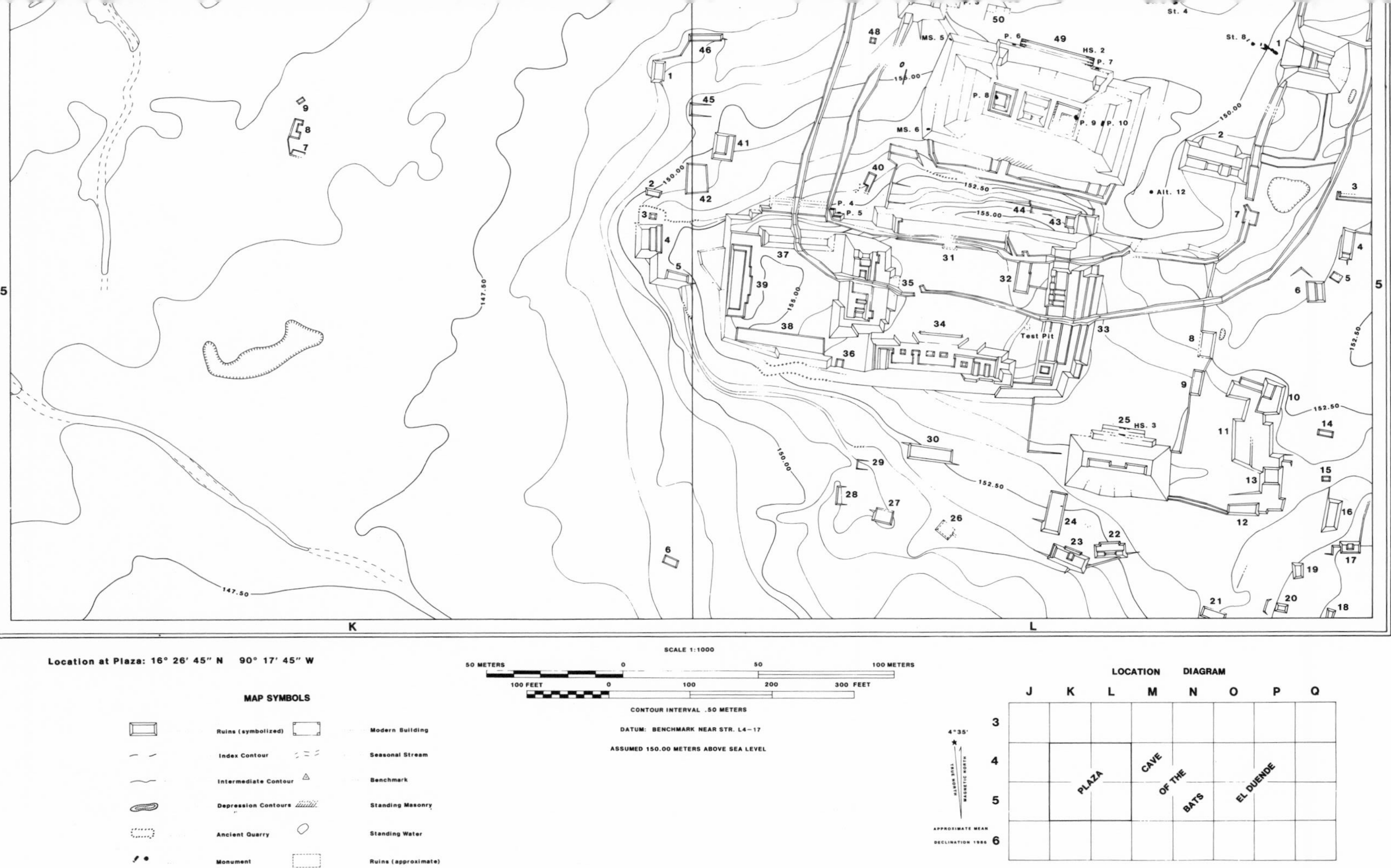

Site Map 1. Dos Pilas map: Plaza sheet. See following pages for details.

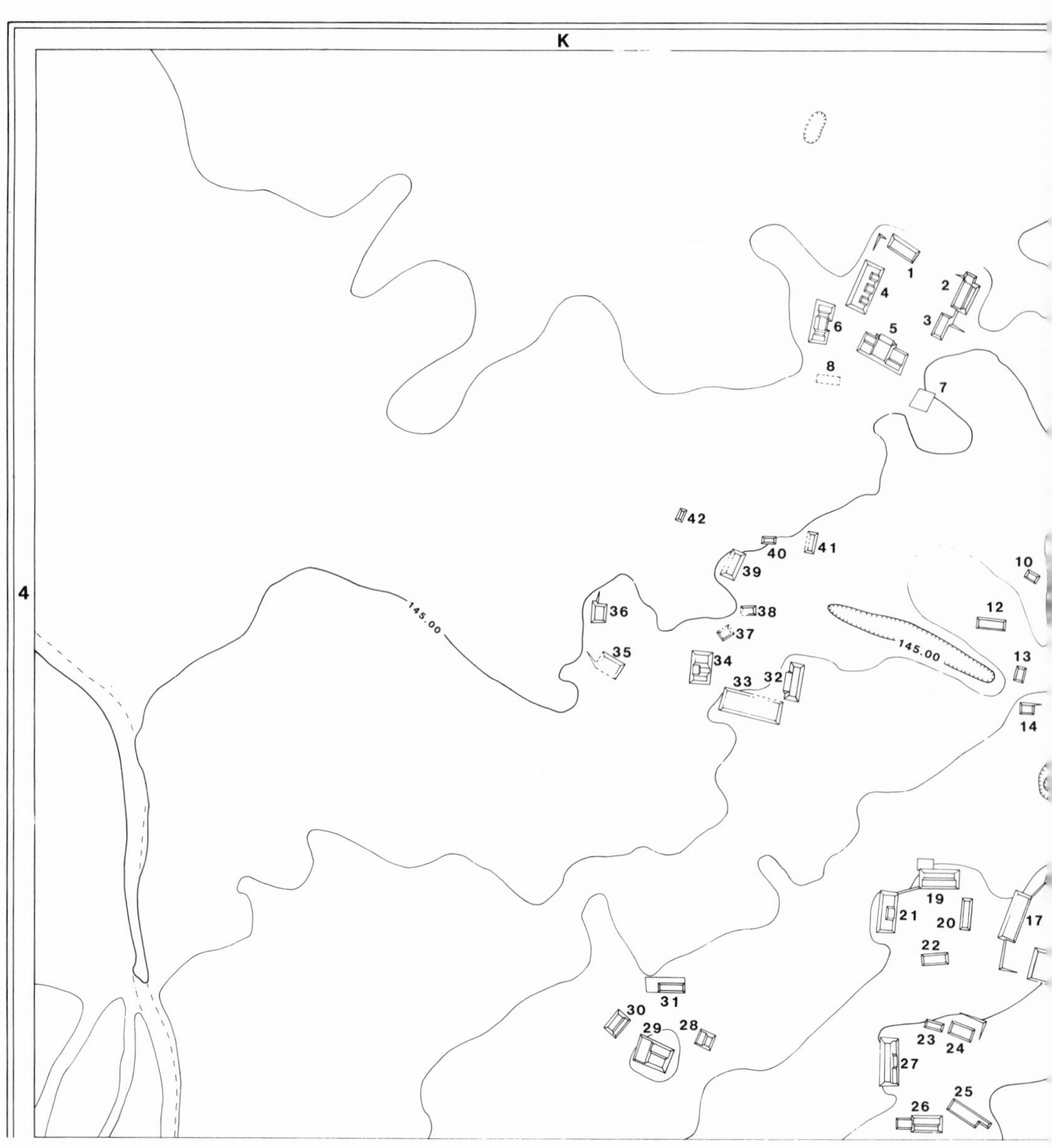

Site Map 1 (continued). Grid K4.

Site Map 1 (continued). Grid L4.

Site Map 1 (continued). Grid K5.

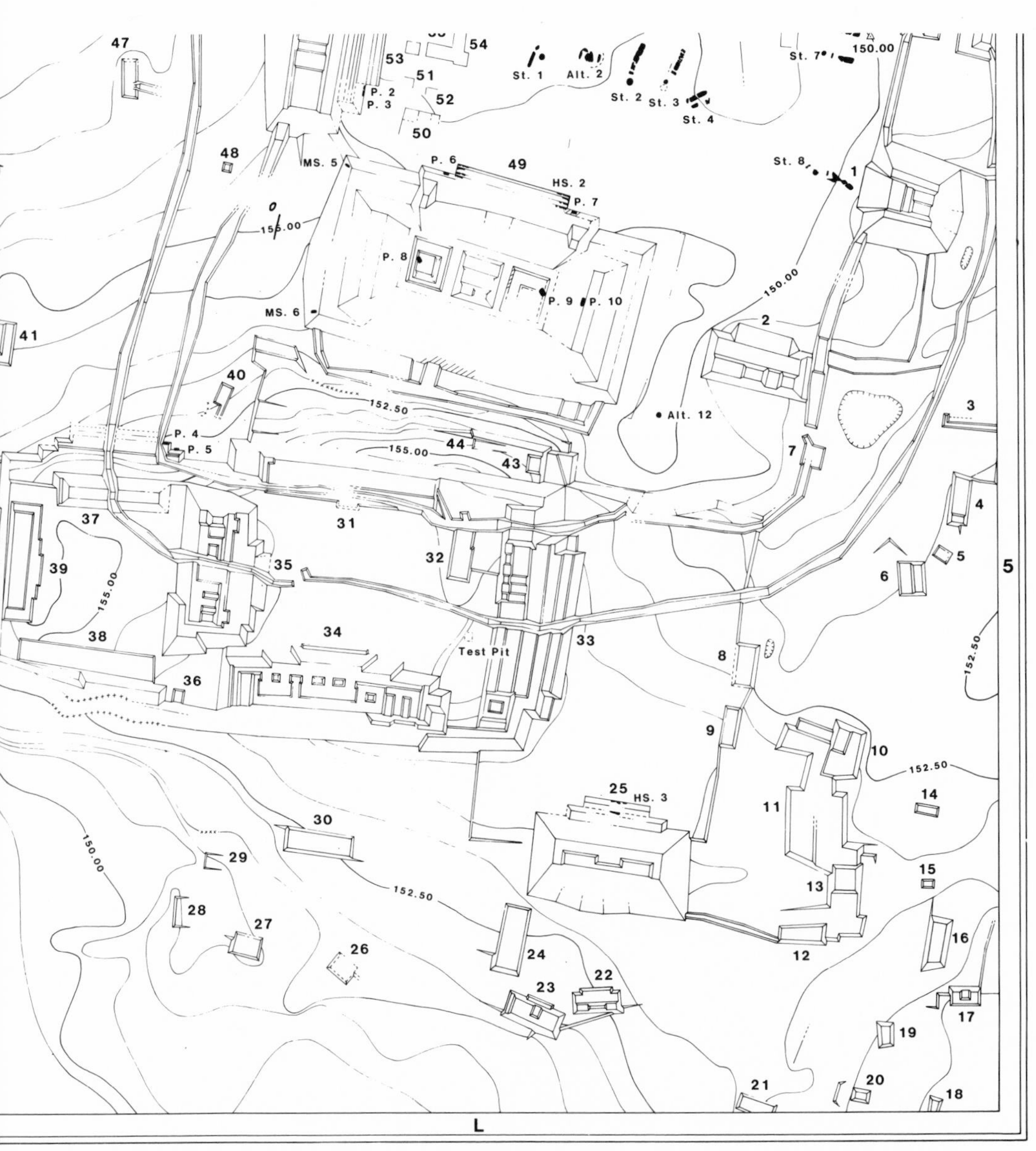

Site Map 1 (continued). Grid L5.

PROYECTO DOS PILAS
Yale University
STEPHEN D. HOUSTON, DIRECTOR

DOS PILAS
DEPARTMENT OF PETEN
GUATEMALA, C. A.

CAVE OF THE BATS
Map 2

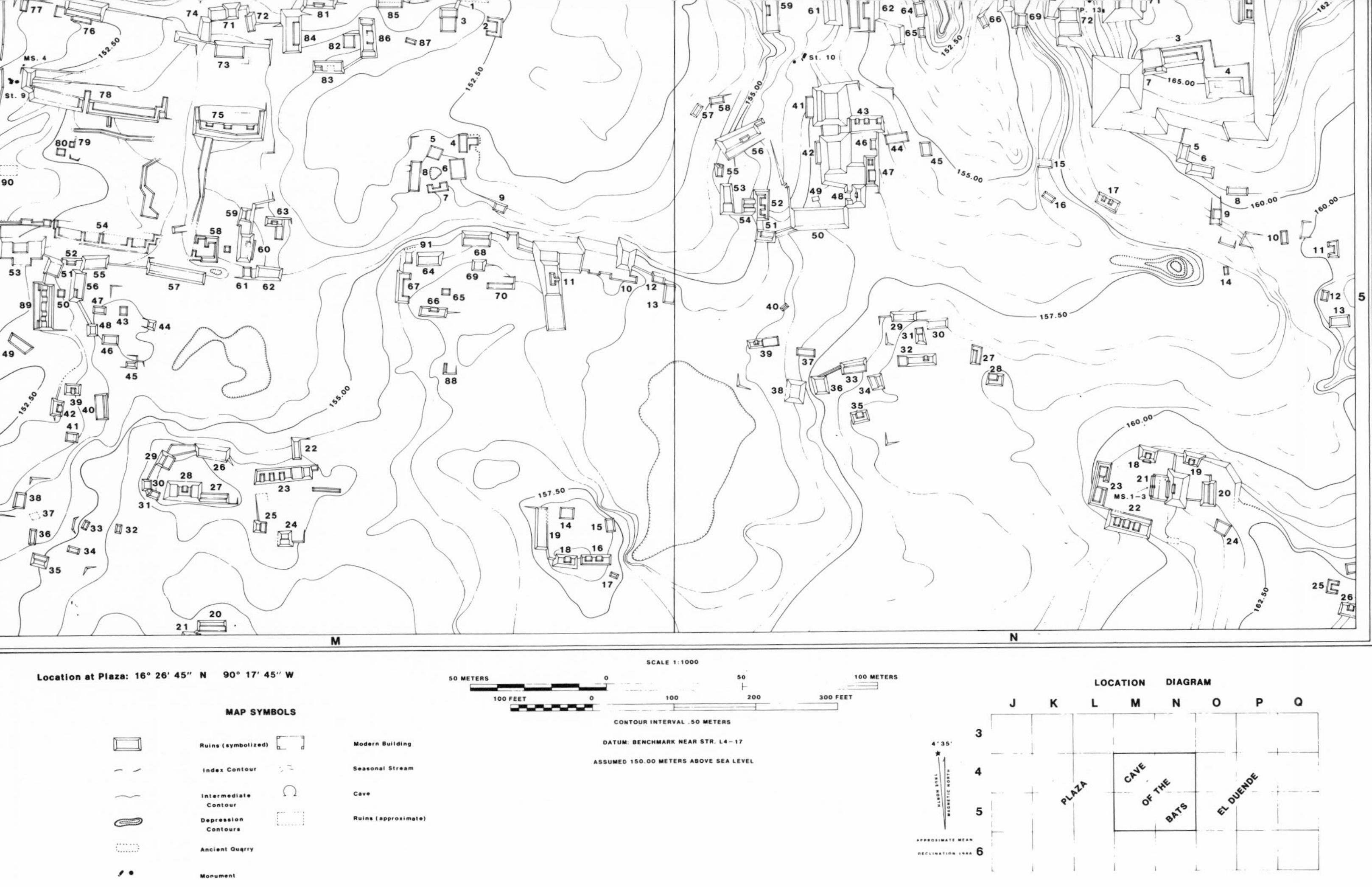

Site Map 2. Dos Pilas map: Cave of the Bats sheet. See following pages for details.

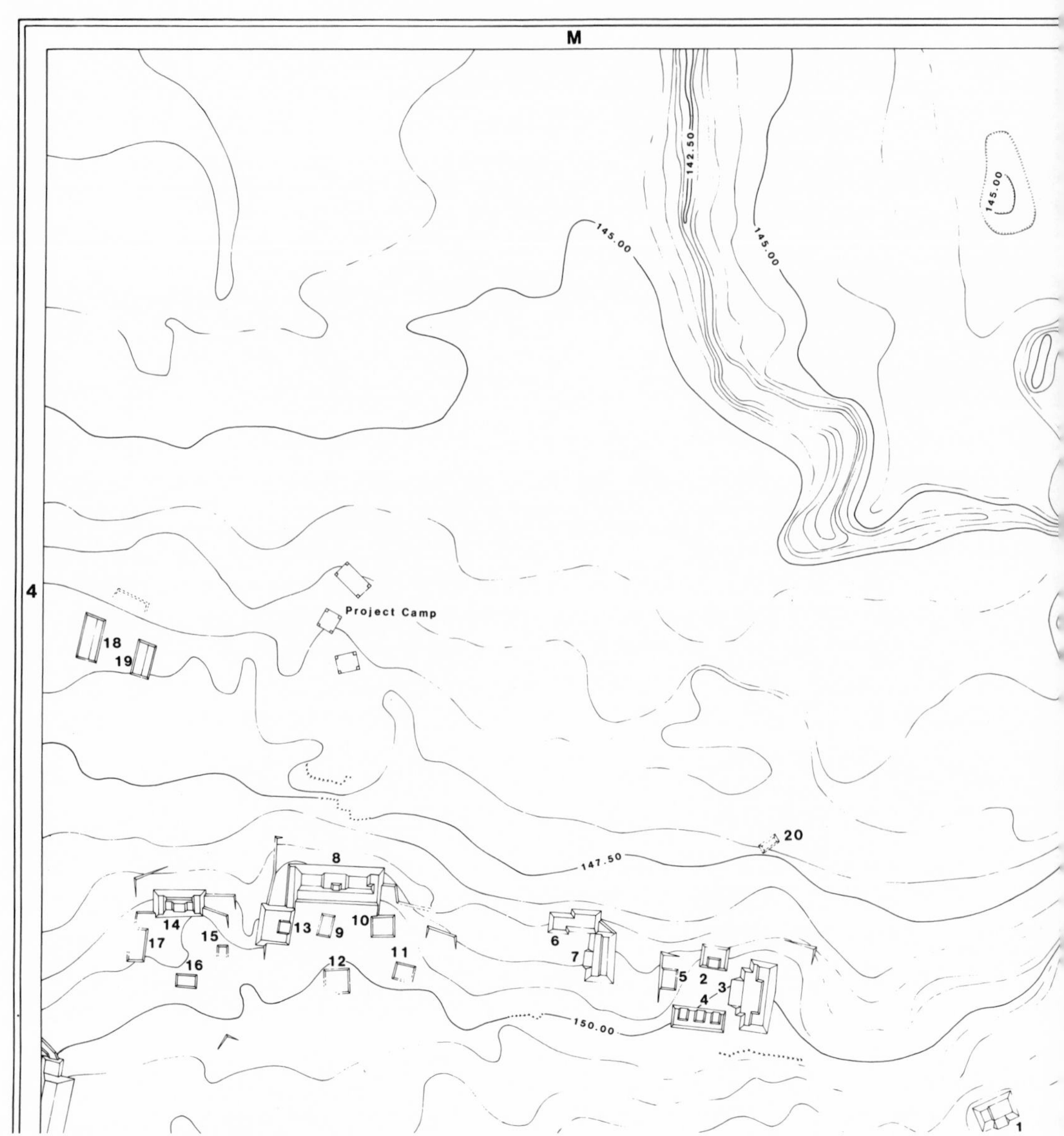

Site Map 2 (continued). Grid M4.

Site Map 2 (continued). Grid N4.

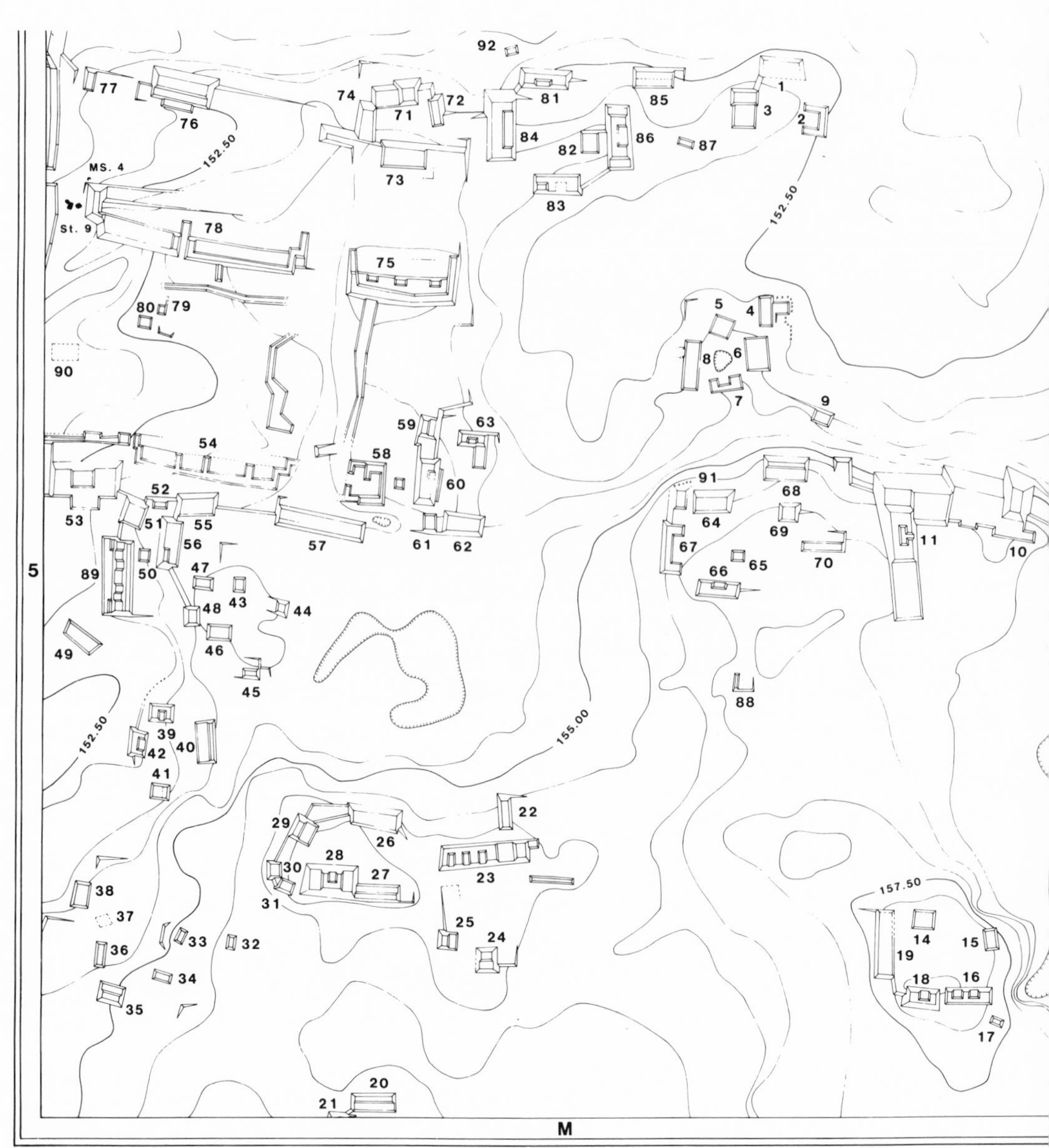

Site Map 2 (continued). Grid M5.

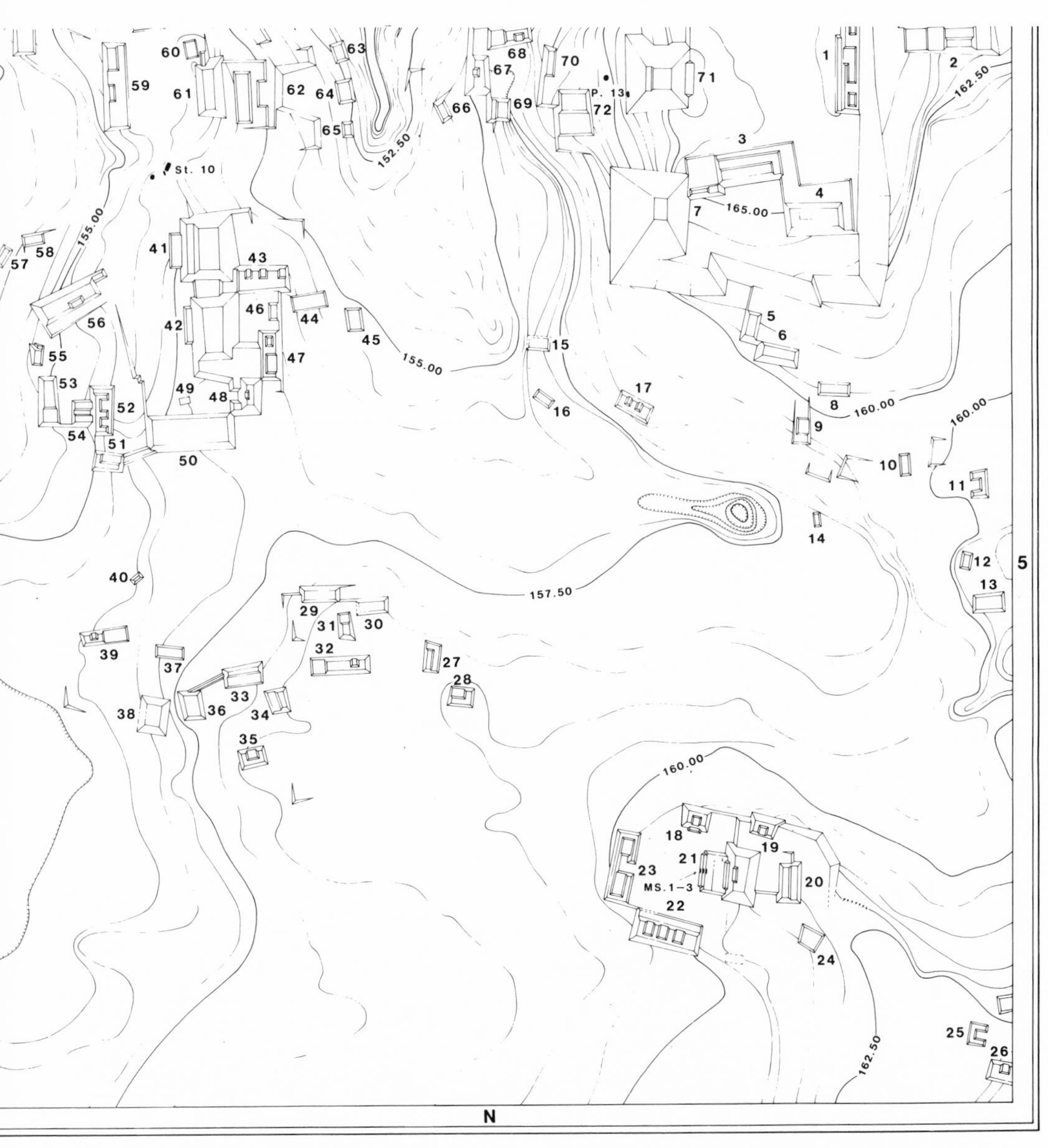

Site Map 2 (continued). Grid N5.

PROYECTO DOS PILAS

Yale University

STEPHEN D. HOUSTON, DIRECTOR

DOS PILAS

DEPARTMENT OF PETEN

GUATEMALA, C. A.

EL DUENDE

Map 3

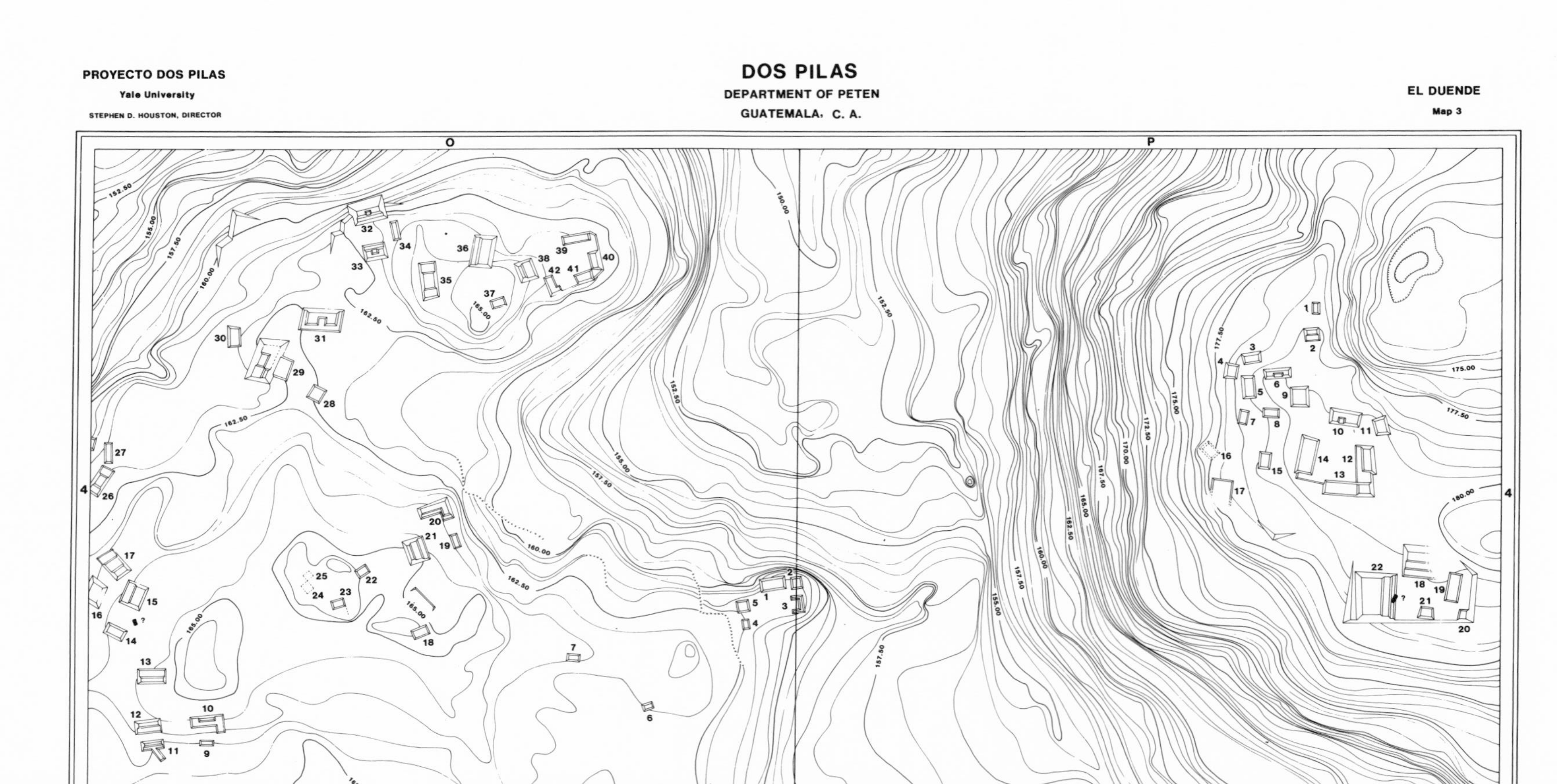

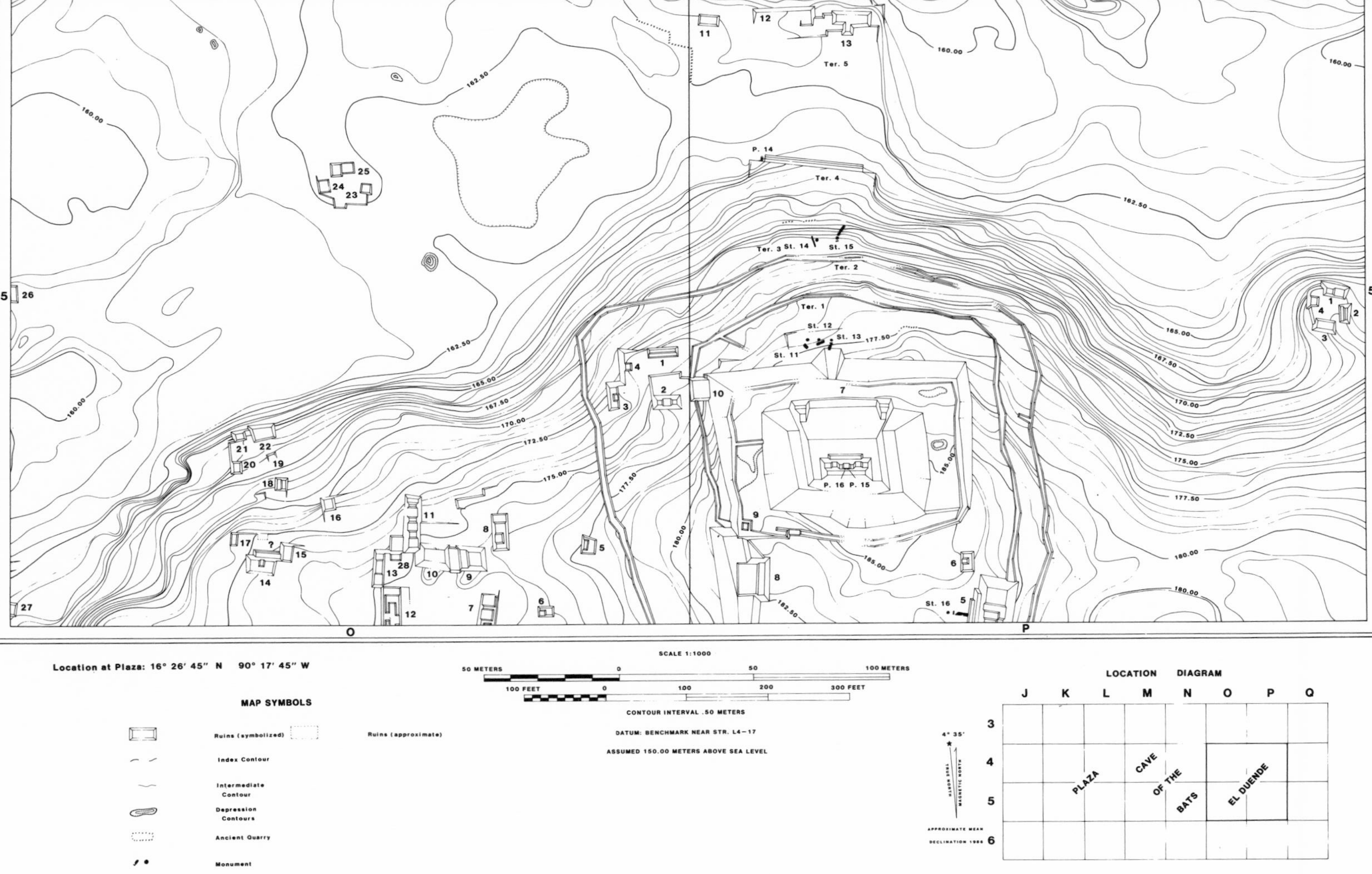

Site Map 3. Dos Pilas map: El Duende sheet. See following pages for details.

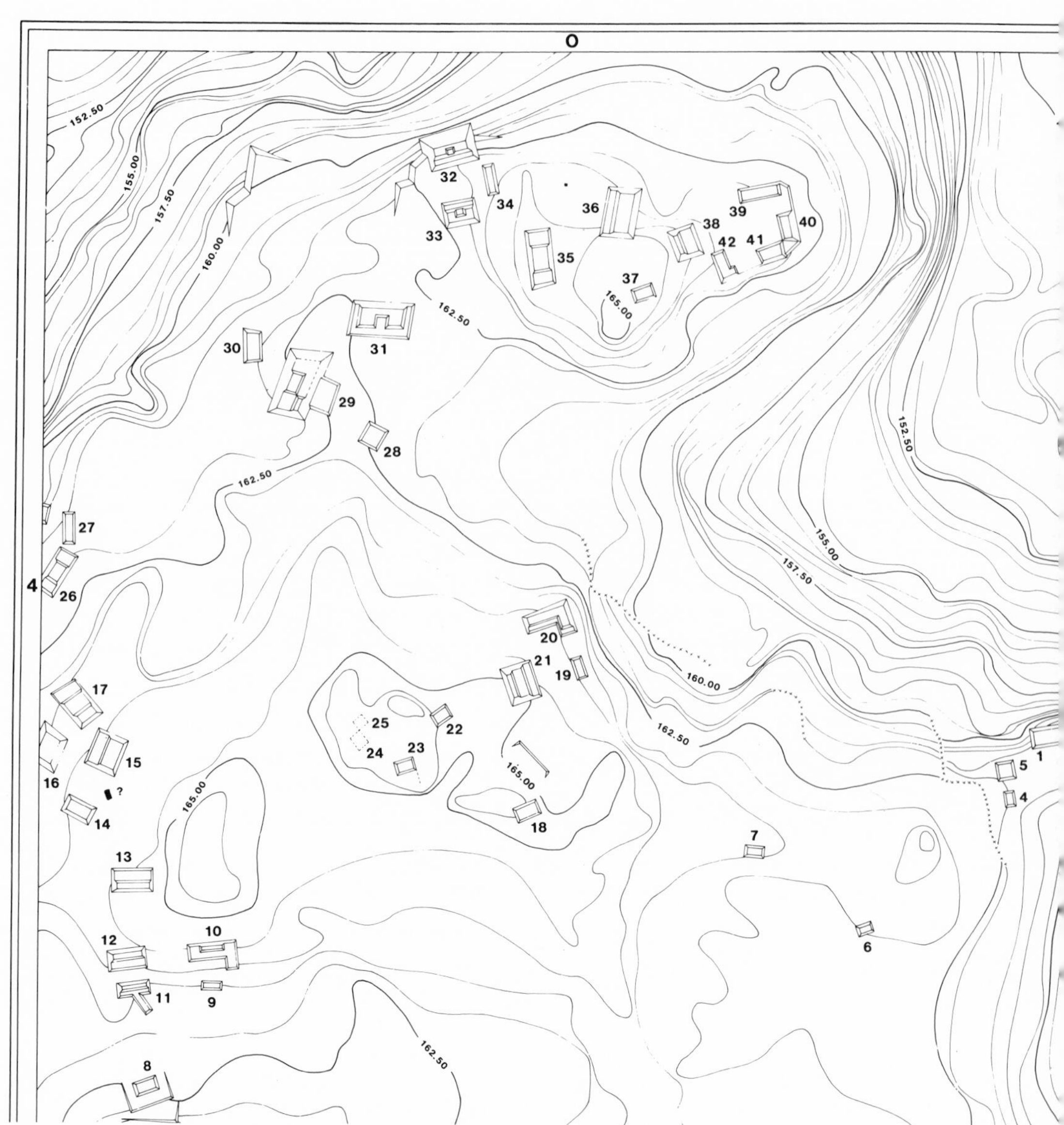

Site Map 3 (continued). Grid O4.

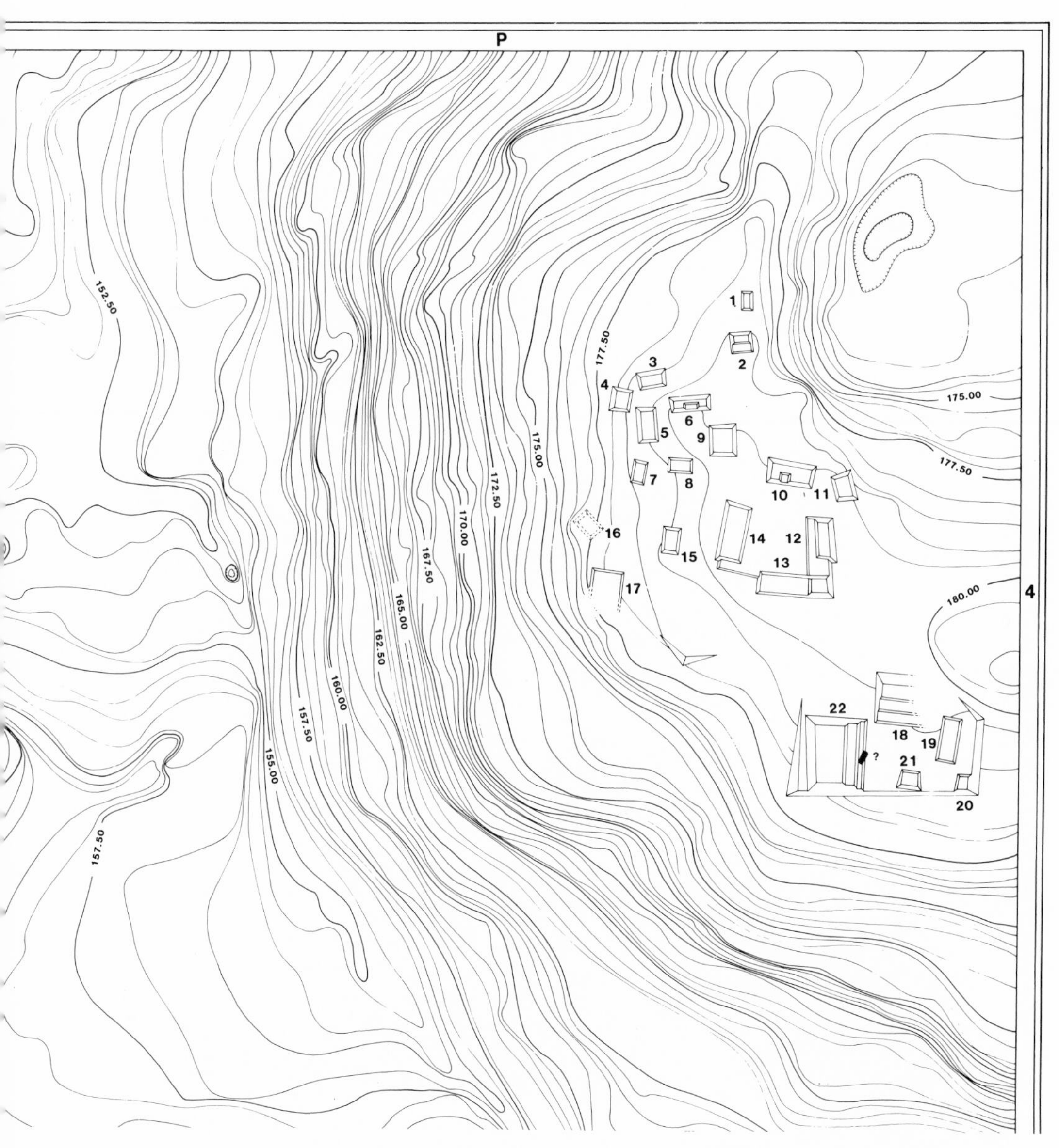

Site Map 3 (continued). Grid P4.

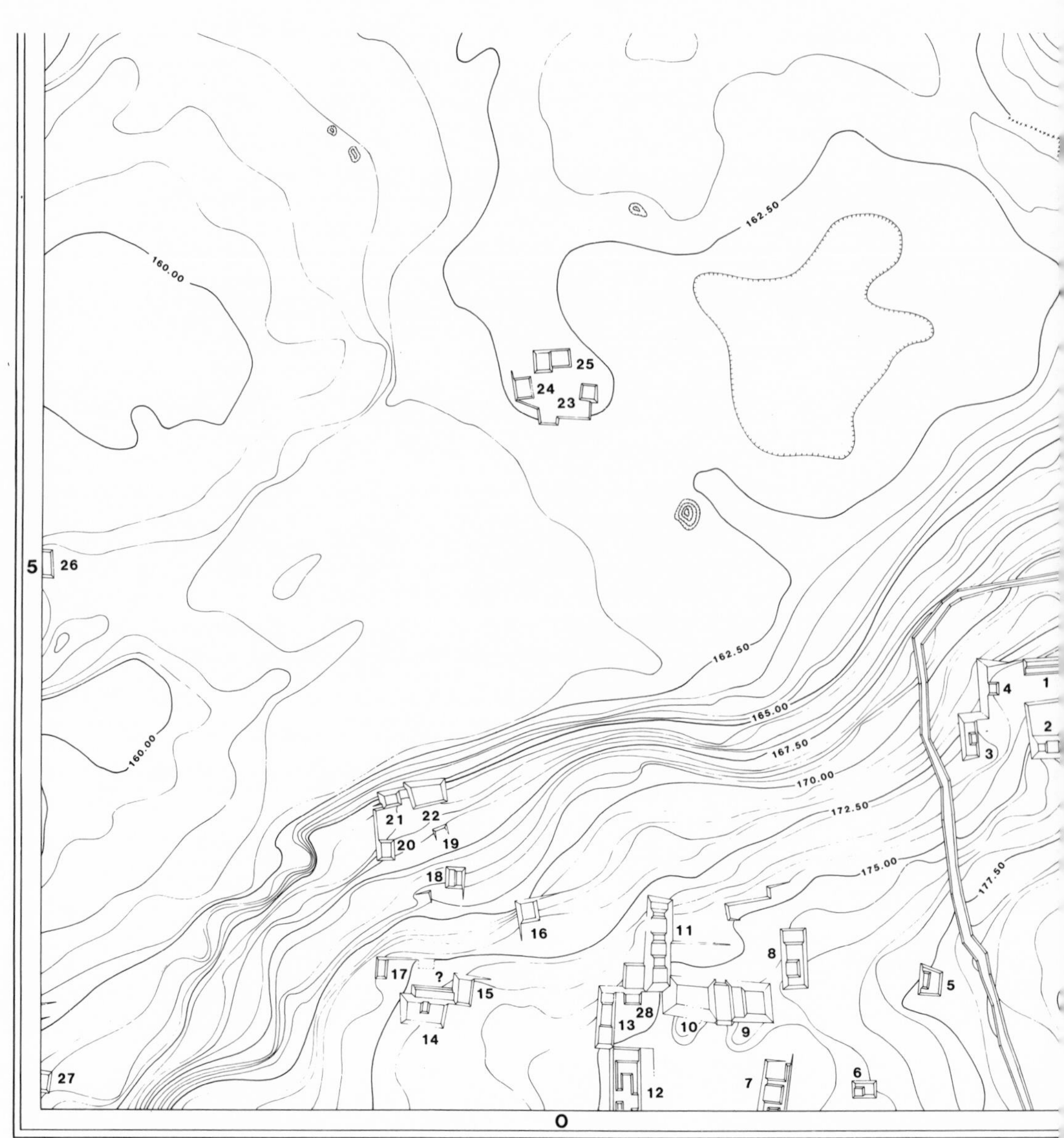

Site Map 3 (continued). Grid 05.

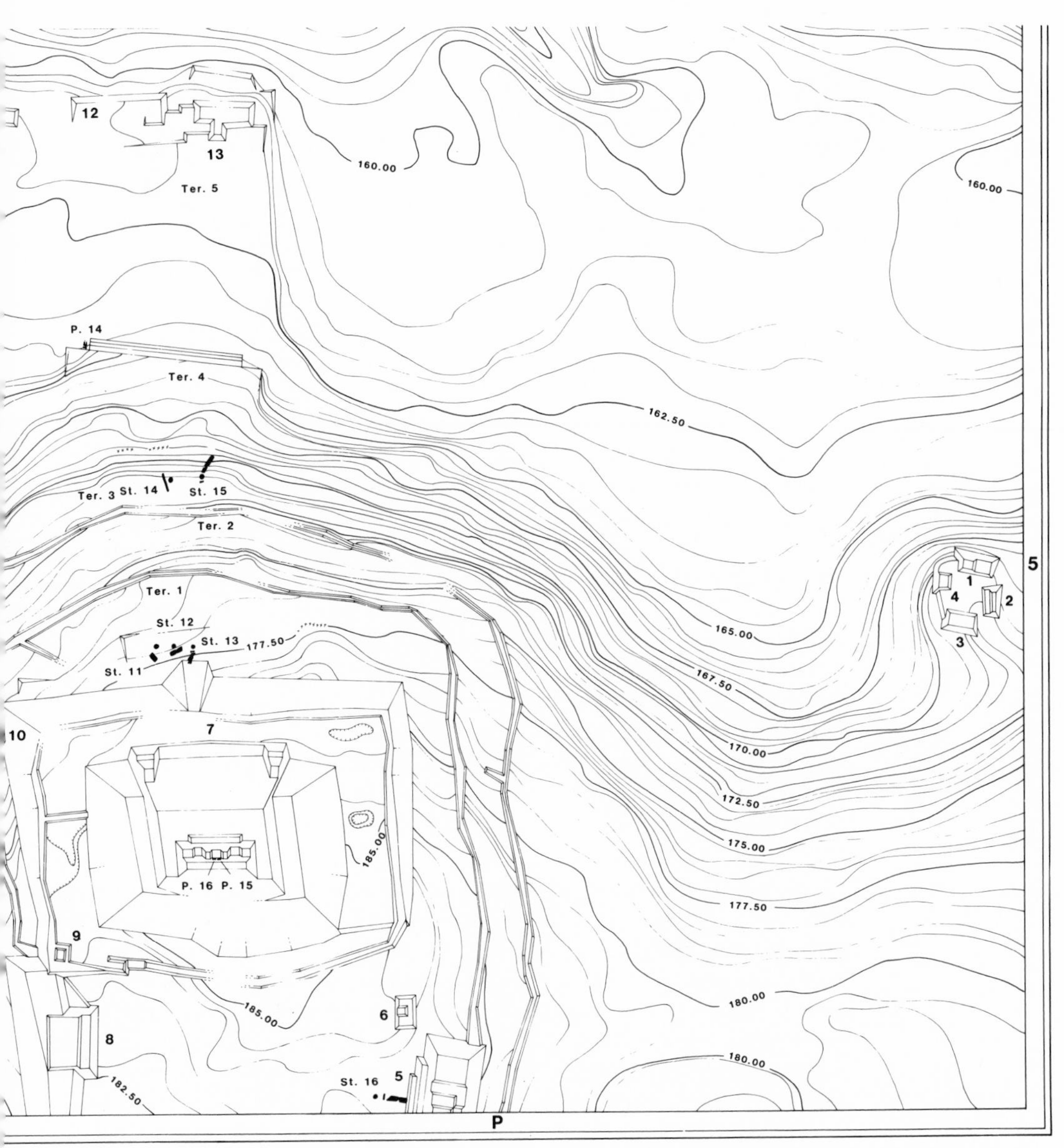

Site Map 3 (continued). Grid P5.

Figure 2-4. Plan view of Dos Pilas.

Pilas, including several investigated by James Brady of the Vanderbilt Petexbatun project.

Water supply at Dos Pilas is very reliable, perhaps a little too much so during the rainy season, when standing water accumulates in poorly drained portions of the site. As mentioned before, the name "Dos Pilas" is inaccurate: there are in reality three clusters of springs at the site, including the eponymous group by the Instituto camp and less reliable ones near Structures N4-30 and O4-2. The water is drinkable, although heavy rains can turn it a muddy hue with suspended sediments. Other streams on the Petexbatun escarpment, such as that near the villages of Petexbatun and Faisán, are sulfurous. All major ruins on the escarpment lie near sources of sweet water, with Dos Pilas being the most amply provisioned. Reliable water supply and high terrain probably attracted the first settlers to Dos Pilas, although political factors most likely probably influenced later settlement.

The distribution of mounds at Dos Pilas is unusual. Unlike many Classic sites, which tend to radial settlement, Dos Pilas follows a linear pattern: it includes at least 492 mounds arranged on an east-west axis, with a minimum area of 71 hectares (Fig. 2-4).[2] The most massive structures at the site, Structures L5-49 and P5-7, appear near the settlement's edges rather than at its midpoint. Settlement between these two structures, and particularly near Structure L5-49, is highly compact. Some patio groups are separated by no more than 10 meters, and yet the areas just beyond these groups lack mounds. A concern for defense perhaps led to such compact settlement.[3]

Most construction at Dos Pilas is now in ruins. Nonetheless, many structural details appear on the surface. These details include the number of rooms, disposition of benches, small patio group outliers (kitchens?), and apparent hearths (as on Structure L4-9, Site Map 1). Such clarity, which is unusual in the Peten, may stem from the thin soil cover, the late date of construction, and the absence of earlier building that "upon erosion, would serve to confuse the surveyor" (Tourtellot 1983a:45). The scarcity of masonry vaulting in the Pasión drainage contributed as well, since vault collapse conceals interior details (Tourtellot 1983a:44–45; 1983b; 1988).

Mounds

The high surface visibility makes it possible to establish a typology of mounds at the site. On the whole, mounds fit easily into the classifications developed for Seibal (Table 2-1; Tourtellot 1983a; 1988). However, some do not. For example, class G, a two-level structure with upper level in the form of a C, appears at Dos Pilas with up to four chambers. The number of rooms is indicated by a superscript; thus, G^3 indicates such a mound with three rooms. Also, some mounds at Dos Pilas combine features from several mound classes, such as a large square structure (M) that supports a small mound with single room (G). A hybrid class, M/G, accommodates this type. A third modification concerns stairways, which are common at Dos Pilas but neglected in the Seibal classification. Stairways occur in two general forms: attached directly to structures or, more usual at Dos Pilas, affixed as doubled outsets (see Loten and Pendergast 1984:11 for a definition of this term). Carved or plain panels flank the outsets, which often display monolithic construction. Mound types with superscripts ^{s} or ^{ss} designate the "direct" and "outset" stairways respectively. Thus, M^{ss} refers to a pyramid with outset stairways. Appendix 2-1 lists by type all mounds on the Dos Pilas plan. Table 2-2 tallies mound type by map quadrant.

In a few cases mounds at Dos Pilas do not even remotely resemble mounds at Seibal. Two types come to mind. The first consists of only three or perhaps four examples (Structures M5-54, M5-75, M5-78, and possibly L5-3). It exhibits a plan much like an elongated U, with angled masonry embellishments on the open terminals of the U. The plan also shows interior platforming as well as supports for a roof. Without exception, this type faces north; in two instances it displays orthostatic masonry as well. Structure M5-58 exemplifies the other type. It resembles some Postclassic structures documented at Mayapan (A. L. Smith

Table 2-1. ***Mound types***

A	Partial structures
B	Adjunct structures
C	Small square structures
D	Medium square structures
E	Rectangular structures
F	Two-level structures
G	Two-level structures with upper level in form of C
H	Interrupted two-level structures
I	Two-level structures with upper level in form of L
J	Three-level structures
K	Three-level structures with upper level in form of C
L	Supporting platforms (not applied at Dos Pilas)
M	Large square structures

Source: Tourtellot 1983a: Table 6.

Table 2-2. *Mound type totals*

Grid	*A*	*B*	*C*	*D*	*E*	*F*	*G*	*H*	*I*	*J*	*K*	*M*	*?*
K4				3	31	5	3						
K5			1		6		1			1			
L4	3		14	2	37	5	2	2		1	1		2
L5	4		8	2	24	6	2	3			1	3	1
M4	1			2	8	5	4						
M5			16	3	38	12	14	2	1	2			4
N4	1		1	4	11	6	2	1	3				1
N5			4		35	7	14	4	2		4	2	
O4			2	3	20	9	2	4		2			
O5	2		2	2	11	2	6	2	1				
P4			1	2	13	1	2	1		2			
P5	1	1		1	5	2	1	1				1	
Total	12	1	49	24	239	60	53	20	7	8	6	6	8

Source: Hybrid types are included in the total for the first type listed in each case; i.e., D/F is counted as D, E/G as E, etc.

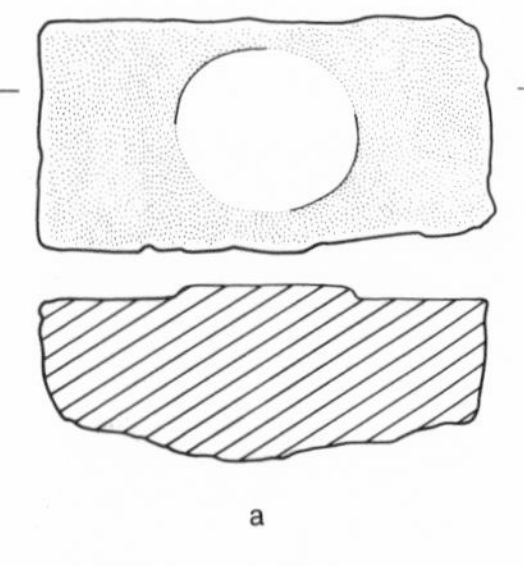

a

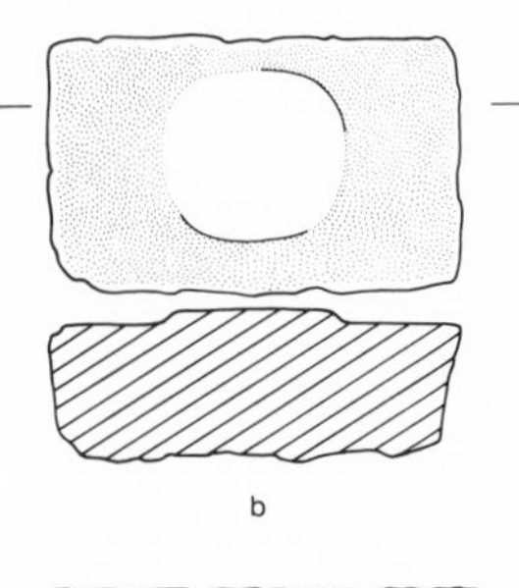

b

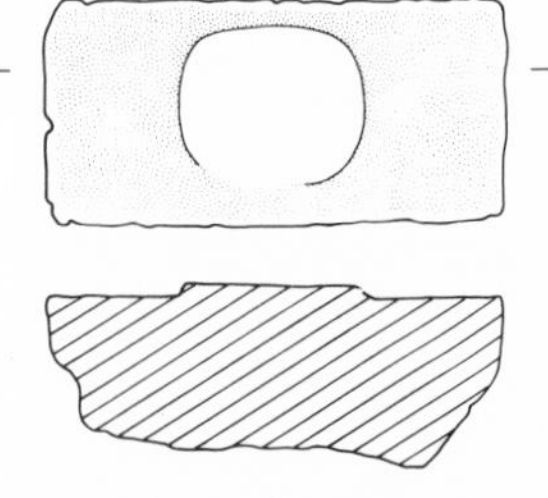

c

Figure 2-5. Miscellaneous Stones 1 (*a*), 2 (*b*) and 3 (*c*). Heights: MS 1, .34 m; MS 2, .38 m; MS 3, .33 m.

1962: Fig. 8*j*) and, more closely, on the island of Cozumel (Type "5a," Freidel and Sabloff 1984:63, Fig. 14), where excavators interpret it as a class of isolated shrines of late date. Nonetheless, excavations by David Stuart have shown that the building at Dos Pilas is a Late Classic structure.

Patio Groups

Mounds are only one unit of Dos Pilas settlement. There are also clusters of mounds known as "patio groups" (Ashmore 1981b:49), courtyards surrounded by structures (Table 2-3).[4] The small structures that accompany such groups presumably served as kitchens or sleeping quarters (Tourtellot 1970:412; 1983b). In addition to patio groups and their variants, there exist groups with less formal arrangements (Ashmore 1981b:48–49). These may represent either functional or fortuitous associations, which are distinguishable only by excavation.

The patio group has subcategories as well. One is a group first defined at Tikal: the "Plaza Plan 2" (Becker 1971). It comprises, among other things, a conspicuous structure on the east side of a patio. This eastern building often contains an important burial or burials, perhaps the focus of ancestor worship. Only one clear example of this group appears on the Dos Pilas plan. This is Group N5-6, which includes a prominent eastern mound (Structure N5-21) adorned with finely dressed stonework. The stonework consists of two items: a stairway decorated with raised disks (Miscellaneous Stones 1, 2, and 3; Fig. 2-5) and a piece of three-member molding that presumably fell from the cornice of a vaulted structure.[5] More recent excavations by Oswaldo Chinchilla of the Vanderbilt project have shown that the group contains an iconographic bench.

Table 2-3. ***Patio groups***

Group	Structures	Navarrete and Luján Muñoz 1963
Grid K4		
K4-1	1–8	
K4-2	9–11, L4-58	
K4-3	16–18, L4-37	
K4-4	19–22	
K4-5	23–27	
K4-6	28–31	
K4-7	32–34, ?37	
Grid K5		
K5-1	3–5	
K5-2	7–9	
Grid L4		
L4-1	4–9	
L4-2	11–15	
L4-3	48–52	
L4-4	39–44	
L4-5	53–55	
L4-6	61–64	
L4-7	28, 68–69	
Grid L5		
L5-1	16–17	
L5-2	22–24	
L5-3	8–9, 25, 33	
L5-4	31–32, 34	Plaza II
L5-5	37–39	
L5-6	41–42	
L5-7	45–46, K5-1	
Grid M4		
M4-1	2–5	
M4-2	6–7	
M4-3	8–13	
M4-4	14–17	
M4-5	18–19	
Grid M5		
M5-1	1–3	
M5-2	4–8	
M5-3	10–13	Plaza III?
M5-4	64–67	Plaza III?

Table 2-3 (*continued*)

Group	*Structures*	*Navarrete and Luján Muñoz 1963*
M5-5	14–19	
M5-6	22–25	
M5-7	26–31	
M5-8	20–21	
M5-9	33–36	
M5-10	39–42	
M5-11	49, 53, 89	
M5-12	47, 55–57	
M5-13	59–63	
M5-14	73, 75	
M5-15	76–78	
M5-16	81–84	
M5-17	85–87	
Grid N4		
N4-1	1–3, O4-26, O4-27	Plaza IV
N4-2	6–8	
N4-3	10–12, 30	
N4-4	16–20	
N4-5	21, 23–24	
N4-6	26–29	
Grid N5		
N5-1	1, 3–4, 7, 71	
N5-2	5–6	
N5-3	8–9	
N5-4	12–13, O5-26	
N5-5	25–26, O5-27	
N5-6	18–24	
N5-7	27–28	
N5-8	29–32	
N5-9	33–36	
N5-10	41–43, 46–56	
N5-11	59–61, N4-14	
N5-12	62–65, N4-13	
N5-13	67–69	
N5-14	70, 72	
N5-15	44–45	
Grid O4		
O4-1	32–34	
O4-2	35–37	
O4-3	38–42	
O4-4	28–31	
O4-5	19–21	
O4-6	1–5	
O4-7	22–25	

Table 2-3 (*continued*)

Group	Structures	Navarrete and Luján Muñoz 1963
Grid O5		
O5-1	23–25	
O5-2	1–4	
O5-3	7, 9–10, 12–13, 28	
O5-4	8, 11	
O5-5	14–15, 17	
O5-6	18–22	
Grid P4		
P4-1	3–9	
P4-2	10–14	
P4-3	18–22	
P4-4	15–17	
Grid P5		
P5-1	1–4	
P5-2	5–6, 8	

Note: The numbers in the "Structures" column correspond to the mounds within the Patio Groups; i.e., 1–8 in Group K4-1 represents Structures K4-1, K4-2, etc. Structures in different grids are identified by a more complete designation.

A variant of Plaza Plan 2 is relatively common at Seibal (Tourtellot 1970: Fig. 84; 1983a: 264, Fig. 14b). In contrast, only three such groups occur at Dos Pilas. In place of a conspicuous structure on the east, the variant has a small, square mound, a pattern attested in Dos Pilas Group L4-4. Another feature distinguishes Group L4-4: it has the only known hieroglyphic bench at Dos Pilas. In this feature and in other details, such as group dimension and arrangement, Group L4-4 resembles strikingly a compound at Copan (Webster and Abrams 1983: Fig. 2). Excavations by Vanderbilt suggest that Group L4-4 was the residence of a royal consort; as such it appears to differ from CV36 at Copan, which may have been the residence of noble scribes (ibid.: 295; Webster 1989).

The other groups at Dos Pilas, Group M5-4 and Group M5-16, correspond more closely to examples at Seibal. They are smaller than Group L4-4, and their eastern mounds accord in position and size with structures at Seibal. At Seibal this variant appears to be late (Bayal or post-10.0.0.0.0; Tourtellot 1983a: 542). Presumably the dates of Groups M5-4 and M5-16 are not far off. The date of Group L4-4 is more problematic, since its bench carries a date some hundred years earlier than the Bayal phase at Seibal. Evidence from Vanderbilt excavations shows that the group underwent considerable modification during its lifetime.

Yet the number of groups in the subcategory is small. Plaza Plan 2, relatively common at Tikal and neighboring centers, is rare at Dos Pilas. Dos Pilas' rulers may well have come from Tikal, but the Dos Pilas site plan scarcely reflects this connection. On another point, the rarity of the Seibal variant suggests that most patio groups at Dos Pilas predate the Terminal Classic. Perhaps this pattern relates to the rapid growth of Seibal's population during the end of the Classic (Tourtellot 1983a: 1036), when sites like Dos Pilas may have contributed many of their residents to the burgeoning center.

Monumental Architecture

Two principles organize Classic architecture: the multiplication of like forms and the continuity of forms from modest structures to pyramids (e.g., Tourtellot 1983a: 520). Groups with doubled or tripled courtyards illustrate the first principle, as in Dos Pilas Groups L5-4, L5-5, O5-3, N5-6, N5-4, and N4-2. The Dos Pilas plaza, in some respects an enormous patio group, exemplifies the second (Site Map 1).[6]

Nevertheless, similar forms may mask differences in function. For example, the "range" structures composing Groups L5-4 and L5-5 doubtless functioned like smaller "range" structures: they were residences, albeit of individuals enjoying exalted rank. But they had other, divergent functions, such as setting the stage for affairs of state and dynastic ritual. The dramatic metaphor is apt. Classic stairways conducted people to the summit and, on occasion, provided highly visible stages for the exhibition, torture, and dismemberment of captives (Miller 1986: 115). Double outset stairways, such as those on Structures L5-35 and L5-25, serve especially well in this regard. They not only incorporate staircases for the display of captives, but supply platforms for attending nobility (cf. Bonampak Room 2, Miller 1986: Plate 2).

The largest structures at Dos Pilas are Structures L5-49 and P5-7, which are associated by their monuments with Ruler 1 and Ruler 2, respectively. More than size distinguishes them: each exhibits a set of lateral terraces, a massive outset stairway framed by solid balustrades, and a set of two dressed panels on its summit. Orientation is to the north. Yet they are also dissimilar in some respects. Structure L5-49 supports three smaller structures, of which the central mound is the tallest. The triadic arrangement recalls slightly the Classic pattern for geneological display, which involves the image of a ruler flanked by his parents (Schele 1978); the discovery in 1990 of mythological texts on the summit recalls patterns in the triadic "Cross Group" at Palenque.[7] In contrast, Structure P5-7 has only one summit mound, and a single continuous room (Hector Escobedo, personal communication, 1990).

Of the two pyramids, Structure L5-49 is the most massive. Yet it cannot compare with the effort that went into constructing the Structure P5-7 complex. The entire hillside below Structure P5-7 has been fashioned into five terraces. Terrace 5 supports a small group of buildings (Structures P5-11, P5-12, and P5-13), two of which (Structures P5-12 and P5-13) are separated by a gap that aligns precisely with the frontal axis of Structure P5-7. One of the most massive stairways in

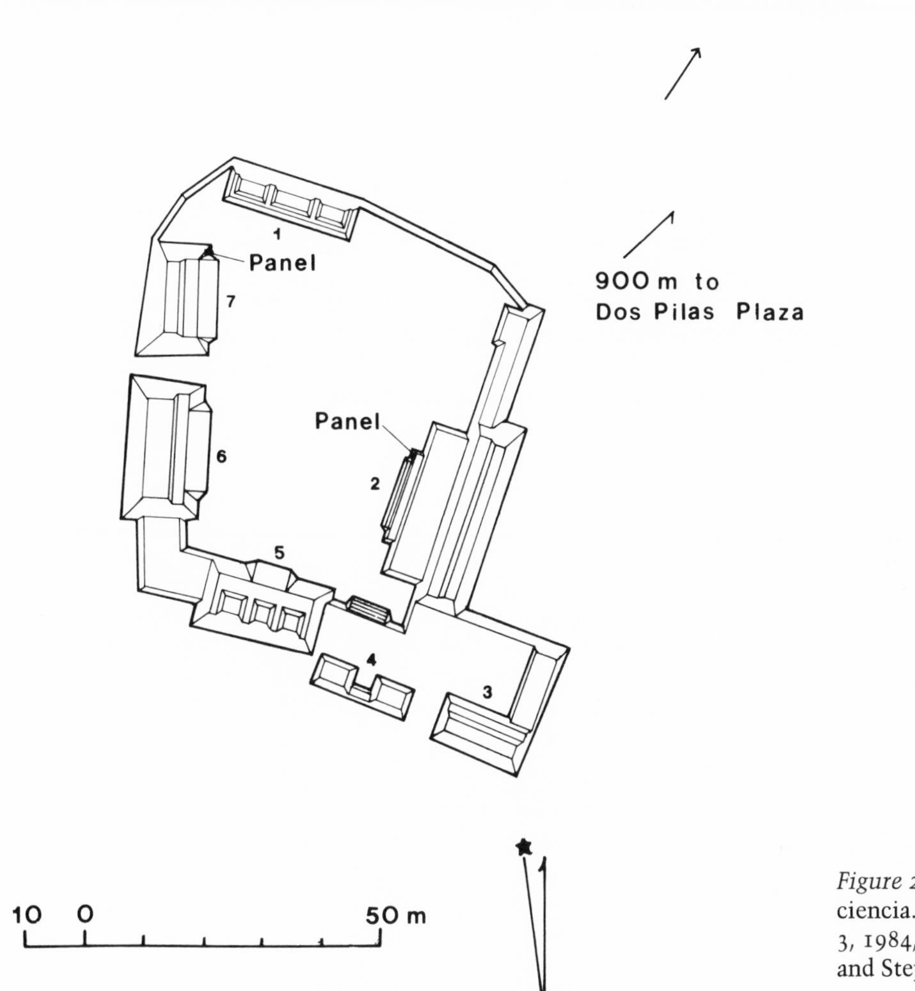

Figure 2-6. Map of La Paciencia. Mapped February 3, 1984, by Boyd Dixon and Stephen Houston.

the Maya area fronts Terrace 4: blocks 2.0 meters long compose the four risers of the stairway. The courses extend 36 meters in length. Structure P5-7 itself rests on a basal platform with front stairway. High, "range-type" structures sit in back, perhaps as functional accessories to Structure P5-7. Nonetheless, the pyramid does not face them.

Another kind of monumental construction deserves mention. In two cases, pyramids of approximately equal size occur next to each other (Structures N5-7 and N5-71 and Structures N5-41 and N5-42). These do not have a consistent orientation, but they do seem to be integral components of large patio groups. The site of La Paciencia, located 900 meters southwest of the Dos Pilas plaza, may contain a similar set of mounds (Structures 6 and 7, Fig. 2-6). The function of these structures is uncertain.

Masonry and Details of Construction

The limestone in buildings at Dos Pilas comes from several quarries, each marked on the plan. A quarry near Structure P5-11 probably provided the monolithic blocks for the Terrace 4 stairway, and more modest quarries supplied Structures L5-38 and M4-8. With the possible exception of Panel 10, which is of extraordinarily dense limestone, all stone monuments at Dos Pilas originated in these quarries, perhaps to be shaped elsewhere, at their final destination (see Haviland 1974).

Stone at Dos Pilas varies greatly in quality. At one extreme, Group K5-2 contains soft and crudely dressed stone perhaps plucked from a field. At the other, Structures L5-49, M4-3, M4-8, and some buildings in Group N5-6 display facing stones dressed with exquisite care. This stone is probably as hard as some facings at Machaquila (I. Graham 1967:55).

Ancient masons at Dos Pilas fashioned facing stones into a number of shapes.[8] Block facings with neat joins (e.g., Structure L5-49) are more common than slab facings (e.g., Structure N5-23), perhaps reflecting differences in date. Of interest here is the three-member molding described above. The form finds its closest parallel at Anonal and in the binder moldings on Bonampak Structure 1, which houses the famed murals (Ruppert, Thompson, and Proskouriakoff 1955:21; Miller 1986:21). More distant parallels occur in the Puuc area of northern Yucatan, where such moldings are common if slightly different in composition; that is, they consist of not one, but three pieces (Kubler 1975:173; Pollock 1980:Figs. 74, 84, 94).[9] It may be that the Dos Pilas molding dates, as does Bonampak Structure 1, to the last forty years of cycle 9 (Miller 1986:38). Links with Puuc chronology are less secure. For one, the molding enjoys long use in the Puuc. For another, northern parallels are in fact of a superficial sort. Pasión masonry is more solid than that of the Puuc, which has weaker bonding between fill and facing.

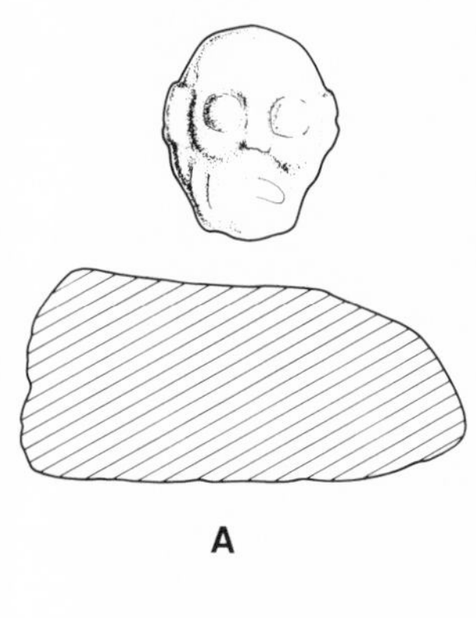

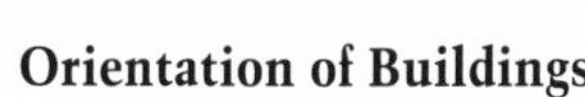

Figure 2-7. Tenoned sculpture from Structure L5-49: Miscellaneous Stones 5(*a*) and 6(*b*). Heights: MS 5, .38 m; MS 6, .22 m.

On occasion facing stones include sculptures, such as the tenoned heads on Structure L5-49 (Fig. 2-7) or the panels flanking doubled outset stairways.[10] Less is known of the internal composition of structures. A looter's trench in Structure O5-10 reveals a heavy rubble core surmounted by packed earth, small pebbles, and buried plaster floor; Vanderbilt investigations show that this structure may be unusual, in that many buildings contain poorly consolidated fill. Elsewhere at Dos Pilas, bedrock forms part of the monolithic staircase in front of Structure P5-7 and probably some of the core of Groups L5-4 and L5-5 (see Tourtellot 1983a:510).

Orientation of Buildings

Architecture throughout Mesoamerica (Aveni 1977:3) shows a consistent orientation east of astronomical north, which is in turn reflected in perpendicular axes. Dos Pilas is no exception. However, unlike structures at Teotihuacan, oriented approximately 15° east of north (Millon 1973:29), and rather more like construction at Tikal (Carr and Hazard 1961:7), mounds at Dos Pilas generally align with

Table 2-4. ***Mound orientation***

Grid	*N*	*NE*	*E*	*SE*	*S*	*SW*	*W*	*NW*
K4	3	3	5	3	3	4	2	3
K5	2		3					
L4	4	1	8	3	5	5	4	2
L5	9	3	5		4		6	
M4	3		3	2	4		6	
M5	14	1	17	1	21		9	
N4	2	2	3		7	1	4	1
N5	15	1	16	1	8		15	
O4	3	1	5	2	6	1	5	4
O5	1		6		7		5	
P4	3		4		5	1	2	
P5	2		2		3		2	1
Total	61	12	77	12	73	12	60	11

the present-day magnetic cardinals, which, of course, have shifted since the structures were built (Table 2-4).[11] Major exceptions include the main plaza, which deviates more than 10° east of actual magnetic north. A slight plurality of mounds at Dos Pilas face east; fewer face south, fewer still north and west.

Late Remains

Late remains at Dos Pilas fall into three groups: (1) reset monuments, (2) walls, and (3) possible "squatter" mounds.[12] Reset monuments occur at all periods of the Classic (Satterthwaite 1958; J. Graham 1989). When the reset monuments are late, the resetting probably took place during the final years of the Late Classic period, or during the Terminal Classic or Postclassic periods, with the latter a less likely possibility in the Pasión drainage because of thin Postclassic occupation (Sabloff 1975:17). Three monuments appear to be reset at Dos Pilas. Hieroglyphic Stairways 2 and 3 show signs of disturbance (Figs. 3-7, 3-8, 3-10). Hieroglyphic Stairway 2 displays an orderly arrangement, but some parts of the inscription are missing, replaced in antiquity by blank blocks. The hieroglyphic stairway of Seibal Structure A-14 went through similar rearrangements (John Graham, personal communication, 1982). Hieroglyphic Stairway 3 apparently lacks a riser, fragments of which may be found in front (Fig. 2-8; Navarrete and Luján 1963:11). The other monument is Stela 10, evidently missing its butt (Houston and Mathews 1985:27). A final stone comes not from a monument, but from the monolithic stairway on Terrace 2. For inexplicable reasons the ancient Maya maneuvered the massive block up a steep rise to Structure P4-22.

Dos Pilas is not alone among Pasión drainage sites in having reset monuments. Arroyo de Piedra Stela 6 is split into lower and upper halves. The lower piece is wedged between the plain Stela 3 and its altar, and the upper fragment forms part of a small masonry structure

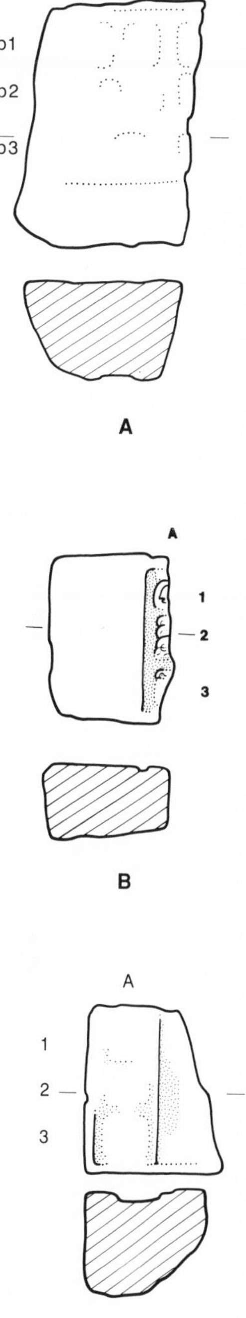

Figure 2-8. Fragments of Hieroglyhic Stairway 3: Miscellaneous Stones 8 (*a*), 9 (*b*), and 10 (*c*). Heights: MS 8, .55 m; MS 9, .37 m; MS 10, .38 m

in the center of the Arroyo de Piedra plaza. This structure served as the foundation for the Late Classic Stela 2, which postdates Stela 6 by approximately one hundred years. Tamarindito has more extensive evidence of resetting. One fragment, illustrated in Figure 2-9, is now a building block, and considerably reduced in size from its original dimensions (cf. J. Graham 1972: Fig. 60). Another monument, the Early Classic Stela 5 (Fig. 3-5), was broken in antiquity, with the middle part later reset into a platform in front of Tamarindito Structure 1.

Another feature on the Dos Pilas plan is an arrangement of concentric walls that circle both the main plaza and Structure P5-7. The walls are of unremarkable size and construction; in only a few places do they exceed a meter in height or width. The stone in the walls is occasionally robbed from structures nearby, such as Structure L5-1 or L5-33, but in most cases resembles fieldstone, or perhaps fill material. Both sets of wall enclose modest areas. The concentric walls around the plaza define slightly more than 4 hectares, those around Structure P5-7 somewhat less, about 3.5 hectares. Most likely, a small work force built these features, or perhaps a large group working for a short time.

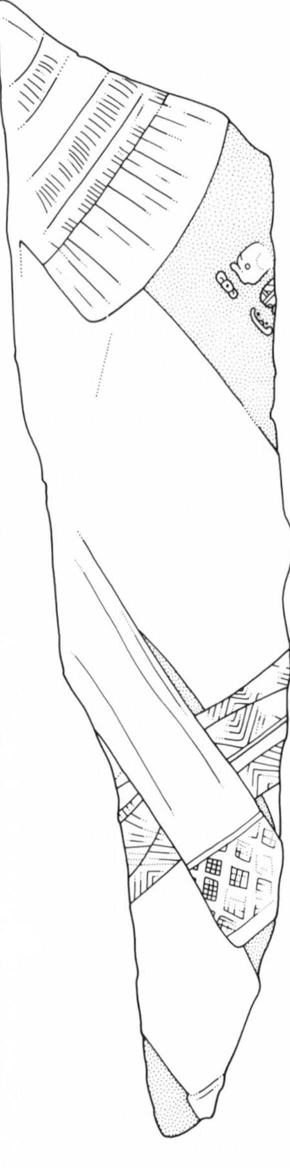

Figure 2-9. Fragment of panel from Tamarindito, recovered from Structure 36. Length: .98 m.

The plans of the walls are similar. Those near the plaza are concentric, with no more than 30 meters between inner and outer walls (Site Map 1). This equals the distance between the outer and second walls around Structure P5-7 and its ancillary buildings, the difference being that a third, inner wall forms a parapet around the platform under Structure P5-7 (Site Map 3). Both sets of walls describe a rectangular rather than a circular ambit, probably to accord with the rectangular plans of the buildings they enclose.

A few entrances pierce the walls. One occurs between Structures L4-17 and L4-25, along with a possible portal, now collapsed. Another entrance lies behind Structure P5-7 and passes through the inner wall. To one side lie connected structures that open within. Some 35 meters to the south (unfortunately off the plan) appears another entrance aligned with the first. As shown by excavations conducted by Hector Escobedo, it features a baffled entrance.

Smaller walls also exist at Dos Pilas. Some connect inner and outer walls (near Structure L5-2), and others connect buildings (Structures L5-12 and L5-25, those behind Structures M5-75 and M5-78). A few attach themselves to one structure only, as do those behind Structure L5-49.

Although the precise date of the Dos Pilas walls is uncertain, their placement demonstrates a late date, probably at the end of the Late Classic period. Some of the walls join structures of probable Late Classic date (e.g., Structures L4-39 and L4-40), but their masonry differs tangibly in quality, suggesting a different epoch of construction. Better evidence for a late date is the manner in which walls pass over important structures, such as those composing Groups L5-4 and L5-5. At the same time they employ stone robbed from these buildings and disrupt spaces presumably important to the Late Classic occupants of Dos Pilas. The bisection of Group L5-3 represents a good example of this disruption.

The walls of Dos Pilas probably served many needs, both in delimiting space (Webster 1980:835) and in regulating movement to and from the area thus defined. More speculatively, the walls may have operated as defensive bulwarks. At no time did the walls exceed the height of a man, but they possibly supported stakes of a sort described for Late Postclassic sites (I. Graham 1967:5) and of a kind likely to intimidate small raiding parties. The walls often make providential use of high ground (e.g., the parapet wall around Structure P5-7); in other places, particularly in Groups L5-4 and L5-5, wall placement seems irrational from the viewpoint of defense.

Small foundations in the Dos Pilas plaza represent the last class of late remains. All are fairly small (less than 10 square meters in area), although orientation varies. Those closest to Structure L4-35 align with larger plaza constructions, a pattern less evident in foundations to the other side of the plaza (Site Map 1). One structure, Structure L5-50, shows signs of internal partition, rather like perishable structures at Mayapan (A. L. Smith 1962:Fig. 10). Presumably, the foundations at Dos Pilas supported houses, which, to judge from their location, postdate the full use of the plaza as a focus for the Dos Pilas dynasty. Excavations of similar foundations at Tikal lend weight to this view (Juan Pedro Laporte, personal communication, 1984), as do large-scale exposures by Joel Palka of Vanderbilt University, who has dated the foundations to the final years of the Late Classic period.

Comparisons of Dos Pilas to Other Pasión Sites

Most sites near Dos Pilas lie on high ground, with Arroyo de Piedra and Aguateca being perhaps the best drained (Figs. 2-10 and 2-11). The lowest site is Punta de Chimino, a group of large mounds only a few meters above Lake Petexbatun. As at Dos Pilas, water supply is generally not a problem. All lie near bodies of water: Aguateca near a lake (during the rainy season) and spring (during the dry); El Caribe some 500 meters from a large perennial spring; La Amelia near a stream. Water sources are less close to El Excavado (Fig. 2-12, just less than 1 kilometer to the south), Tamarindito (Fig. 2-13, 1 kilometer to the northeast), and Arroyo de Piedra. The eponymous *arroyo de piedra*, or "stone gully," in fact courses close to an hour's walk from the site. It is far closer to a complex of walls and destroyed mounds termed "Santo Tomás" (Fig. 2-14), lying 280 meters southeast of the stream.

Few doubt that Seibal is the largest site in the Pasión drainage.[13] Moreover, it has received more thorough investigation than other ruins. Hence its record is better and the disparities with neighbors more evident. There is another problem in comparing Seibal with Dos Pilas and its neighbors: estimates of Seibal's area seem extraordinarily high (Mathews and Willey 1991:Fig. 5), perhaps because of confusions between site core and hinterland. For these reasons—one practical, the other analytic—the following remarks on size, density, and site composition in the lower Pasión drainage lean to the impressionistic. They make no pretensions to discussing changes through time, the study of which depends on extensive excavation.

Seibal, Dos Pilas, and Altar de Sacrificios are not the only large sites in the lower Pasión drainage. Itzan and Tamarindito occupy a

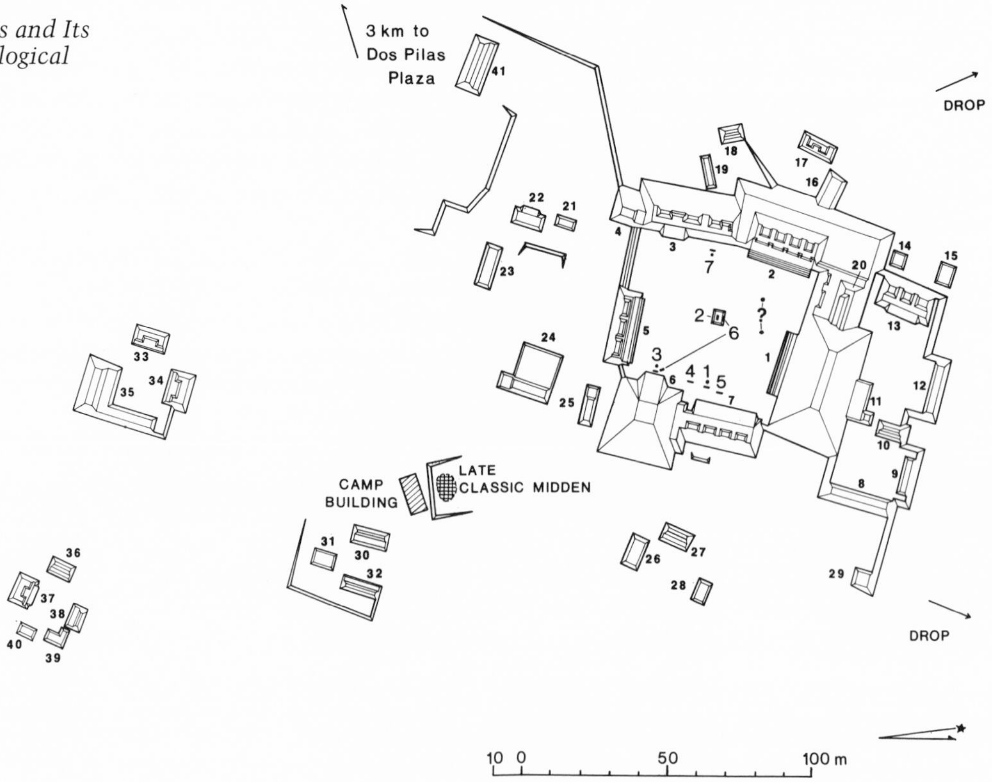

Figure 2-10. Map of Arroyo de Piedra. Mapped in February 1984 by Boyd Dixon and Stephen Houston.

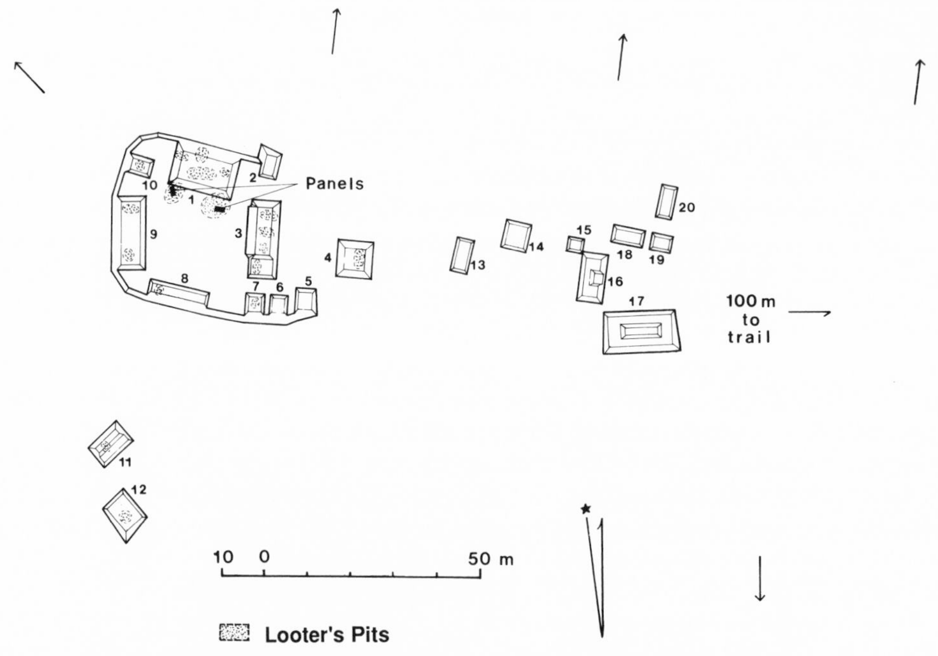

Figure 2-12. Map of El Excavado. Mapped April 18, 1984, by Stephen Houston and Leopoldo Moro.

Figure 2-11. Map of Aguateca. Mapped in February–March 1984 by Boyd Dixon and Stephen Houston.

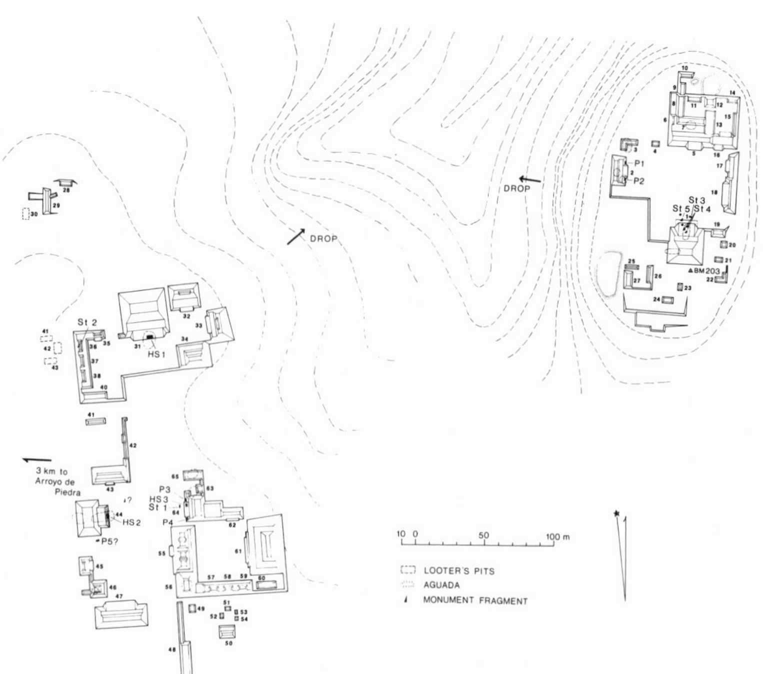

Figure 2-13. Map of Tamarindito. Mapped February 1984 by Boyd Dixon, Stephen Houston, and Alejandro Córdoba.

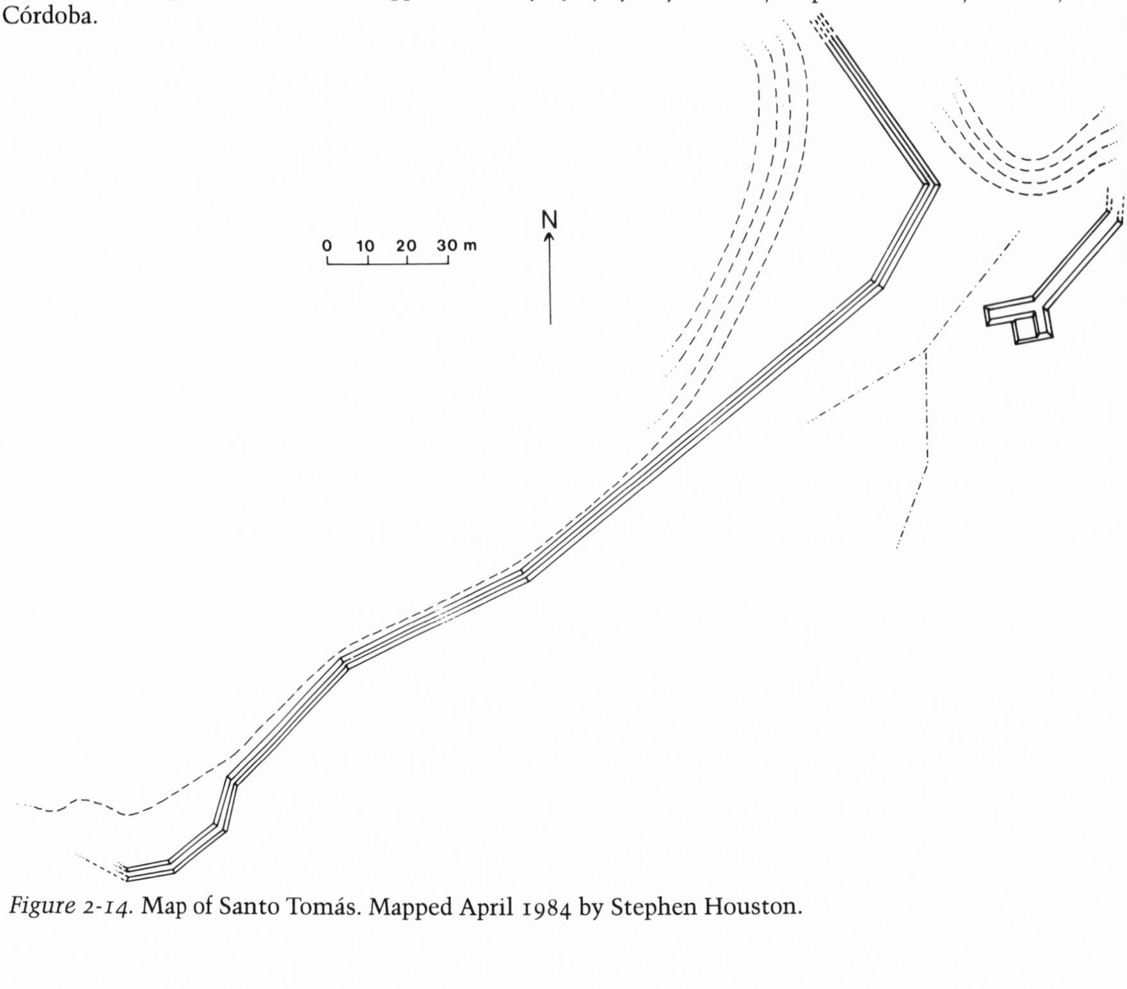

Figure 2-14. Map of Santo Tomás. Mapped April 1984 by Stephen Houston.

minimum of 15 hectares each, excluding outliers.[14] Aguateca is far larger, with a minimum area of 71 hectares, again with substantial outliers to the west.[15] Smaller sites include Arroyo de Piedra, with 7 hectares, La Paciencia with close to 3 hectares, and El Excavado with 2 hectares.[16] Minimum structure counts for these sites are: Aguateca, 157; Punta de Chimino, 82; Tamarindito, 65; Arroyo de Piedra, 60; Itzan, 36; El Excavado, 20; and La Paciencia, 13.[17] The actual figures for these sites, particularly Tamarindito and Aguateca, are probably much higher. However, Aguateca does seem to differ in settlement density. It stands out in the number of house mounds and patio groups close to the plaza, beyond which density diminishes rapidly.

The density of Aguateca settlement relates to other features. For one, Aguateca is alone among the Pasión sites in possessing a *vía*, an avenue delineated by architecture rather than walls or parapets. Similar features mark Yaxha (Hellmuth 1972) and two sites in Quintana Roo, Chichmuul and Chacchoben (Harrison 1981:281). All appear to be of Late Classic date. The dense construction along the Aguateca *vía* flanks a processional way leading to what was a probable palace. The remarkable surface visibility at the site (cf. Dos Pilas and Seibal) reveals tandem chambers with benches and multiple entrances.

But what most marks Aguateca is its elaborate system of walls and unusually defensible position. Aguateca's walls resemble those at Dos Pilas in their poorly dressed stone. They differ, however, in their greater length, with an aggregate extension of over 3.78 kilometers. Also, their arrangement is less mechanically concentric. They do not describe full circles, but rather loop from the escarpment edge to the fissure running through the site.[18] More subtly, the walls accommodate established architecture to a greater degree at Aquateca than at Dos Pilas. This is most apparent around the plaza, although some walls clearly obstruct the *vía*. Relatively little time may separate walls and monumental construction at Aguateca.

The arrangement of the Aguateca walls merits further comment (see Fig. 2-11). Virtually all mounds lie within the eastern perimeter wall, which then ends abruptly in flat terrain. The inner walls, however, contain all monumental construction. They terminate only upon reaching the fissure. The walls are more complex to the south of the plaza. There, the slope is gentle, but for depressions near the walled entrance to the fissure. Two other walls appear to the southeast, beneath the escarpment cliff. They meet near Aguateca's perennial water source, possibly for reasons related to defense. Another set of walls traverses the mesa north of the "palace" (Structures 132 and 133), posing an obstacle to ready access from the north.[19]

Again, walls may serve several functions, but at Aguateca they were most likely defensive. As at Dos Pilas and Santo Tomás, the walls bear little similarity to *sacbeob*, or Maya roads: they are high, narrow, and concentric, to say nothing of the fact that they often lead to precipices. In addition, they are little like the boundary walls at some northern Maya sites (Bullard 1952; Vlcek, Garza, and Kurjack 1978:Fig. 11.4; Folan, Kintz, and Fletcher 1983; Freidel and Sabloff 1984:87). What they do resemble, in arrangement if not in bulk, are the walls circumscribing several Maya sites (Andrews and Andrews 1975:12;

Armillas 1951; Baudez and Becquelin 1973; Garza and Kurjack 1980: 1:65–66; Harrison 1981:284; Matheny 1970:5; Pollock and Strömsvik 1953: Fig. 1; Puleston and Callender 1967; Rice and Rice 1981; Sáenz 1972; Sanders 1960:175, 263; Shook 1952; Strömsvik and Longyear 1946; Webster 1976; 1978; 1979; 1980).

The best parallels are with walls in northern Yucatan. At Cuca (Kurjack and Andrews 1976:319; Webster 1980:838) and Mayapan (M. Jones 1952), walls enclose substantial areas, but in similar arrangement to Dos Pilas: two concentric walls circling monumental buildings. Moreover, the Yucatec walls do not heed prior construction. The walls at Cuca ignore preexisting settlement, and, again like Dos Pilas, consist of slipshod masonry. Walls at Ake and Chunchucmil similarly appear over existing community plans. A final parallel comes from Mayapan, where walls occasionally cross hillslopes without regard to contours (Shook 1952:9). Such can be seen on Dos Pilas Groups L5-4 and L5-5. It is almost as if walls occasionally conformed more to an inflexible template than to practical necessity.

CONCLUSIONS

In conclusion, Dos Pilas is very much a Pasión site. Relatively little can be traced directly to Tikal and the northeastern Peten, where the Dos Pilas dynasty may well have originated (Chapter 4). C-shaped structures, which are common at Dos Pilas and Seibal, exemplify this: Late Classic in the Pasión, elsewhere they date to the Postclassic (Tourtellot 1983a:623; cf. J. Johnson 1985: Figs. 1 and 4). If parallels are to be found they are rather with Yucatan, although most likely at a late date.

Inscriptions show that the Late Classic rulers of Dos Pilas were deeply preoccupied with warfare (Chapter 4; Houston and Mathews 1985). Nonetheless, the only probable defensive features at the site postdate the zenith of the local dynasty. This fact supports reevaluations of the conduct and aims of Late Classic warfare, which some believe to have been a ritually restricted enterprise (Demarest 1978; Freidel 1986a).

Many of the results in this chapter come from surficial reconnaissance. As a result of preliminary work by the Vanderbilt University Petexbatun Project (Arthur Demarest, Director), rather more can now be said about the chronology of Dos Pilas. Late material has been found in the Dos Pilas plaza near a "squatters'" settlement, but the majority of the site appears firmly to be Late Classic in date, with only a handful of Early Classic sherds and a somewhat larger quantity of Preclassic material coming from caves under Dos Pilas (James Brady, personal communication, 1990; Antonia Foias, personal communication, 1990). On the whole, the correspondence to epigraphy, which attests to a limited range of dates, is remarkably close. The community of Dos Pilas seems to have flourished quickly, and then disintegrated into a smaller, ephemeral village, which must have contrasted starkly with the ruined pyramids and stripped facades of structures built only a short time before. Future excavations by Vanderbilt will show more precisely what happened to Dos Pilas and when.

Appendix 2-1. Structure Numeration, Comments, and Concordance

Structure	Type	Elevation	Patio Groups	Orientation	Comments	Navarrete and Luján Muñoz 1963	Houston and Mathews 1985
Figure 2-4: Grid K4							
K4-1	E		1	SW			
K4-2	F	145.42	1	NW			
K4-3	E	145.22	1	NW			
K4-4	G[3]		1	SE			
K4-5	D/F		1	NE			
K4-6	E/G	145.51	1	E			
K4-7	D		1				
K4-8	E		1				
K4-9	E		2	S			
K4-10	E		2				
K4-11	E		2				
K4-12	E	146.22					
K4-13	E						
K4-14	E						
K4-15	E						
K4-16	E		3	SW			
K4-17	E		3	SE			
K4-18	D		3	NE			
K4-19	F	146.76	4	S			
K4-20	E	147.24	4	W			
K4-21	G		4	E			
K4-22	E		4	N			

Note: The numbers in the Patio Group column represent the final number of a Patio Group designation; i.e., Structure K4-1 forms part of Patio Group K4-1. If most of the Patio Group lies in another grid and hence carries a different grid reference, a more complete description appears in this column; i.e., Structure K5-1 occurs within Patio Group L5-7.

Appendix 2.1 (*continued*)

Structure	*Type*	*Elevation*	*Patio Groups*	*Orientation*	*Comments*	*Navarrete and Luján Muñoz 1963*	*Houston and Mathews 1985*
K4-23	E		5	SW			
K4-24	E		5	SW			
K4-25	E	147.48	5				
K4-26	E/F	147.72	5	N			
K4-27	F	147.63	5	E			
K4-28	F	146.71	6	NW			
K4-29	E/F	146.72	6	NE			
K4-30	F		6	SE			
K4-31	E		6	S			
K4-32	E[s]	146.09	7	W			
K4-33	E	145.45	7	N			
K4-34	G	145.91	7	E			
K4-35	E	145.54					
K4-36	E			E			
K4-37	E		7?				
K4-38	E						
K4-39	E	145.27					
K4-40	E						
K4-41	E						
K4-42	E						

Figure 2-4: Grid K5

Structure	*Type*	*Elevation*	*Patio Groups*	*Orientation*	*Comments*	*Navarrete and Luján Muñoz 1963*	*Houston and Mathews 1985*
K5-1	E	149.67	L5-7	E			
K5-2	E	150.7					
K5-3	C		1				
K5-4	J	153.35	1	E			
K5-5	E	152.76	1	N			
K5-6	E						

K5-7	E		2	N		
K5-8	G	147.03	2	E		
K5-9	E	146.96	2			

Figure 2-4: Grid L4

L4-1	E	145.6				
L4-2	E					
L4-3	A	145.64				
L4-4	F?	147.08	1			
L4-5	G		1	S		
L4-6	E	146.00	1	SW		
L4-7	C		1			
L4-8	C		1			
L4-9	E	146.17	1	W	Hearth?	
L4-10	A					
L4-11	H	147.39	2	S		
L4-12	H	148.39	2			
L4-13	E	147.74	2	E		41
L4-14	C	147.9	2		Destroyed	
L4-15	E	148.71	2	N?		40
L4-16	?			W	Ballcourt	6
L4-17	?	155.74		E	Ballcourt	5
L4-18	E				Destroyed	
L4-19	C	149.37				
L4-20	E	149.54				
L4-21	E					
L4-22	C	149.18			Foundation	
L4-23	E	149.54			Foundation	
L4-24	E	149.23			Foundation	
L4-25	E[s]	151.39		SE		7
L4-26	C	149.16			Foundation	
L4-27	C	149.26			Foundation	
L4-28	C	145.26	7	S		
L4-29	C	149.31			Foundation	
L4-30	C	149.25			Foundation	
L4-31	C	148.20			Foundation	
L4-32	E[3]	150.36			Destroyed	
L4-33	E	149.15			Foundation	

Appendix 2.1 (*continued*)

Structure	*Type*	*Elevation*	*Patio Groups*	*Orientation*	*Comments*	*Navarrete and Luján Muñoz 1963*	*Houston and Mathews 1985*
L4-34	E	149.18			Foundation		
L4-35	J[ss]	153.75		SE		1	1
L4-36	E						
L4-37	C	K4-3					
L4-38	F			E			
L4-39	E?	148.26	4	NE			14
L4-40	F	148	4	NW			13
L4-41	K	148.5	4	E	HB. 1		15
L4-42	E		4	SW			
L4-43	D	148.74	4	SW			12
L4-44	E	146.77	4		Destroyed		16
L4-45	E			S			
L4-46	C						
L4-47	G	147.01		SW			11
L4-48	E		3				
L4-49	E		3	W			
L4-50	E[s]	147.75	3	W			
L4-51	E		3				
L4-52	E	147.87	3	E			
L4-53	E	147.59	5	N			10
L4-54	E	147.06	5	S			8
L4-55	F	147.08	5	E			9
L4-56	D				Destroyed		
L4-57	A	145.88					
L4-58	F		K4-2	NW			
L4-59	E				Destroyed		
L4-60	E	145.7					
L4-61	E	146.1	6	E			
L4-62	E	145.9	6	N?			
L4-63	E		6	SW			
L4-64	E	145.81	6	SE			

L4-66	C				Destroyed		
L4-67	E				Destroyed		
L4-68	E	145.53	7	N	Destroyed		
L4-69	E	145.33	7	E			

Figure 2-4: Grid L5

L5-1	M^{s}	159.57		W			4
L5-2	F^{s}	153.67		N			3
L5-3	?			N			
L5-4	E	152.05		E			
L5-5	C						
L5-6	F	152.72		W			
L5-7	C				Destroyed		36
L5-8	E		3	W			
L5-9	E		3	W			
L5-10	H	154.37					
L5-11	E?	154.47					
L5-12	E	154.45		N			
L5-13	D	154.48		W?			
L5-14	E						
L5-15	E	153.49					
L5-16	E	154.66	1	E			
L5-17	G	155.18	1	N			
L5-18	E						
L5-19	E	154.62					
L5-20	E						
L5-21	E						
L5-22	F/H^{s}		2	N			33
L5-23	G^{s}	153.14	2	NE			32
L5-24	E		2	E			31
L5-25	M^{ss}	160.10	3	NE	HS. 3	3	30
L5-26	D						
L5-27	E	151.39					
L5-28	A	150.65					
L5-29	A						
L5-30	E	153.17					
L5-31	F^{s}	158.09	4	S			26
L5-32	E	157.8	4				27
L5-33	K^{ss}	158.14	3	E			29

Appendix 2.1 (*continued*)

Structure	*Type*	*Elevation*	*Patio Groups*	*Orientation*	*Comments*	*Navarrete and Luján Muñoz 1963*	*Houston and Mathews 1985*
L5-34	F^{ss}	158.59	4	N			28
L5-35	F^{ss}	160.20	4	E			25
L5-36	C						24
L5-37	E	156.90	5	S			22
L5-38	E	155.17	5	N			23
L5-39	H^{ss}	155.39	5	E			21
L5-40	E	151.7					
L5-41	H	151.27		N			17
L5-42	E	151.04	6				18
L5-43	C	154.77		W			
L5-44	A			S			
L5-45	A	150.23	7	N			
L5-46	E	149.75	7	S			
L5-47	E	149.11					
L5-48	C						
L5-49	M^{ss}	167.22		NE	Summit structure	2	2
L5-50	E?	149.68			Foundation		
L5-51	C?	149.57			Foundation		
L5-52	C?	149.45			Foundation		
L5-53	C	149.24			Foundation		
L5-54	E	149.26			Foundation		
Figure 2-5: Grid M4							
M4-1	E^{s}			SE			
M4-2	G	150.06	1	S			
M4-3	F/G^{ss}	151.56	1	W			
M4-4	G^{3}	150.91	1	N			
M4-5	E		1	E			

M4-6	E?	149.23	2	S		
M4-7	F[s]	150.3	2	W		
M4-8	F/G	151.59	3	S		63
M4-9	E	150.19	3			
M4-10	D		3			
M4-11	E		3		Destroyed	
M4-12	D	150.6	3	N	Destroyed	
M4-13	G	150.02	3	E		60
M4-14	G/H	150.42	4	S		57
M4-15	A	149.6	4	W		
M4-16	E		4	N		59
M4-17	E	149.81	4	E	Destroyed	58
M4-18	F	147.25	5	SE		
M4-19	F	147.13	5	NW		
M4-20	E				Destroyed	

Figure 2-5: Grid M5

M5-1	E		1	S	Destroyed
M5-2	G	153.27	1	W	
M5-3	D/E	153.85	1	E	
M5-4	E	153.39	2		
M5-5	C	153.28	2	S	
M5-6	E	153.96	2	W	
M5-7	G	154.18	2	N	
M5-8	E	153.95	2	E	
M5-9	E	154.21			
M5-10	E/M	158.39	3	S	
M5-11	E/G	157.52	3	E	
M5-12	E	156.37	3	S	
M5-13	E	156.86	3	W	
M5-14	C		5	S	
M5-15	E		5	W	
M5-16	G[2]	158.93	5	N	
M5-17	E		5		
M5-18	G	158.99	5	N	
M5-19	E	158.93	5	E	
M5-20	F	156.45	8	S	

Appendix 2.1 (*continued*)

Structure	*Type*	*Elevation*	*Patio Groups*	*Orientation*	*Comments*	*Navarrete and Luján Muñoz 1963*	*Houston and Mathews 1985*
M5-21	J	156.76	8	E			
M5-22	E		6				
M5-23	G[3]	156.84	6	S			
M5-24	F	157.86	6	N?			
M5-25	F		6	E			
M5-26	E	156.89	7	S			
M5-27	F		7	N			
M5-28	G/H	157.99	7	N			
M5-29	F	157.13	7	SE			
M5-30	D		7	E			
M5-31	D		7	NE			
M5-32	E						
M5-33	E		9				
M5-34	E	155.08	9				
M5-35	F	155.24	9	N			
M5-36	E	154.86	9	E			
M5-37	E				Destroyed		
M5-38	E	154.33		E			
M5-39	G	153.92	10	S			
M5-40	F	154.63	10	W			
M5-41	C	153.48	10	N			
M5-42	G	154.32	10	E			
M5-43	C						
M5-44	C						
M5-45	E						
M5-46	E						
M5-47	E	154.51	12				
M5-48	E						
M5-49	E	153.23	11				
M5-50	C						
M5-51	C			S			

M5-52	E			S		
M5-53	H^s	153.47	11			
M5-54	?	154.96				
M5-55	E	154.76	12	S		
M5-56	I	154.53	12	E		
M5-57	E	154.36	12	S		
M5-58	?	154.7		W		
M5-59	F		13	E		
M5-60	G^s	155.35	13	E		
M5-61	C		13			
M5-62	E	153.97	13	N		
M5-63	E/G	154.83	13	S		
M5-64	E	156.55	4	S		
M5-65	C		4			
M5-66	G	157.18	4	N		
M5-67	G	156.94	4	E		
M5-68	F	156.97		S		
M5-69	C	157.18				
M5-70	F	157.45		N		
M5-71	C/E	153.45		S		
M5-72	E			W		
M5-73	E	154.57	14	S		
M5-74	E	153.5		E		
M5-75	?	155.17	14	N		
M5-76	F^s	153.38	15	S		72
M5-77	E		15			71
M5-78	?	154.33	15	N		73
M5-79	C					
M5-80	C					
M5-81	G	154	16	S		
M5-82	C	153.87	16	W		
M5-83	H	153.94	16	N		
M5-84	G	154.37	16	E		
M5-85	F	153.17	17	S		
M5-86	G/H	154.13	17	E		
M5-87	E		17			
M5-88	E	157.15				
M5-89	J^3	153.17	11	W		
M5-90	E				Destroyed	
M5-91	C	156.11	4			
M5-92	C					

Appendix 2.1 (*continued*)

Structure	*Type*	*Elevation*	*Patio Groups*	*Orientation*	*Comments*	*Navarrete and Luján Muñoz 1963*	*Houston and Mathews 1985*
Figure 2-5: Grid N4							
N4-1	E	161.06	1	S			
N4-2	F	161.36	1	E			
N4-3	E	161.58	1	NE			
N4-4	I?	164.42		S			
N4-5	E	163.7		S			
N4-6	H	166.27	2	W			
N4-7	F[s]	167.35	2	S			
N4-8	G	163.12	2	W			
N4-9	E	156.02					
N4-10	E		3	S			
N4-11	F	161.7	3	N			
N4-12	G	160.99	3	W			
N4-13	E		N5-12	SW			
N4-14	F/G	157.26	N5-11	S			
N4-15	E	155.18					
N4-16	E[s]	156.25	4	S			
N4-17	E	156.48	4	W			
N4-18	I?	156.84	4	N			
N4-19	F?	156.23	4	E			
N4-20	F	155.99	4	E			
N4-21	I?		5	NW			
N4-22	A	155.48					
N4-23	C		5				
N4-24	E	147.98	5	NE			
N4-25	D	147.16					
N4-26	D		6				
N4-27	?		6				
N4-28	D		6				
N4-29	D		6				
N4-30	E		3				

Figure 2-5: Grid N5

N5-1	F/G	167.21	1	W	
N5-2	E/F	164.76		N	
N5-3	H	166.77	1	N	
N5-4	K?	167.13	1	N	
N5-5	E	161.14	2	E	
N5-6	E	161.17	2	N	
N5-7	M	171.43	1	E?	
N5-8	E	160.69	3	S	
N5-9	G	160.24	3	E	
N5-10	E				
N5-11	G	160.42		W	
N5-12	E	160.92	4	E	
N5-13	E	161.23	4	N	
N5-14	E				
N5-15	E				Destroyed
N5-16	E				
N5-17	G^2	159.11		NE	
N5-18	G^s	161.89	6	S	
N5-19	G	163.56	6	S	
N5-20	F	162.85	6	E	
N5-21	K^{ss}	164.18	6	W	MS. 1
N5-22	F/G	161.59	6	N	
N5-23	G	161.61	6	E	Standing masonry
N5-24	C	161.98	6		
N5-25	G	162.34	5	E	
N5-26	G	163.69	5	N	
N5-27	H	159.44	7	E	
N5-28	I	159.83	7	N	
N5-29	E	158.92	8	S	
N5-30	E		8	S	
N5-31	H	159.1	8	W	
N5-32	E/G	159.51	8	N	
N5-33	F	153.31	9	S	Connecting walls
N5-34	F	159.52	9	W	
N5-35	G	159.14	9	N	

Appendix 2.1 (*continued*)

Structure	*Type*	*Elevation*	*Patio Groups*	*Orientation*	*Comments*	*Navarrete and Luján Muñoz 1963*	*Houston and Mathews 1985*
N5-36	E	158.18	9	E			
N5-37	E	158.0					
N5-38	E	157.96			Looted		
N5-39	E/G	156.62		N	Hearth?		
N5-40	C						
N5-41	F^s	161.03	10	W			
N5-42	E^s	161.25	10	W			
N5-43	G^3	157.09	10	N			
N5-44	E	156.03	15	S			
N5-45	E	155.93	15	W			
N5-46	C		10				
N5-47	G^2?		10				
N5-48	K?	159.36	10	W			
N5-49	C		10				
N5-50	E	158.73	10	N			
N5-51	I		10				
N5-52	G^2	157.08	10	E			
N5-53	E/H	155.32	10	E			
N5-54	G	156.97	10				
N5-55	E	154.76	10	E			
N5-56	K	156.85	10	SE			
N5-57	E						
N5-58	E						
N5-59	H	157.43	11	E			
N5-60	E		11	W			
N5-61	E	158.80	11	W			
N5-62	E/?	156.42	12	E			
N5-63	E		12	W			
N5-64	E	153.35	12	W			
N5-65	E	153.51	12	W			
N5-66	E	154.46					

N5-67	G	158.71	13	E	
N5-68	E/G	159.1	13	S	
N5-69	E		13	N	
N5-70	E	161.10	14	E	
N5-71	M[s]	170.30	1	W?	
N5-72	F	162.57	14	N?	

Figure 2-6: Grid O4

O4-1	E	162.11	6	S	
O4-2	D	161.79	6		
O4-3	G	161.94	6	W	
O4-4	E	162.40	6	E	
O4-5	D	161.22	6	E	
O4-6	E				
O4-7	E				
O4-8	E	163.21			
O4-9	E	163.99			
O4-10	H	165.12		S	
O4-11	F	165.91			
O4-12	F	165.45		S	
O4-13	F	167.77		N	
O4-14	E	164.88			
O4-15	F	165.23		NW	
O4-16	E	164.3			Looted
O4-17	J	163.94		NW	
O4-18	E			NW	
O4-19	E		5	SW	
O4-20	F/H		5	SE	
O4-21	J	166.03	5	NE	
O4-22	E		7		
O4-23	E		7		
O4-24	C		7		Destroyed
O4-25	C		7		Destroyed
O4-26	H	162.8	N4-1	NW	
O4-27	E	162.05	N4-1	W	
O4-28	D	162.88	4	SE	
O4-29	H[s]	164.36	4		
O4-30	E	162.63	4		

Appendix 2.1 (*continued*)

Structure	*Type*	*Elevation*	*Patio Groups*	*Orientation*	*Comments*	*Navarrete and Luján Muñoz 1963*	*Houston and Mathews 1985*
O4-31	G/H	163.88	4	S			
O4-32	F/G	163.62	1	S			
O4-33	F/G	164.15	1	N			
O4-34	E	162.62	1	W			
O4-35	H	165.32	2	E			
O4-36	F	165.49	2	W			
O4-37	E	165.23	2				
O4-38	F	164.81	3	E			
O4-39	E	163.37	3	S			
O4-40	E	163.64	3	W			
O4-41	E	163.62	3	N			
O4-42	E	163.91	3	E			
Figure 2-6: Grid O5							
O5-1	F	174.11	2	S			
O5-2	G?	177.4	2				148
O5-3	G		2	E			
O5-4	C		2				
O5-5	H	177.99		E			
O5-6	I	176.23		S			
O5-7	G[3]?	176.01	3	W			159
O5-8	G	176.94	4	W			154
O5-9	E	177.76	3				155
O5-10	E	177.56	3		Looted		
O5-11	E[2]	175.41	4		Looted		
O5-12	G?	176.41	3	E	Near cave		
O5-13	H	175.05	3	E			
O5-14	G	174.34	5	N			
O5-15	E		5				

O5-16	C	171.66			
O5-17	E		5		
O5-18	F	169.20	6	W	
O5-19	A		6		
O5-20	E		6	E	
O5-21	E		6	S	
O5-22	E	165.17	6	S	
O5-23	D		1	W	
O5-24	E		1	E	
O5-25	D/E		1	S	
O5-26	E	161.62	N5-4	W	
O5-27	A		N5-5	S	
O5-28	E	174.67		S	

Figure 2-6: Grid P4

P4-1	E	179.18			
P4-2	F	179.72		S	
P4-3	E	178.84	1	S	
P4-4	E	178.31	1	E	
P4-5	E	179.55	1	E	
P4-6	G	179.62	1	S	
P4-7	E	179.17	1		
P4-8	E	179.31	1	N	
P4-9	D	179.68	1	W	
P4-10	G	180.70	2	S	
P4-11	E	180.14	2	SW	
P4-12	H	180.46	2	W	
P4-13	E	180.41	2	N	
P4-14	E	180.50	2	E	
P4-15	E	179.55	4		
P4-16	E		4		Destroyed
P4-17	D	179.87	4		Destroyed
P4-18	J	180.82	3	S	
P4-19	E	179.96	3		
P4-20	C	179.76	3		
P4-21	E	179.45	3	N	
P4-22	J	181.28	3	E	Stair block

Appendix 2.1 (*continued*)

Structure	*Type*	*Elevation*	*Patio Groups*	*Orientation*	*Comments*	*Navarrete and Luján Muñoz 1963*	*Houston and Mathews 1985*
Figure 2-6: Grid P5							
P5-1	H	171.81	1	S			
P5-2	F	172.68	1	W			
P5-3	E	172.28	1	N			
P5-4	E			E			
P5-5	F^{ss}	186.34	2	NW			151
P5-6	G	184.91	2	W			150
P5-7	M^{s3}	202.54		N	"Duende"		146
P5-8	E/F	186.48	2	E			149
P5-9	D	184.36			1 room		
P5-10	B	177.62					147
P5-11	E	162.15					
P5-12	A	162.4		S			
P5-13	E	163.23		S			

3. The Monumental Sculpture of Dos Pilas: A Summary

THE SCULPTURES OF DOS PILAS can be studied in two ways, as physical objects of a certain shape and iconographic design, and as historical documents. Here we explore their intrinsic properties as artifacts, including the form, material, and iconographic meaning and composition of monuments at Dos Pilas. This chapter summarizes more detailed remarks made elsewhere (Houston 1987:34–217) and is not intended to be a thorough treatment of iconography at the site. Rather, it sketches trends that can be understood in relation to information in the next chapter.

But first we need to discuss the numbering of monuments at Dos Pilas. Most epigraphers follow one of two systems, that proposed by Vinson and Grieder (although presented without explicit numeration; Vinson 1960; Grieder 1960), and another used by Navarrete and Luján (1963). Others have supplemented Navarrete and Luján's list, although occasionally with inconsistencies (e.g., two monuments termed "Stela 22," Houston and Mathews 1985:Fig. 2). The main problem with these schemes is that they are contradictory, inaccurate, and unwieldy, labeling wall panels as "stelae" and using both a numeric and an alphabetic series to identify altars (Navarrete and Luján 1963:23). Clearly, a new system is in order.

Table 3-1 presents a new numbering (Houston 1987:Table 2), along with a concordance with other schemes, including a revised numbering by Ian Graham (personal communication, 1989). The list introduces two new classes of monument. The first is "panel," a term applied to sculpture that is set into masonry as architectural ornament. The second is "miscellaneous stone," referring to stray blocks of uncertain association or unusual form. Miscellaneous stones form a residual category from which monuments may be reassigned to new classes.

DOS PILAS MONUMENTS: PHYSICAL CHARACTERISTICS

The masons who blocked out the monuments of Dos Pilas generally used a hard limestone, probably quarried locally (Navarrete and Luján 1963:Fig. 37; "Type 2," according to the Seibal Project system,

Note: I wish to thank Prof. Laura Junker of Vanderbilt University for her generous help with my statistical research.—S.C.S.

Table 3-1. *Monument numeration and concordance*

New[a]	*VG*[b]	*NL*[c]	*IG*[d]	*IG*[e]	*HM*[f]
Stelae					
St. 1	St. 17	St. 1			
St. 2	St. 16	St. 2			
St. 3	St. 15	St. 3			
St. 4	St. 14	St. 4			
St. 5	St. 13	St. 5			
St. 6	St. 12	St. 6			
St. 7	St. 11	St. 7			
St. 8	St. 10	St. 8			
St. 9	St. 3	St. 17		St. 9	
St. 10	St. 9	St. 21		St. 12	
St. 11			St. 22		
St. 12			St. 23		
St. 13			St. 24		
St. 14			St. 25		
St. 15			St. 26		
St. 16					St. 27
Altars					
Alt. 1		Alt. 1			
Alt. 2		Alt. A			
Alt. 3		Alt. 2			
Alt. 4		Alt. 3			
Alt. 5					
Alt. 6		Alt. 4			
Alt. 7		Alt. 5			
Alt. 8		Alt. 6			
Alt. 9		Alt. 7			
Alt. 10		Alt. 8			
Alt. 11		Alt. 9			
Alt. 12		Alt. B			
Alt. 13					
Alt. 14					
Alt. 15					
Alt. 16					
Alt. 17					
Alt. 18					
Alt. 19					
Panels					
Pan. 1		St. 9			
Pan. 2	St. 18	St. 10			
Pan. 3					
Pan. 4		St. 11		Pan. 7	
Pan. 5					
Pan. 6	St. 5	St. 12		Pan. 3	

Table 3-1 (*continued*)

New[a]	*VG*[b]	*NL*[c]	*IG*[d]	*IG*[e]	*HM*[f]
Pan. 7	St. 4	St. 13		Pan. 4	
Pan. 8	St. 8	St. 14		Pan. 5	
Pan. 9	St. 7	St. 15		Pan. 6	
Pan. 10	St. 6	St. 16		St. 10	
Pan. 11	St. 2	St. 18		BCS[g] 1	
Pan. 12	St. 1	St. 19		BCS 2	
Pan. 13		St. 22		St. 13	
Pan. 14					
Pan. 15					
Pan. 16					
Pan. 17					
Pan. 18					
Pan. 19					
Hieroglyphic stairways					
HS 1		HS 1			
HS 2		HS 2			
HS 3		HS 3			
HS 4					
Hieroglyphic bench					
HB 1					HB. 1
Miscellaneous stones					
MS 1					
MS 2					
MS 3					
MS 4					
MS 5					
MS 6					
MS 7					
MS 8					
MS 9					
MS 10					
MS 11					
MS 12					
MS 13					
MS 14					

[a]New designations by Houston.
[b]Designations by Vinson (1960) and Grieder (1960).
[c]Designations by Navarrete and Luján (1963).
[d]Designations by Ian Graham (1967 and personal communication, 1983).
[e]Designations by Ian Graham (personal communication, 1989).
[f]Designations by Houston and Mathews (1985).
[g]Ball Court Sculpture.

Table 3-2. ***Chronological ordering of stelae from Dos Pilas***

Stela	*Dedicatory Date*	*Style Date*
9	9.12.10. 0. 0?	9.17.0.0.0 + 2k
1	9.13.15. 0. 0	9.17.0.0.0 + 2k
11	9.14. 5. 0. 0	9.17.0.0.0 + 2k
14	9.14. 5. 3. 4	9.17.0.0.0 + 2k
16	9.14. 6.10. 2?	Late Classic
15	9.14.10. 4. 0	9.15.0.0.0 + 2k
8	9.14.15. 5.15?	9.16.0.0.0?
5	9.15. 0. 0. 0	9.17.0.0.0? (Front) 9.15.0.0.0? (Back)
2	9.15. 5. 0. 0?	9.14.0.0.0?
4	9.15.11. 0. 0?	9.17.0.0.0 + 2k
12		9.16.0.0.0?
6		9.17.0.0.0?
3		Late Classic
7		Late Classic
10		Late Classic
13		Late Classic?

Key to column headings: HT = height; HLC = height above lowest carving; MTH = maximum thickness; MW = maximum width; REL = relief; B = border; D = design.

A. L. Smith 1982). They may also have used a softer limestone, as in Panels 11 and 12, although more likely such stone softened from its original condition because of continual exposure to rain. The one monument of fine-grained and dense limestone is Panel 10, evidently of nonlocal material (Fig. 3-1). The fact that the panel was recarved in antiquity testifies to the rarity and desirability of its stone.

A variety of instruments were used for carving. Pecking with mauls served to rough out the sculptures, which still bear vestiges of such marks. Finer touches were made with smaller implements, possibly stone or tooth chisels, which left grooves some .01 meter wide, as on Panel 10. There is some evidence that these chisels resembled dental tools, with different blades or teeth (perhaps peccary tusks) mounted at either tip—the Mixtecs used similar instruments (Karl Taube, personal communication, 1988), and a recently discovered panel from the Classic Maya site of Emiliano Zapata shows such a chisel in use on a sculpture (D. Stuart 1990c). Vigorous grooving perpendicular to the outlines of carving helped accentuate breaks between flat and molded surfaces. An abrasive provided a final finish.

Table 3-2 and Figures 3-2 and 3-3 chart the physical characteristics of Dos Pilas stelae. Of all variables, the most uniform is thickness, which in only one case exceeds .50 meter (cf. C. Jones and Satterthwaite 1982:121).[1] The uniformity probably reflects an interest in reducing the number of bedding planes within a stone, since such planes are natural points of cleavage that jeopardize the physical integrity of a sculpture. This concern did not prevent the accidental splitting of some Dos Pilas monuments.

Table 3-2 *(continued)*

HT	*HLC*	*MTH*	*MW*	*REL*	*B*	*Class*	*D*	*Glyph Blocks*
>2.64		.27	.90	.015	+	FLR	M, CB	18
5.4		.38	1.44	.02	+	FB	M, CB, W	>19
	3.13	>.37	.77	.025	+	F	M	12?
	4.78	.39	1.31	.04	+	F	M, CB, D, W	30
	>5.55	.40	1.07	.015	+	F	M	36
	>5.35	.42	.95	.025	+	F	M, CB, D, W	>46
	>4.95	.42	1.22	.10	–	FB	M	>118
	3.77	.55	1.10	.03	–	FBLR	M, CB	>108
>6.85		.38	1.19	.05	–	FB?	M, CB	>40
	3.81	.40	1.34	.10	–	F	M, CB	>20
	2.36	.38	1.13	.03	+	F	M, CB	>38
>4.89		.40	1.63	.07	–	F	M	>43
	>4.92	.37	1.19	.05	–	F	M	>5
	>3.87	.38	.96	.09	–	F	M	>39
	>2.64	.40	.81	.03	+	F	M	0?
	1.94	.23	.79	.03	+	F	M	?

Key to body of table: k = katun; + = present; – = absent; F = front; B = back; L = left; R = right; M = male; CB = captive, in base panel; W = water bird; D = dwarf.

Dos Pilas stelae show a number of impressionistic trends. There is a gradual increase in height, building up to a peak during the reigns of Rulers 2 and 3 (see the following discussion on statistics and Chapter 4 for an overview of Dos Pilas history). Most of the larger stelae and all those of Ruler 3 lack borders around figural carving.

The reasons for such trends are unclear. Increases in size of monument may have accorded with changes in taste. But there may also have been improvements in technical ability, which permitted sculptors to present more information on stelae, and in ever more grandiose treatments. In either case, the earliest Petexbatun stelae, Arroyo de Piedra Stela 6 (Fig. 3-4) and Tamarindito Stela 5 (Fig. 3-5) are among the smallest, and considerably less massive than Aguateca Stela 7 (Fig. 3-6), which is the latest.

Several stelae at Aguateca record some of the same dates and rulers as do monuments at Dos Pilas (I. Graham 1967:9). The principal difference between the sites is formal, in height of monument. Contemporary stelae at Dos Pilas are far higher than those at Aguateca. Yet, when monuments cease to be erected at Dos Pilas, stelae at Aguateca begin to be carved at impressive scale, with one stela attaining a height above lowest carving of 4.60 meters (Stela 7; ibid.:26). The change in stela height may express the greater importance of Aguateca after the apparent decline of Dos Pilas. Other factors, such as improvements in technique, may also have contributed to the change.

Early sculptors at Dos Pilas, especially those associated with Ruler 1, evidently devoted less effort to stelae than to outset glyphic stairways. These stairways, which first appear in the Pasión drainage at the

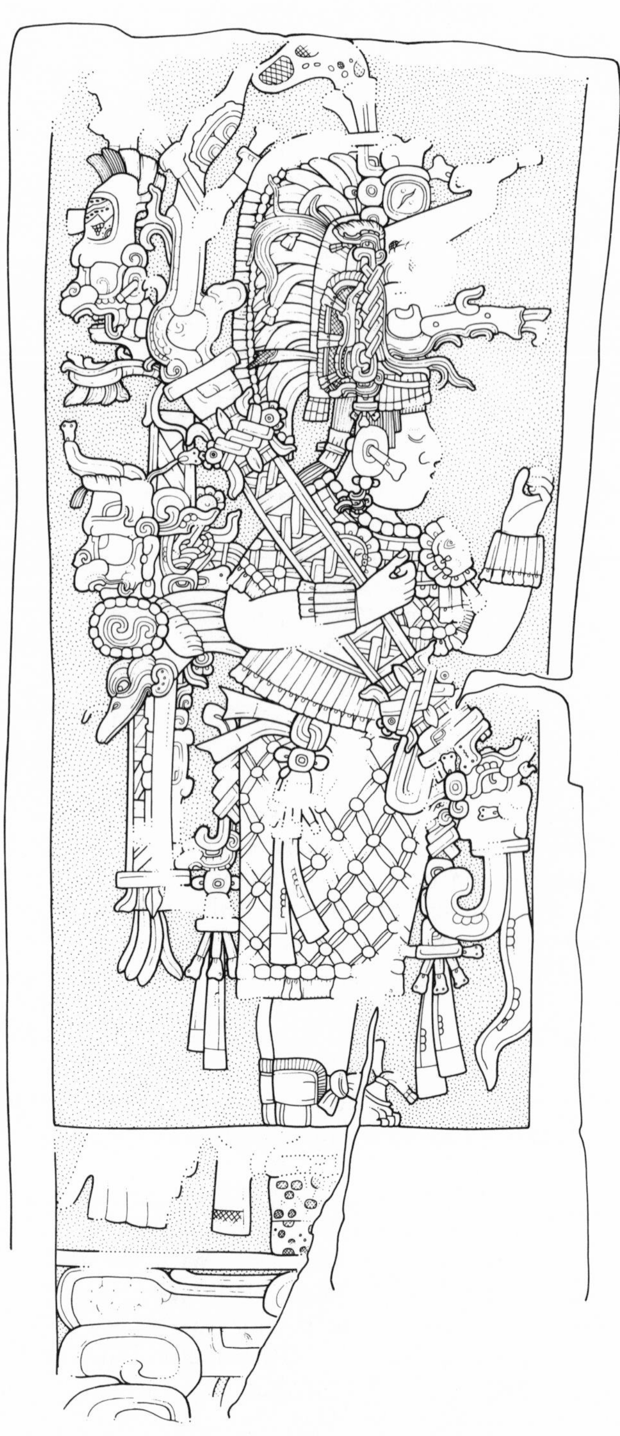

Figure 3-1. Dos Pilas Panel 10. Width: 1.26 m. Height not clear.

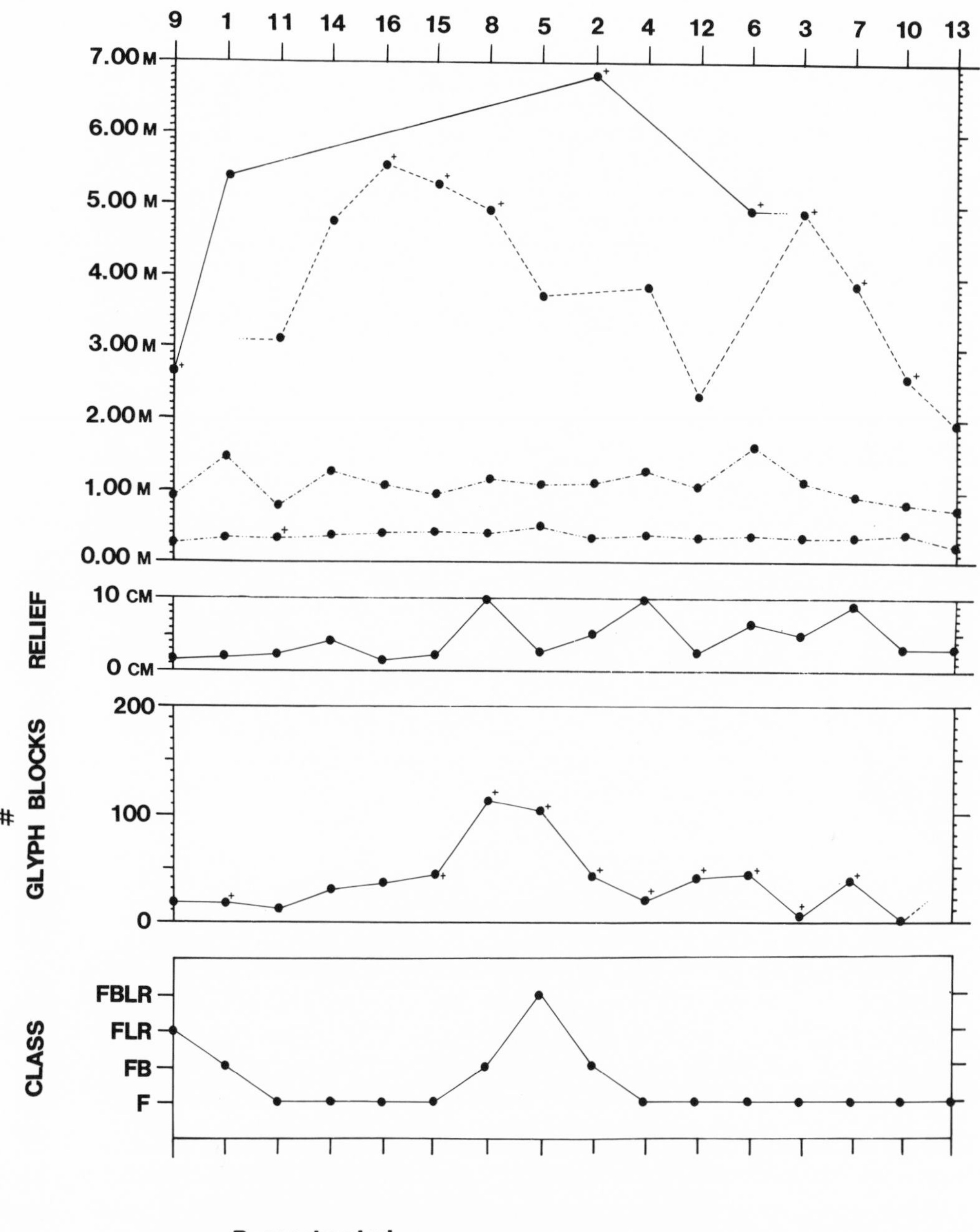

Figure 3-2. Physical characteristics of Dos Pilas stelae. In upper register, solid line indicates height of monument; dashed line, height of sculpture; dash/dot line, maximum width; and dash/double-dot line, maximum thickness.

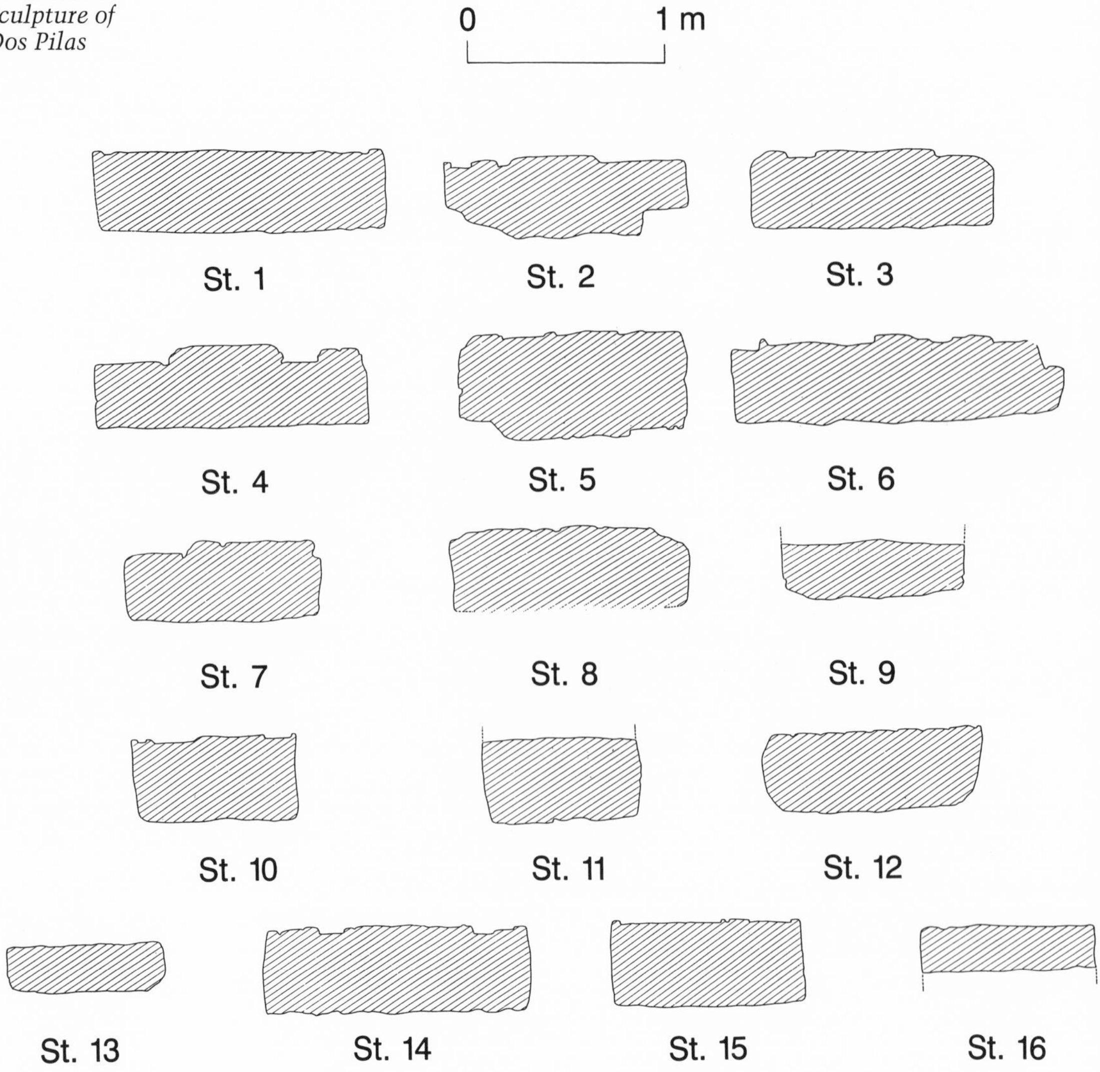

0 1 m

St. 1 St. 2 St. 3

St. 4 St. 5 St. 6

St. 7 St. 8 St. 9

St. 10 St. 11 St. 12

St. 13 St. 14 St. 15 St. 16

Figure 3-3. Sections through Dos Pilas stelae. Location of section below top of stela, in meters: Stela 1, 2.00; Stela 2, 2.00; Stela 3, ca. 3.21; Stela 4, 2.27; Stela 5, 1.00; Stela 6, 2.50; Stela 7, 2.00; Stela 8, 2.70; Stela 9, 1.47; Stela 10, .70; Stela 11, 1.20, taken from tip of butt; Stela 12, .30; Stela 13, 1.84; Stela 14, 1.20; Stela 15, 1.20; Stela 16, 5.35.

site of Itzan, represent an enormous investment, since they are by considerable degree more massive than stelae.[2] The earliest examples at Dos Pilas, Hieroglyphic Stairways 2 and 4, consist of thick risers that are asymmetrical in plan (e.g., Figs. 3-7 and 3-8). Later examples, Hieroglyphic Stairways 1 (Fig. 3-9) and 3 (Fig. 3-10), show evidence of more

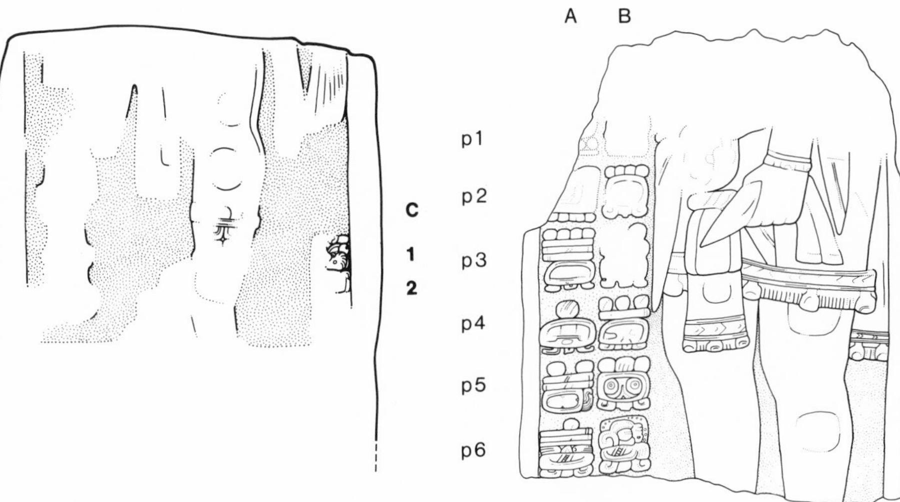

Figure 3-4. Arroyo de Piedra Stela 6. Width: .87 m.

Figure 3-5. Tamarindito Stela 5. Height: .82 m.

Figure 3-6. Aguateca Stela 7. Height of carving: 3.7 m. Reproduced with permission from Publication 33, Middle American Research Institute, Tulane University, New Orleans, Louisiana (I. Graham 1967:Fig. 17).

judicious use of stone, employing relatively thin risers of even thickness and height.

Table 3-3 and Figure 3-11 exhibit a chronological ordering of altars at Dos Pilas. The ordering is necessarily tentative and, to some extent, hypothetical, since it derives from the dates of associated stelae.[3] Thickness varies little over time, although diameter tends to correlate positively with increased monument height. This trend is particularly pronounced during the reign of Ruler 3, who commissioned Stelae 2, 8, and 5 (Fig. 3-12), and perhaps the reign of Ruler 4, who caused Stela 4 to be erected.

Table 3-4 and Figures 3-13 and 3-14 supplement information on stelae and altars with data on panels. The charts indicate that height above lowest carving varies considerably, dipping from Panels 6 and 7 to the roughly coeval Panels 8 (Fig. 3-15) and 9 (Fig. 3-16), and then rising to accommodate Panels 12 (Fig. 3-17), 10 (Fig. 3-1), and 11 (Fig. 3-18), which are within the range of stelae. Without question, the latest panels are high for the class. The other shifts in height, however, stem from the inclusion of tall and wide wall panels in the chart. The former are set into floors, the latter above them.

Hieroglyphic stairways, benches, and miscellaneous stones are not presented in tabular form for the reasons that these monuments are either unique at the site (e.g., Hieroglyphic Bench 1) or inclusive of blocks displaying great formal heterogeneity (e.g., Hieroglyphic Stairway 1).

A clear trend in figural carving at Dos Pilas is the increasing im-

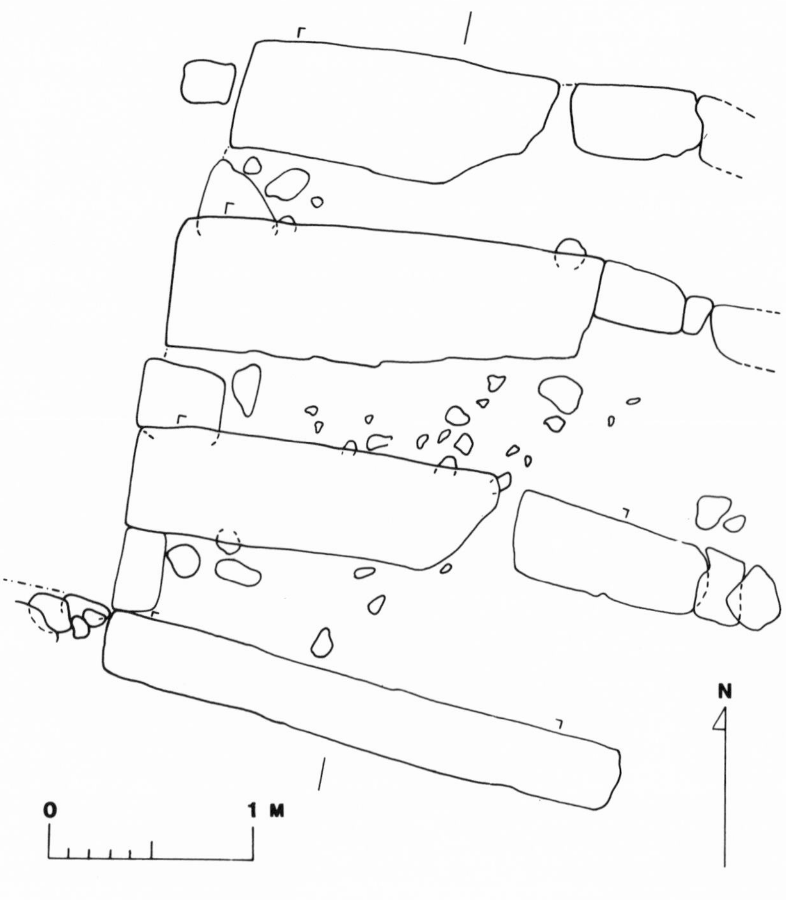

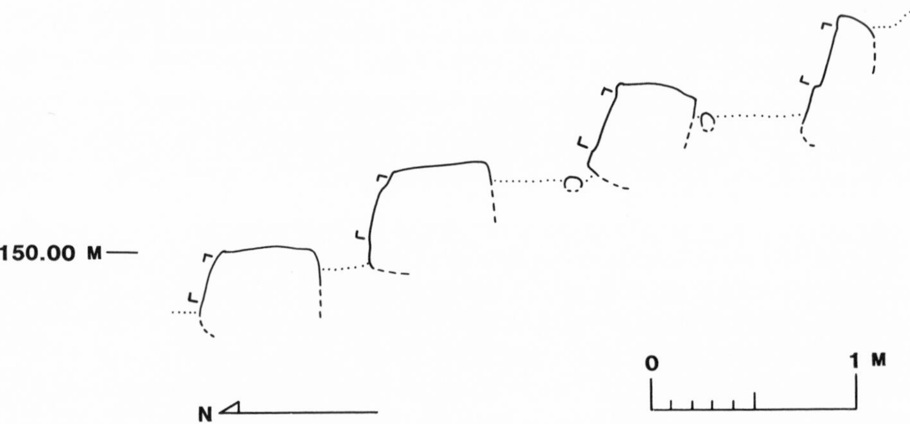

Figure 3-7. Dos Pilas Hieroglyphic Stairway 2, west: plan and section.

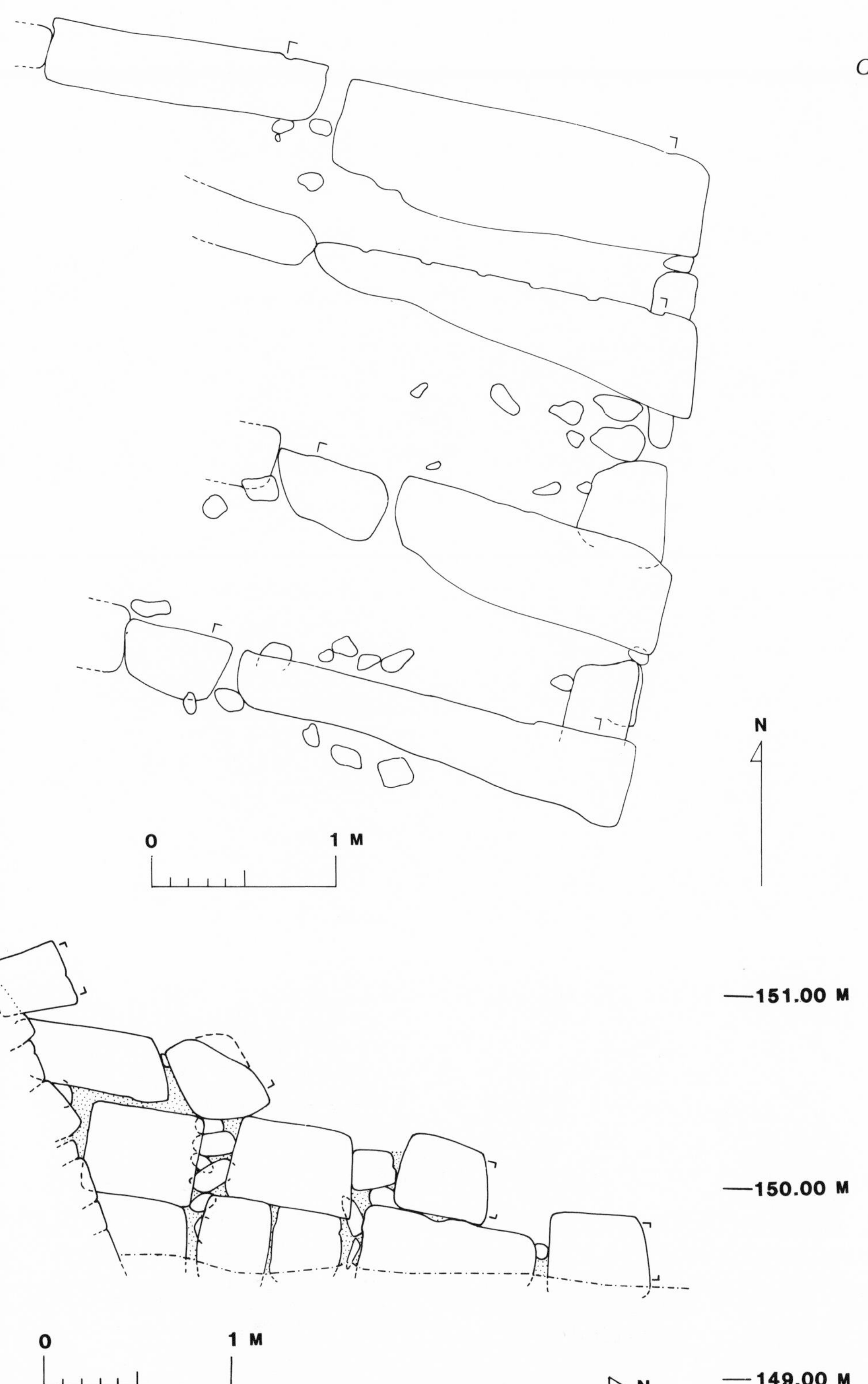

Figure 3-8. Dos Pilas Hieroglyphic Stairway 2, east: plan and section.

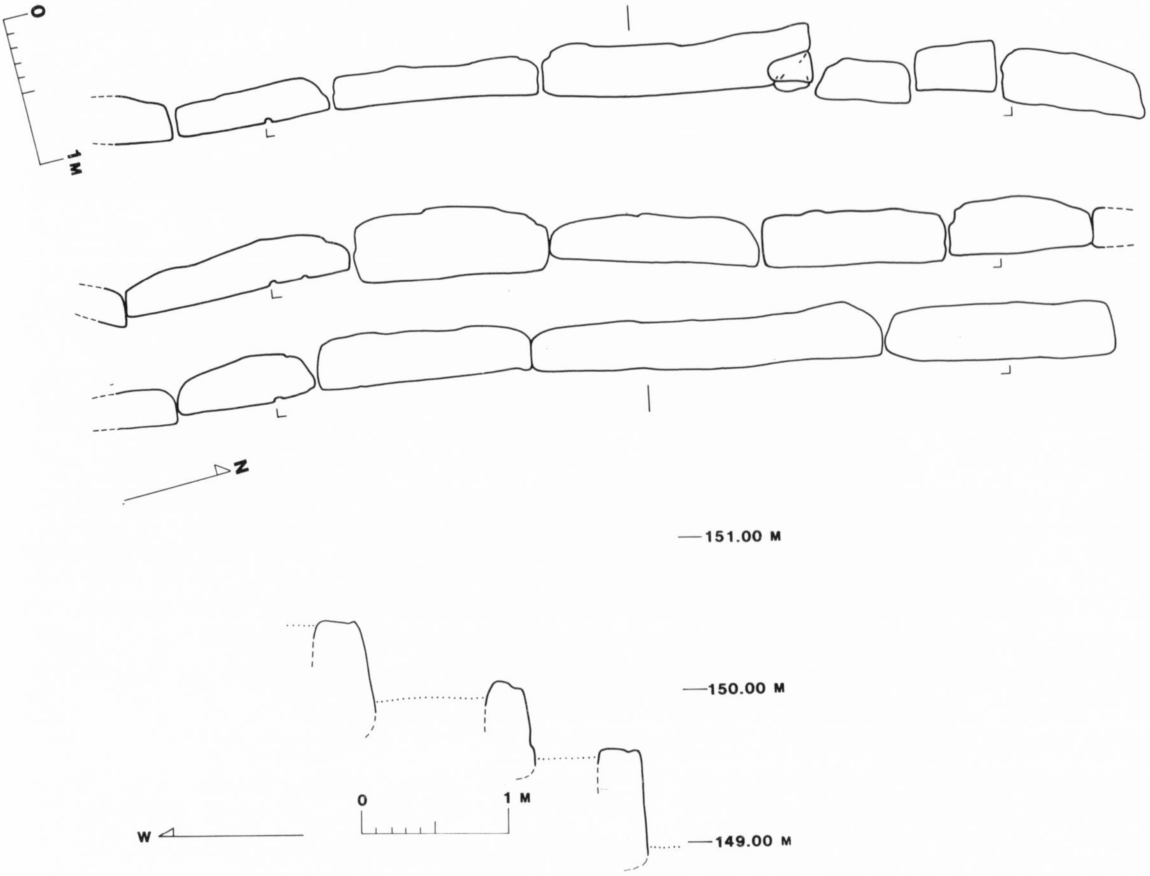

Figure 3-9. Dos Pilas Hieroglyphic Stairway 1: plan and section.

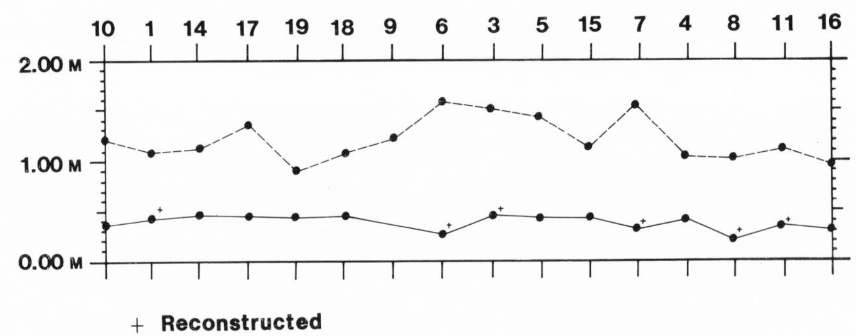

Figure 3-11. Physical characteristics of Dos Pilas altars. Dashed line indicates diameter, solid line thickness.

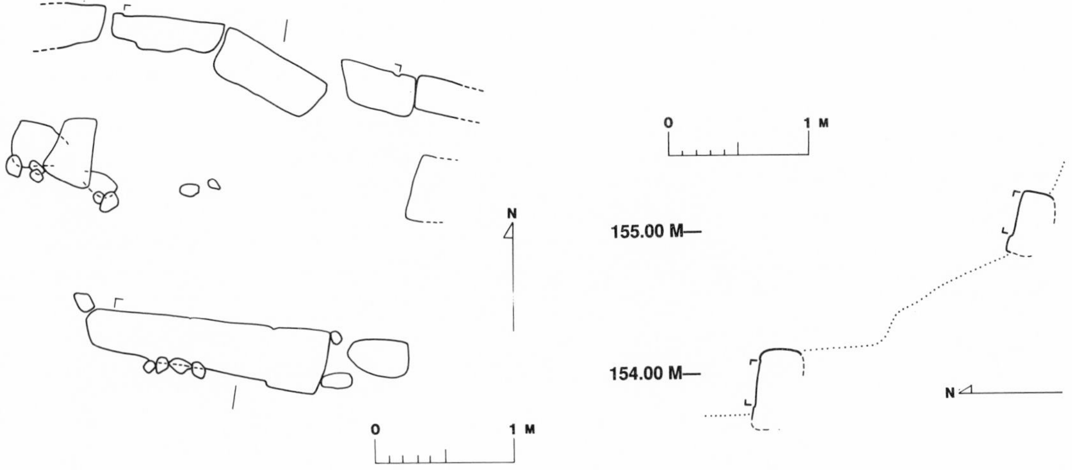

Figure 3-10. Dos Pilas Hieroglyphic Stairway 3: plan and section.

Table 3-3. *Chronological ordering of altars from Dos Pilas*[a]

Altar	*Associated Monument*		*DIA*	*MTH*	*REL*
10	St. 9	(9.12.10. 0. 0?)	1.20?	.37	.03
1	St. 1	(9.13.15. 0. 0)	1.10	>.40	
14	St. 11	(9.14. 5. 0. 0)	1.12	.45	
17	St. 14	(9.14. 5. 3. 4)	1.37	.43	
19	St. 16	(9.14. 6.10. 2?)	.86	.40	
18	St. 15	(9.14.10. 4. 0)	1.10	.45	
9	St. 8	(9.14.15. 5.15?)	1.25		
6	St. 5	(9.15. 0. 0. 0)	1.63	>.28	
3	St. 2	(9.15. 5. 0. 0?)	1.50	>.45	
5	St. 4	(9.15.11. 0. 0?)	1.41	.42	
15	St. 12	(9.16. 0. 0. 0, SD)	1.16	.40	
7	St. 6	(9.17. 0. 0. 0, SD)	1.55	>.30	
4	St. 3	(Late Classic)	1.02	.40	
8	St. 7	(Late Classic)	1.02	>.18	
11	St. 10	(Late Classic)	1.13	>.35	.01
16	St. 13	(Late Classic?)	.96	.30	

[a]Chronological ordering by associated stela.
Key to headings: DIA = diameter; MTH = maximum thickness; REL = relief.
Key to body of table: St. = stela; SD = style date.
Note: Altars 2, 12, and 13 are omitted because they do not accompany datable monuments.

Figure 3-12. Dos Pilas Stela 5: front (*a*) and back (*b*). Height of carving: 3.77 m.

Table 3-4. *Chronological ordering of panels from Dos Pilas*[a]

Panel	*Dedicatory Date*	*HLC*	*MTH*	*MW*	*REL*	*Glyph Blocks*
6	(ca. 9.12.13.17.7)	1.63	.31	.94	.02	16
7	(9.12.13.17.7)	1.22	.30	.96	.02	12
8	(Late Classic)	.80	.21	1.21	.015	48
9	(Late Classic)	.82	.20	1.18	.015	48
1	(Late Classic)	.37	.14	.68	.025	?
2	(Late Classic)	.98	.15	.71	.04	3
3	(Late Classic)	1.65	.12	1.03	.025	?
12	(9.15.0.0.0?, SD)	>2.81	.38	1.06	.08	>7
10	(9.16.0.0.0 + 2k, SD)	?	.38	1.26	.03	?
11	(9.18.0.0.0?, SD)	>2.92	.34	1.05	.06	13

[a] Chronological ordering by date and by associated monument.

Key to headings: HLC = height above lowest carving; MTH = maximum thickness; MW = maximum width; REL = relief.

Key to body of table: k = katun; SD = style date.

Note: Panels 4, 5, 13, 14, 15, 16, and 17 cannot be dated on present evidence. Panels 18 and 19, both wall panels of Late Classic date, were found too recently to be included here.

portance of three-dimensionality, which is, however, difficult to demonstrate statistically (see following section on statistics; Spinden 1913). Stela 9, for example, is apparently the earliest complete stela at the site. Its carving is shallow and its relief low, yet the carved edges are beveled, suggesting plasticity and rounded form. Later stelae, and particularly those associated with Ruler 2 (including Arroyo de Piedra Stela 2), display deeper relief and modeling, although still with chamfered outlines. The latest stela with a reliable date, Stela 4, departs from beveling and attains rounded and undercut carving. At this time relief is at its highest.

For obscure reasons, sculptors at Dos Pilas reused some monuments, a pattern also occurring at other Maya sites (Proskouriakoff 1950:103; Satterthwaite 1958; Justeson and Mathews 1983:Fig. 1; I. Graham 1982:145). Panel 10, for example, exhibits a fragment of imagery near its base (Fig. 3-1). The features of this earlier carving, which was partly obliterated during the second episode of sculpting, indicate an early date, possibly of the Early Classic period or Hiatus. Another monument, Altar 11 (Fig. 3-19), which may also be recarved, is considerably later than Panel 10 and may date to the final years of the Late Classic period.

Once carved, some Dos Pilas monuments were moved or their arrangement disturbed. This is hardly surprising: the Classic Maya frequently built on older structures, and this passion for remodeling affected monuments such as double outset stairways, which form integral parts of construction. Remodeling may account for the disruption of Hieroglyphic Stairway 2 and the monolithic stairway north of Structure L5-37. The repositioning of other monuments, such as Stela 10, is less easily explained, since these carvings do not form part of structures.[4]

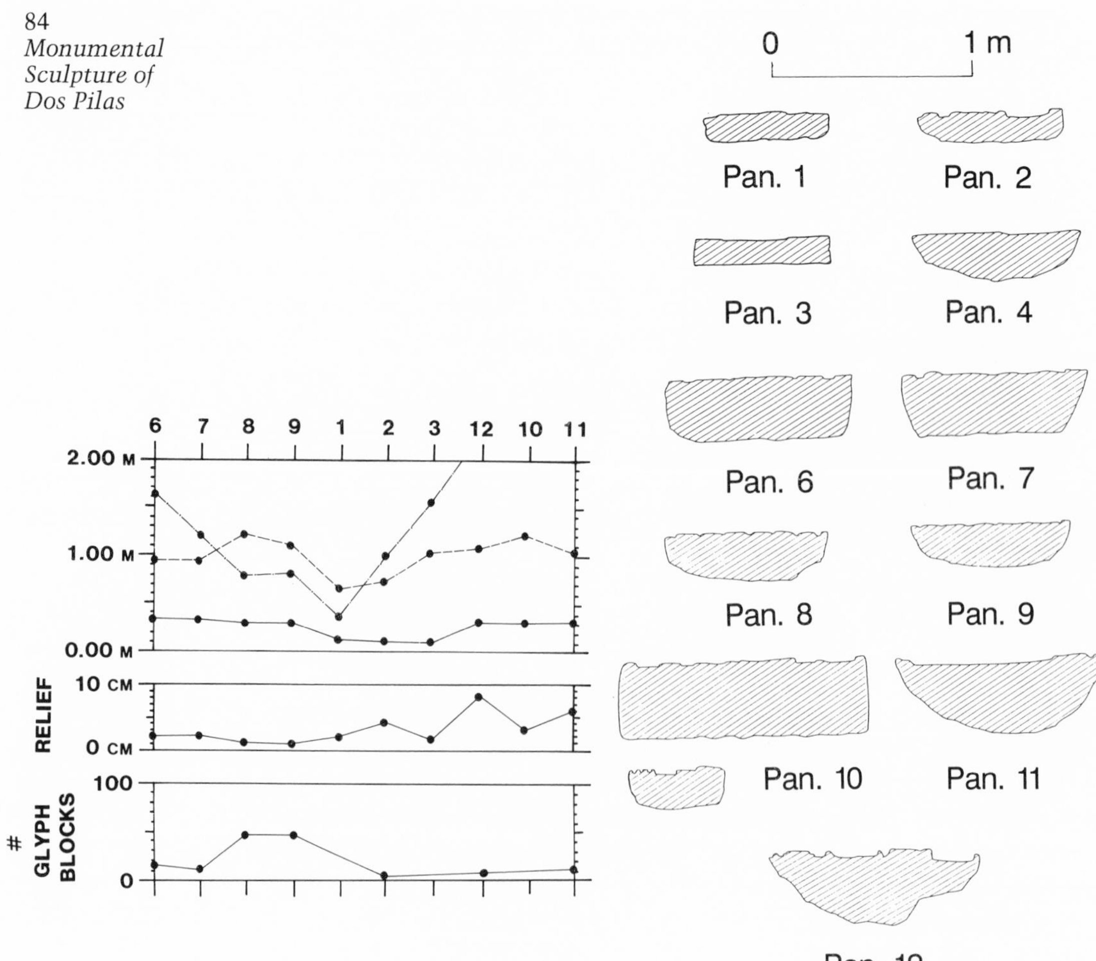

Figure 3-13. Left: Physical characteristics of Dos Pilas panels. In upper register, solid line indicates maximum thickness; dashed line, maximum width; and dash/dot line, height.

Figure 3-14. Right: Sections through Dos Pilas panels.

One of the intriguing aspects of Dos Pilas sculpture is the absence of references to sculptors, whose names have been identified at other sites, some in the Pasión drainage (Figs. 3-20 and 3-21; Stuart 1986). The reasons for this omission are unclear, although it may hint that sculptors were of lesser status at Dos Pilas than at other sites.

STATISTICAL TRENDS IN THE STELAE OF DOS PILAS AND RELATED SITES
by Stacey C. Symonds

Statistical analysis of stelae from Dos Pilas and related sites (Aguateca, Altar de Sacrificios, Machaquila, Tikal, and other, smaller sites in the lower Pasión region) yields a set of emerging patterns (Symonds 1990).[5] That these patterns are still not entirely certain is a function of sample size. Some sites have only two or three stelae, making it impossible to confirm trends at individual centers. Yet the combined data

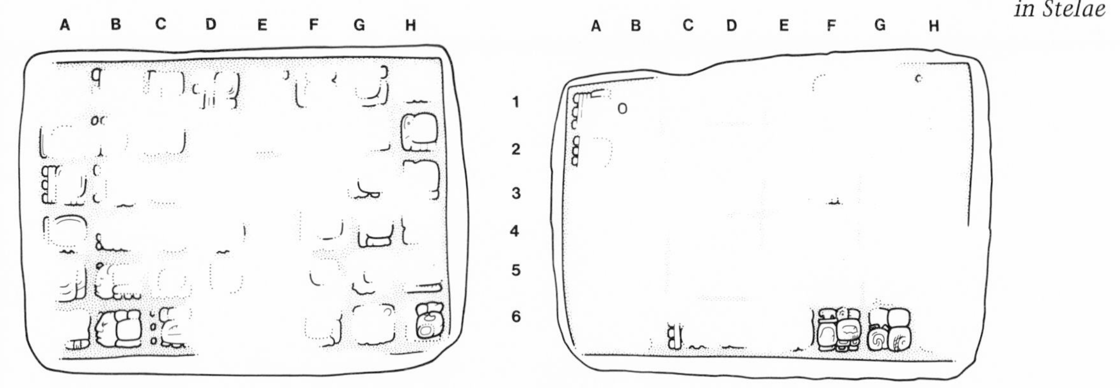

Figure 3-15. Left: Dos Pilas Panel 8. Height of carving: .80 m.
Figure 3-16. Right: Dos Pilas Panel 9. Height of carving: .82 m.

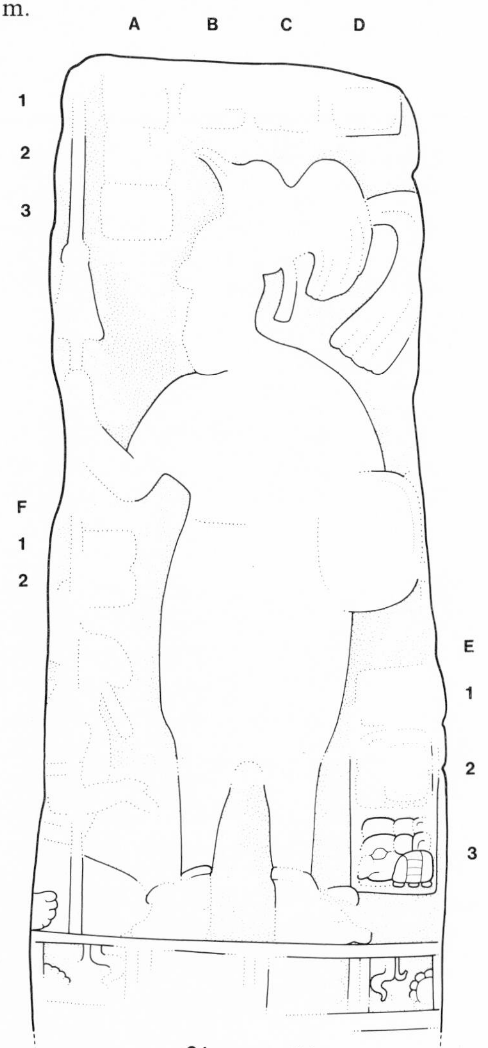

Figure 3-17. Left: Dos Pilas Panel 12. Height of carving: 2.81 m.
Figure 3-18. Right: Dos Pilas Panel 11. Height of carving: 2.92 m.

Figure 3-19. Dos Pila Altar 11. Diameter: 1.13 m.

provide useful material for regional comparisons (Table 3-5). Eventually, with a fuller sample and more comprehensive statistical treatment, Classic Maya stelae will serve not only as markers of chronology but also as the basis for a statistically significant seriation of Maya sculpture.

The most important trend noted thus far is the overwhelmingly strong correlation between date and width and between date and height. A clear and unequivocal pattern is that height increases with time. For all sites in the survey, this correlation is significant at the .01 level. However, when the data from Tikal are removed, the correlation loses its validity (most probably because the removal of these data constitutes the removal of one-third of the sample). Only the relationship between width and date remains significant, although at the .05 level. I suspect that the strong deviation of Machaquila from regional patterns may have affected correlations for the rest of the Pasión. Removal of the Machaquila data restores the significance of the correlation between both width and height and date.

Although not a Pasión site, and as such only loosely connected with Dos Pilas (see Chapter 4), Tikal has by far the strongest correlations for width and height. In comparison, Dos Pilas shows no significant correlations. Tikal has a much larger data set (thirty-seven stelae as opposed to Dos Pilas' sixteen) and covers a longer time span. These factors doubtless influenced my statistical seriation. However, the general, impressionistic trend (increasing height and width over time) seems to be the same for monuments at Tikal and at the Petexbatun sites. T-tests, on the other hand, show that the actual dimensions of

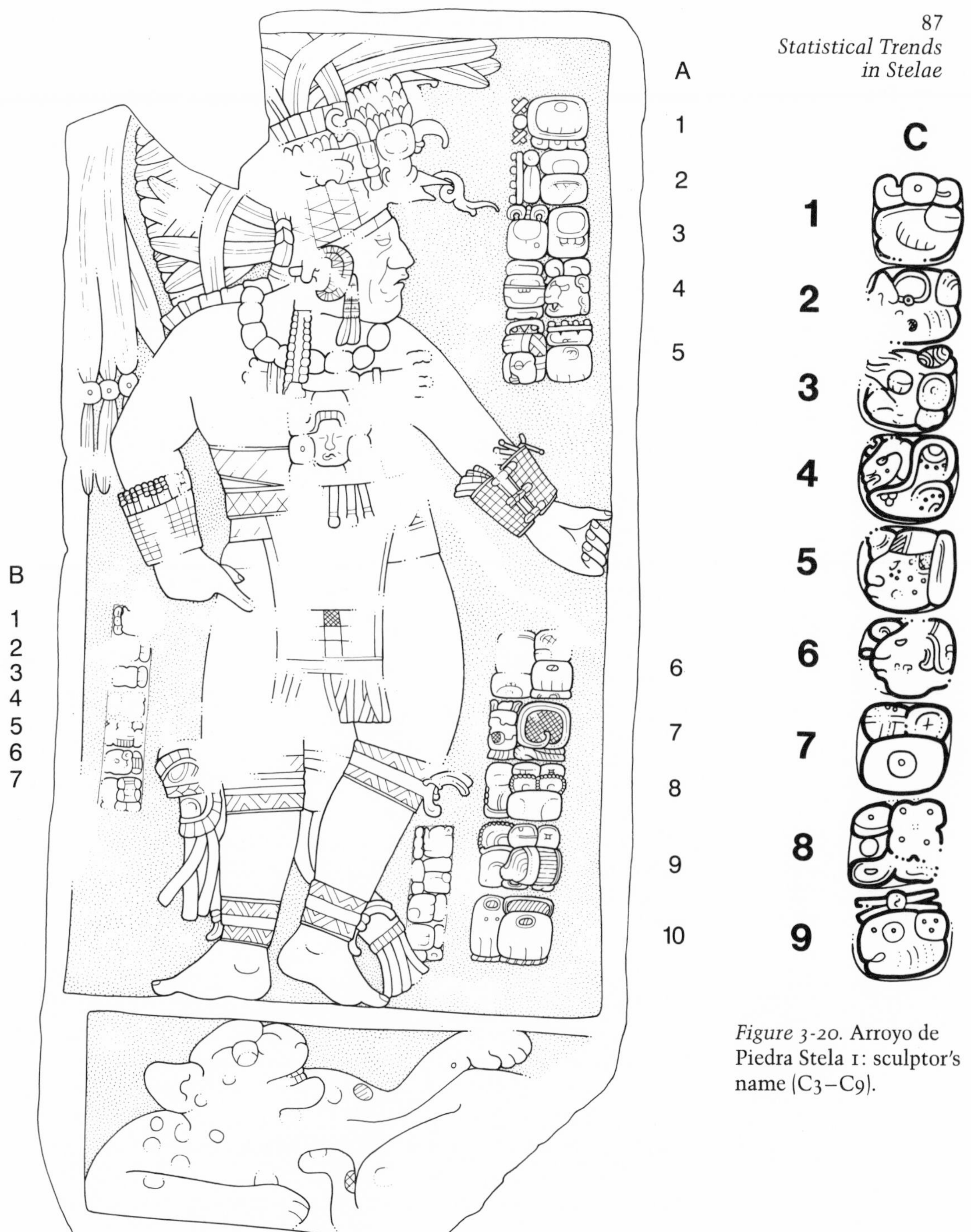

Figure 3-20. Arroyo de Piedra Stela 1: sculptor's name (C3–C9).

Figure 3-21. La Amelia Panel 2. Height of carving: 1.69 m. Sculptor's name at B1–B7, C1–C4.

Table 3-5. ***Correlation significance of size-determinant variables with date, arranged by site***

	Thickness	*Width*	*Relief*	*Height*
All sites	(−).105	.000	(−).054	.000
All sites but Tikal	(−).469	.032	(−).926	.348
All sites but Tikal and Machaquila	.097	.001	.723	.009
Tikal	.209	.000	.313	.000
Altar de Sacrificios	(−).105	.000	(−).054	.000
Machaquila	(−).014	(−).005	(−).008	(−).070
Dos Pilas	.160	.108	(−).308	.891

the monuments at Tikal and Dos Pilas differ for all size-determinant variables (thickness, width, height, relief). Two other possibilities need to be tested: (1) date categories arranged by ruler and (2) categories defined in terms of artists' lifetimes. Unfortunately, the second option will be difficult to evaluate at Dos Pilas, since the site lacks artists' signatures.

Intersite comparisons are also revealing. Machaquila, for example, exhibits trends that are altogether different from those at other sites in the study. The only variable whose means approximate those of the other Pasión monuments is relief. Stelae at Machaquila show a strong correlation of time with both thickness and width, but in contrast to the situation at other sites in the survey, the correlation is negative. The monuments become thinner and narrower toward the end of the Classic period. Another significant difference is that at Machaquila height fails to correlate with time. In addition, stelae at Machaquila show a marked pattern in which relief decreases over time. Altar de Sacrificios may also exhibit this pattern, but at the .05 level of significance.

Were different sources of stone used at Machaquila? Did Maya stoneworking technology change over time? Or are the patterns detected here simply the result of differences in carving styles and masons' preferences? It is to be hoped that additional data and the examination of different categories will confirm trends in the technological and morphological evolution of Pasión monuments.

DOS PILAS MONUMENTS: ICONOGRAPHY

Despite occasional anomalies, monumental iconography at Dos Pilas is uniform and formulaic, with almost complete emphasis on the ruler rather than on secondary figures and background. (The tableaux on Hieroglyphic Stairway 1 [Fig. 3-22] and Panel 19 [Fig. 3-23] are notable exceptions.) The overwhelming majority of stelae show rulers in the same position and with similar headgear and costume. The salient difference seems to be in the deity masks worn by the rulers. These masks correlate with glyphic compounds apparently referring to the places where the deities reside, and, indeed, to particular locations

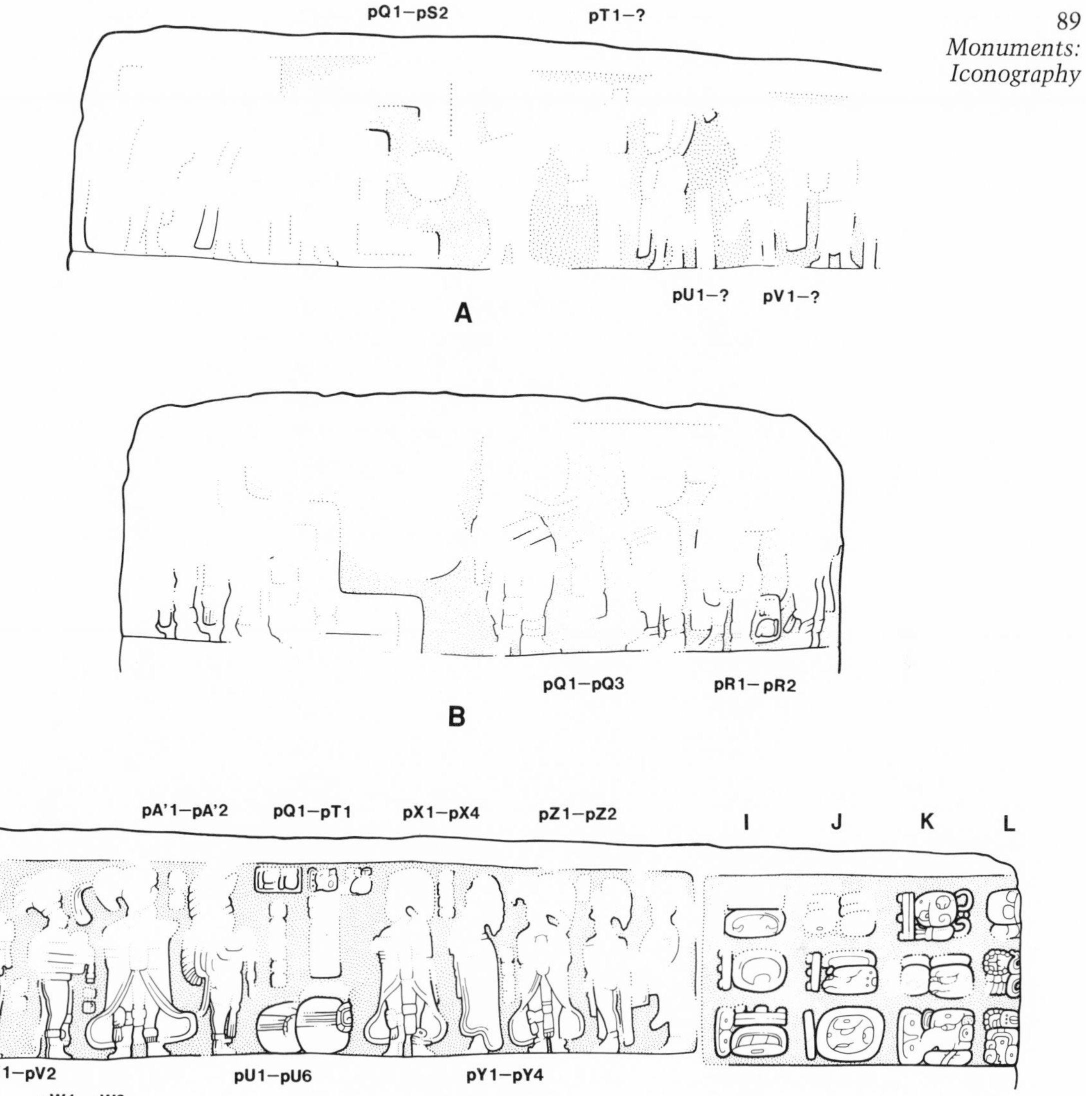

Figure 3-22. Tableaux on Dos Pilas Hieroglyphic Stairway 1: *a*, Step I; *b*, Step II; *c*, Step III. Height: Step I, .55 m; Step II, .50 m; Step III, .51 m.

within Dos Pilas (Stuart and Houston 1990). Another difference may be in the "God K scepters," which, like some stelae at Copan (David Stuart, personal communication, 1986), perhaps possessed personal epithets or descriptive titles. The uniformity of Dos Pilas stelae is nowhere more apparent than on the terraces north of Structure P5-7. All legible monuments on the terraces refer to Ruler 2, who most likely commissioned the massive pyramid behind the sculptures. The stelae show masked representations of Ruler 2, all displaying closely similar costumes, shields, and God K scepters (Figs. 3-24 and 3-25). Two of the stelae on the terraces (Stelae 14 and 15), and another behind Structure P5-7 (Stela 16, Fig. 3-26) record "shell-star" or Venus war events (Lounsbury 1982). The other monuments, now eroded, may have contained similar messages.

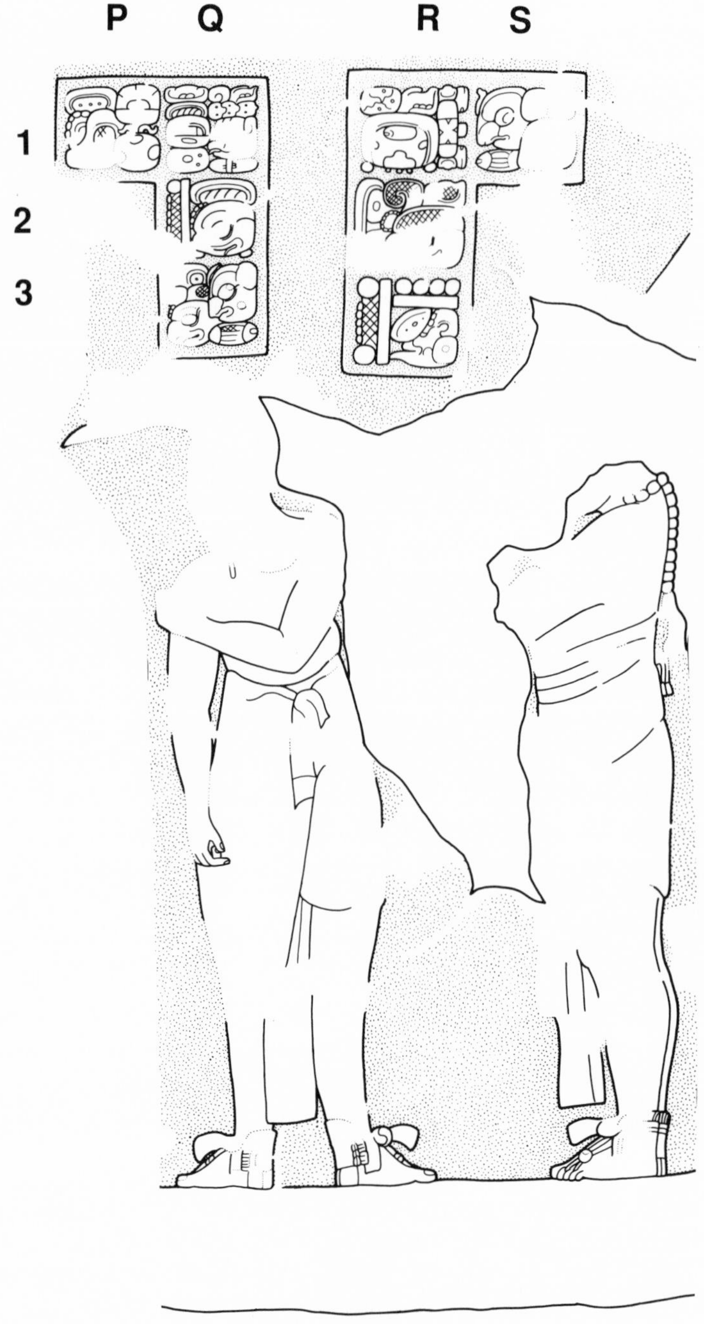

Figure 3-23. Detail of Dos Pilas Panel 19. Drawing by David Stuart, courtesy of Petexbatun Regional Archaeological Project, Vanderbilt University.

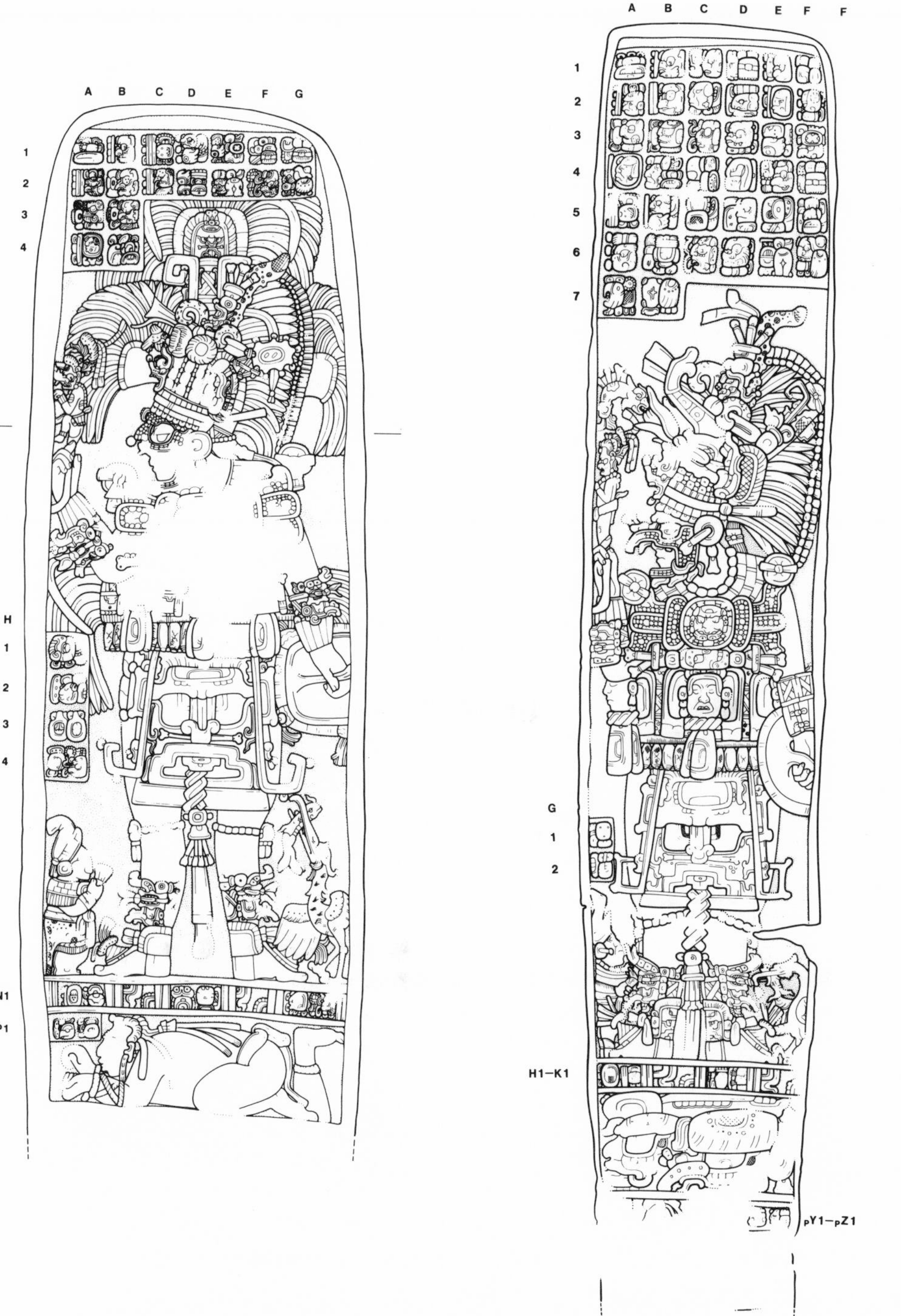

Figure 3-24. Left: Dos Pilas Stela 14. Height of carving: 4.78 m.

Figure 3-25. Right: Dos Pilas Stela 15. Height of carving: >5.35 m.

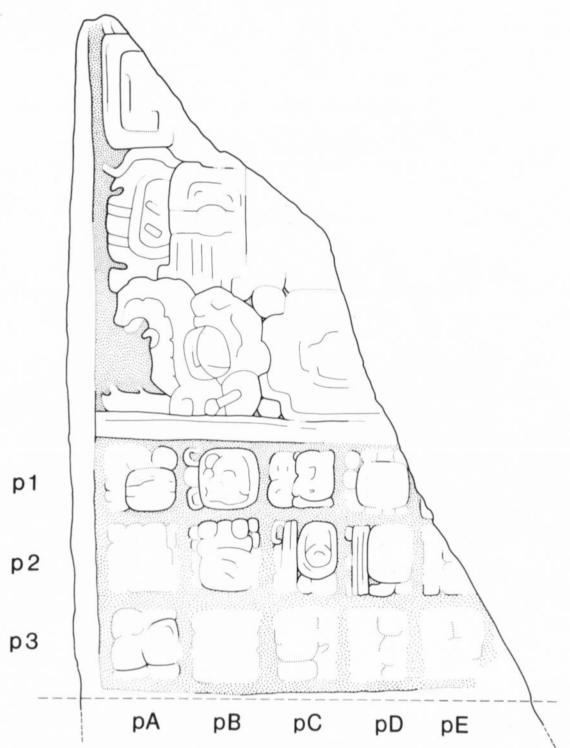

Figure 3-26. Right: Dos Pilas Stela 16. Height of carving: >5.55 m.

Figure 3-28. Above: Dos Pilas Stela 2. Height of carving: >6.85 m. Reproduced with permission from Publication 33, Middle American Research Institute, Tulane University, New Orleans, Louisiana (I. Graham 1967).

But how, in general, is such iconography to be understood? One clue comes from a common Maya glyph, which occurs also on the monuments from El Duende. First interpreted as an "auxiliary verb" (Josserand, Schele, and Hopkins 1985), this sign in fact records a word for "dance," *ak'ot* (Nikolai Grube, personal communication, 1990). The decipherment is an important one, for it suggests that a large number of Maya portraits—and particularly those showing individuals dressed in masks and supporting elaborate backracks—depict dancing lords (Fig. 3-27; Houston 1985). The emphasis on dance is one that is documented throughout Classic Maya art and in Colonial sources (e.g., Houston and Stuart 1989b). Conceivably, many of the open spaces in Maya sites, such as palace courtyards and plazas, served as floors for ritual dances. Rulers at Dos Pilas often appear with captives, usually displayed in abject posture beneath the feet of the lord. In all cases the captives are specific individuals named by glyphic captions. Most are stripped of costume, save for the ragged kilts peculiar to captives. A few, particularly Yich'ak Balam of Seibal, wear more extensive ornament, including circular earspools with wide perforations. The ornament not only underlines the importance of these individuals, but attests to a ritual in which Maya lords were adorned with jewelry prior to their sacrifice (Bricker 1986:195; David Stuart, personal communication, 1990). This practice recalls the rich dress and clothing accorded special captives and sacrificial victims in Aztec society (Durán 1971:175).

Despite the martial allusions at Dos Pilas, battle dress occurs on only a few sculptures. The best example is Stela 2, which projects an image laden with Teotihuacanoid elements (Fig. 3-28). Such elements

Figure 3-27. Dos Pilas Stela 11. Height of carving: 3.13 m.

often accompany battle gear (Schele 1984). In addition, Stela 2 exhibits a square shield, much like those grasped by lords on Panels 11 and 12. At other sites, such as Tonina (Becquelin and Baudez 1982: Figs. 158, 160-162) and Bonampak (Miller 1986: Pl. 2), square shields appear in war scenes or serve as mats for kneeling captives. The objects seem, then, to be direct accessories of war.

Ranking within Dos Pilas society is reflected in dress. Rulers 2 and 3 wear a distinctive outfit consisting of jaguar kilt, broad collar, feathered headdress, belt attachment with three celts, and "epaulettes." Virtually the same costume appears on a subsidiary figure on Panel 19, although with a paperlike headdress and less braiding (Fig. 4-19). This figure, who kneels to let blood from the midsection of a high-ranking child, contrasts with the child's guardians, who wear simple kilts and relatively little jewelry. Presumably, sumptuary laws played an important role at Dos Pilas during the Classic period.

CONCLUSIONS

Monuments at Dos Pilas show decided changes through time, such as subtle shifts in form, some demonstrable statistically. They also show a set of images that reflect the more general preoccupations of the Classic Maya elite. In formal terms, thickness is more or less constant throughout the Late Classic period, although changes in width and height correlate closely with the passage of time. Regional differences, particularly with sites such as Machaquila, can be pronounced, perhaps because sculptors are using different quarries or methods of carving, or because their style is more closely linked with that of areas beyond the Pasión drainage. A strong suspicion is that many of these changes correlate with particular events or the accession of new rulers.

Iconography at Dos Pilas tends to be both uniform and formulaic, with rulers being strongly engaged in the presentation of ceremonial dances involving the impersonation of supernatural figures. Many such rites may represent attempts by rulers to associate themselves with supernaturals such as *naguales* or *wayob* (Houston and Stuart 1989b). But sculptural form and iconographic conventions are merely the medium through which the lords of Dos Pilas expressed their concerns. We must turn now to the historical messages in glyphic texts, which give more precise meaning to the patterns detected here.

4. The History of Dos Pilas and Its Lords

THE TRUE IMPORTANCE of Dos Pilas and the Pasión region lies not so much in the quantity of its texts—there are at least 225 carved monuments in the area—as in their quality. Unusually full inscriptions occur in many competing centers, particularly those from Dos Pilas and neighboring sites near Lake Petexbatun, allowing scholars to examine relationships between autonomous and semiautonomous elites of the Late Classic period (ca. A.D. 550–850). Of all the sites, Dos Pilas has one of the largest epigraphic records (sixteen stelae, nineteen altars, nineteen panels, fourteen miscellaneous stones, four hieroglyphic stairways, one hieroglyphic bench) and also a highly influential family, who were among the most active participants in the dynastic politics of the Pasión drainage. This chapter explores the historical significance of the dynasty by discussing, first, the historiographical problems of working with Classic Maya texts and, second, the details of Dos Pilas history, including the identifying title, or Emblem Glyph, of the royal family, the overall dynastic sequence, and the broader meaning of events at the site.

CLASSIC MAYA TEXTS AS HISTORICAL SOURCES

To date, relatively few epigraphers have evaluated Maya texts as sources of Classic history (Houston 1989:3–7). In part, this is because many decipherments are recent, and specialists have had little time to ponder the implications of new readings. Another reason is that only a few epigraphers have a background in historical method, the majority being trained as linguists or archaeologists (Wood 1990:81–82). This can present a problem, for the prudent epigrapher should never take glyphs at face value: they are without question stereotyped, restricted in scope, and edited for appropriate religious and political content (Nicholson 1971:64). Egyptologists detect a similar pattern in Egyptian hieroglyphs, where "decorum" helps define and rank "the fitness of pictorial and written material on monuments, their content and their captions" (Baines 1983:576). In Egypt as in Mesoamerica, no public information is ever the result of spontaneous, unpremeditated declaration.

Equally certain is the proposition that, as dynastic records, hieroglyphic inscriptions seldom if ever show evidence of impartiality—the notion that history constitutes a balanced reconstruction of the past is, after all, a fairly recent invention. Rather, the inscriptions contain statements of propaganda. Much like other sources of history in Mesoamerica (Mary E. Smith 1983:260; van Zantwijk 1985:9; Gillespie 1989:xxvii), glyphic texts contain historical biases and local points of view. Lavish care went into their carving and presentation, but for essentially pragmatic reasons: the writing conferred legitimacy on an individual, a government, a course of action, and, in Mesoamerica as elsewhere (A. F. Wright 1979:240), fused religious belief and political legitimacy. Naturally, the ultimate aim was to lend authority to existing structures of control (Altheide and Johnson 1980:4).

Disentangling reliable from unreliable accounts is no easy task. But we can take heart from similar efforts in Central Mexico, where the following points have been made (Nicholson 1971:67–70). First, "clearly mythological, legendary, novelistic, romantic, and/or folkloristic" records are readily identifiable, particularly in migration legends and the mythological foundations of dynasties (ibid.:64). As a result, these can be distinguished from contemporary records (Classic, Postclassic, or early Colonial in date), which require more serious attention as historical documents. Second, most histories are plainly biased in their presentation of information, typically emphasizing the glories and successes of a particular community, town, or dynasty. Nonetheless, a composite and fairly accurate history can be assembled from the texts of rivals or allies, who often recorded different impressions of an event or period (ibid.:68). Finally, Central Mexican documents often display a surprising degree of fidelity to the sequence and nature of historical events; some documents, for example, such as the Codex Mendoza (Ross 1978:23), do not conceal defeats and other reversals of fortune (Nicholson 1971:69). Thus, the traditional methods of historiography—the evaluation of the credibility of sources and the construction of a comprehensive, reliable narrative from them (Gottschalk 1958:28)—are well within the grasp of the Mesoamerican ethnohistorian.

What are the lessons for historians of the ancient Maya? The most important one is that we should evaluate periods and events individually, as any good historian would. If corroborative inscriptions are scanty, or an event seems anomalous and unlikely (a mythological account, for instance), then the textual record should be viewed with skepticism and caution. But if other accounts exist, a composite history comes within our grasp, and the level of confidence in inscriptions rises accordingly.

Not all scholars will be convinced that historiographical method can be applied to Classic Maya texts. To a point, theirs is a reasonable reservation, since epigraphers can seldom be entirely certain that a ruler acceded on a particular date, or that a battle took place on another. However, skeptics should also place some faith in the "composite" approach and in the overall value of the historical texts. With careful sifting, glyphs can provide both a firm dynastic chronology (Houston 1989:22–23) and a reasoned view of what happened to certain members of the Maya elite during the Classic period.

Yet it would be a mistake to focus too narrowly on a purely historiographical approach. In many cases, the distortions and rhetorical clichés are every bit as interesting as the objective truths they are thought to conceal. For example, Maya texts clearly fit into historical genres, ranging from lists of royal successions to tabulations of deaths (e.g., Fig. 4-3; Houston 1991). Just as some Mixtec or Central Mexican documents emphasize genealogy, creation, or migration, so do many Classic Maya texts focus on events that are "like-in-kind," probably with the goal of providing an appropriate historical context for a peak event, the culmination of a particular inscription. In such instances, history is likely to be "paradigmatic" (Cooper 1983a), with events selected for rhetorical effect and molded by literary traditions; such descriptions are not idiosyncratic by nature, but are rather phrased in acceptable, well-worn ways, as, indeed, is much dynastic self-presentation (Winter 1981:7). Several scholars go so far as to argue that these paradigms originate in oral performance (Vansina 1985:34–39), in which the "transmission of historical tradition was . . . subordinated to the demands of the form and context of . . . performance" (Gillespie 1989: xxvii). This is a persuasive argument, for there is ample evidence that most Precolumbian texts were intended not so much to be read as to be sung and performed (e.g., Monaghan 1990).

THE DOS PILAS EMBLEM GLYPH

Three decades ago Heinrich Berlin (1960:26–27; 1977:90) identified an Emblem Glyph, which he attributed not so much to Dos Pilas as to the Lake Petexbatun region to the east of the escarpment on which Dos Pilas lies. Berlin had noticed that the Emblem (Fig. 4-1) enjoyed an unusually broad distribution: it served as the principal Emblem of Dos Pilas, Aguateca, and La Amelia, and also appeared at Seibal. Other researchers, among them Joyce Marcus (1976:63–68; 1983: Fig. 8; 1984: Fig. 6), suggested that Berlin's discovery pointed to a "Petexbatun confederacy": a political association of "lower-order" centers rather than the more typical grouping of subordinate towns serving a "primate" city. Berlin also noticed the appearance of the Tikal Emblem at Dos Pilas, raising the possibility that Dos Pilas and its neighbors recorded part of Tikal's "missing history," an epoch between 9.8.0.0.0 and 9.12.9.17.16 (Coggins 1975; C. Jones and Satterthwaite 1982: Table 5). According to this interpretation, Dos Pilas harbored an expatriate branch of the Tikal dynasty, which later reverted to its site of origin.

These views were reasonable for the time, but additional research points to other conclusions. In the first place, a Petexbatun confederacy is tenable only in the sense that the Dos Pilas dynasty seems to have controlled more than one center. Other sites near Lake Petexbatun, such as Arroyo de Piedra, apparently fell only briefly under the hegemony of Dos Pilas (Houston 1987:295). To describe them as components of a confederacy misrepresents a complex pattern of autonomy and subordination. Further, the very term "confederacy" connotes equality of partnership in a collective political enterprise, a concept that finds little support in Petexbatun epigraphy. In the main,

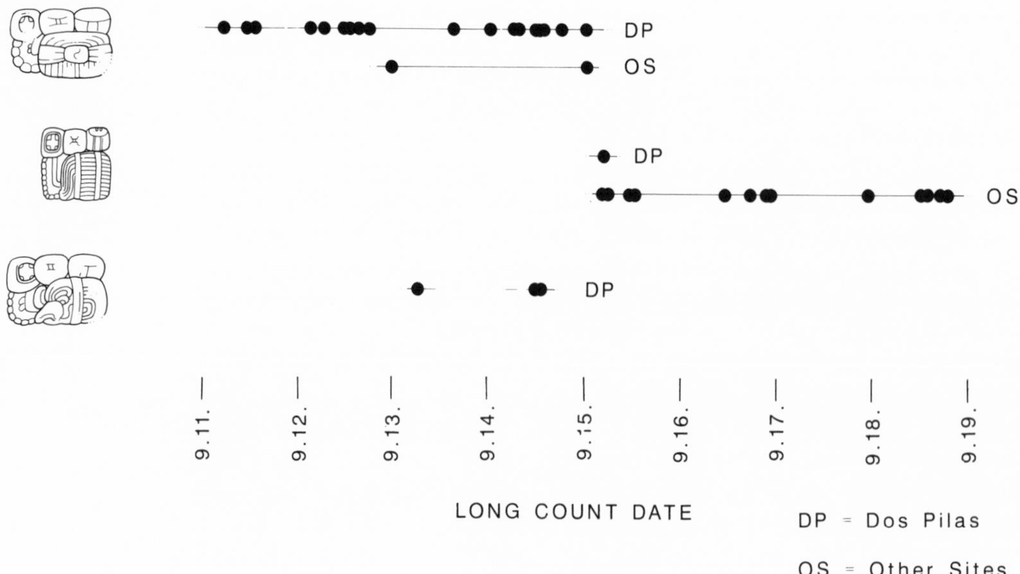

Figure 4-1. Examples of the Dos Pilas Emblem Glyph.

local texts document dynastic competition and ephemeral alliance rather than sustained "confederation," a description perhaps more appropriate to the politics of northern Yucatan (Freidel and Schele 1989).

In the second place, the Emblem of Dos Pilas and Aguateca is, for all intents and purposes, identical to that of Tikal. The glyph conforms to the range of variation of the Tikal Emblem (T569ms), albeit with an increasing preference through time for a particular form of the sign (i.e., T716; see Fig. 4-1; Houston and Mathews 1985 : Fig. 3). Thus, Berlin was in error when he distinguished between a Tikal and a local, "Petexbatun," Emblem. They are simply variants of the same sign.

What are we to make of this? At the very least, it presents a problem of nomenclature. Michael Closs argues that the Pasión version of the Emblem should be described as a "Tikal Emblem glyph" (Closs 1985), an opinion that, as will be seen below, is more or less correct. Nonetheless, I very much favor the term "Dos Pilas Emblem," for the reason that the history of Dos Pilas is on the whole distinct from that of Tikal.

Until recently, many scholars believed that Dos Pilas inscriptions filled the lacunae in Tikal's monumental record, a view best labeled the "missing history hypothesis" (e.g., Coggins 1975). Yet the Dos Pilas dynasty existed independently of Tikal's (Houston 1987 : 275–286). Early members of the dynasty perhaps occupied the Petexbatun region during the time of the Hiatus or later, and their descendants formed a continuous succession of rulers before, during, and after the enthronement of Ruler A of Tikal, at which time Tikal began again to record its history in hieroglyphs. If there was contact between the areas (and evidence suggests that there was), it occurred between different lines of rulers.

But the problem remains of determining the relationships between sites using the Dos Pilas/Tikal Emblem and of discerning the ultimate connection with Tikal. At this juncture, we must define three concepts. The first is "polity," a unit over which Classic rulers exercised real or imagined dominion. Peter Mathews and John Justeson have argued that Emblem Glyphs refer indirectly to such polities, although within the context of royal appellatives (1984). More recent decipherments by David Stuart and others suggest that the entire glyph is to be read, in paraphrase, "holy or divine lord (of) X" (David Stuart, personal communication, 1988). The second concept is "dynasty," an elite descent group ruling over a polity. The third is "toponym," the place name of a particular site controlled by the dynasty, or even of sectors within a site (e.g., "El Duende" at Dos Pilas; see Pohl and Byland 1990 for comparable evidence from the Mixtecs). Stuart and I have proposed the existence of such toponyms, which frequently appear at the end of texts, following an expression meaning "It happened (within)" (D. Stuart 1990a; Stuart and Houston 1990). Toponyms not only enable the epigrapher to establish where certain events took place, but also often form the "main signs" of Emblem Glyphs (the "X" in the preceding paraphrase). Heinrich Berlin has come independently to some of these conclusions (1987:17).

Thus, a dynasty may rule several centers, each identified by its respective toponym. A polity (to which an Emblem alludes) in turn encompasses these centers. In more concrete terms, the Dos Pilas dynasty evidently controlled a polity that embraced more than one site. The toponyms of three of these centers, Dos Pilas, Aguateca, and Seibal, are known (Aguateca Stelae 1:D10a, 2:G6b, 7:F2, I. Graham 1967:Figs. 3, 5, 17): T?:556 for Dos Pilas, T176:200:173 for Seibal, and T74:184:299:529 for Aguateca, with some slight variation in affixation and configuration of signs. The implications of these toponyms are discussed more fully elsewhere (D. Stuart and Houston 1990), but for the moment one thing is clear: the Dos Pilas dynasty inscribed monuments at several sites, each of which contributed importantly to the history of the family (Fig. 4-2). Other Pasión toponyms, possibly surviving to the present, are Akul (see below) and Chakha, documented at Altar de Sacrificios, Arroyo de Piedra, and Tamarindito; Chakha may correspond to the modern Chacrío, which flows northeast of Dos Pilas.

The notion of a toponym and its relation to Emblem Glyphs also helps clarify the connection between the Dos Pilas and the Tikal dynasties, which appear to have used the same Emblem. Mounting evidence suggests that the use of toponyms precedes Emblem usage; that is, only toward the end of the Early Classic period, when dynasties spread over several distinct centers, did Emblems begin to convey a meaning beyond "holy lord of such-and-such a place" (Houston and Johnston 1987). At this point, Emblem Glyphs became more generalized to include a conception of dominion over multiple centers. Consequently, the Dos Pilas Emblem which clearly originated as a toponym at Tikal, must ultimately have derived from that center. And, more pertinent here, it must have been adopted in the Pasión region *after* its meaning became generalized at Tikal. This internal evidence

Figure 4-2. Right: Probable toponyms of the Pasión area: *a*, Aguateca; *b*, Altar de Sacrificios; *c*, Dos Pilas; *d*, Machaquila; *e*, Seibal; *f*, Tamarindito.

Figure 4-3. Above: Tikal Miscellaneous Text 28; reference to Ruler 2 indicated by bracket. Drawing by Annemarie Seuffert, courtesy Tikal Project, The University Museum, University of Pennsylvania (Neg. #68-5-84).

suggests, first, that the Dos Pilas dynasty either came from Tikal or at least claimed derivation from it and, second, that the dynasty laid claim to the title sometime after the middle of the Early Classic period. As with the Mexica Aztec, it is possible that the rulers of Dos Pilas were *invited* from a more exalted site, in this case Tikal, as a ploy by local groups to acquire a prestigious bloodline. The "Woman of Tikal" may have been invited to Naranjo for precisely the same reason: to lend prestige to a dynasty buffeted by ill fortune (Houston 1987).

Nonetheless, available data suggest that Dos Pilas' relationship to Tikal was complex. It has been established that the Dos Pilas dynasty was distinct from Tikal's, although almost certainly the former stemmed from the latter. We also know that the families were in contact with one another during the middle of the Late Classic period: the name of Tikal Ruler A's father, the so-called Shield Skull, appears both on Dos Pilas Hieroglyphic Stairway 2 (David Stuart, personal communication, 1989) and on the newly discovered Hieroglyphic Stairway 4, and an incised text from Tikal Burial 116 (Fig. 4-3) commemorates the death of Dos Pilas Ruler 2 (who, incidentally, is identified by the *toponym* of his site, the one feature to distinguish him from a Tikal lord [Proskouriakoff 1973:173]).[1]

But there is also evidence of turbulence in the relationship. Hieroglyphic Stairway 2 at Dos Pilas records a battle at the site of Tikal during the first years of Dos Pilas' history. And a later record on the same monument refers to war against the site of Dos Pilas, apparently in connection with Ruler A's father. Hieroglyphic Stairway 4, a recent find by Stacey Symonds of the Vanderbilt Petexbatun project, provides much firmer evidence for warfare between Tikal and Dos Pilas: after an initial reverse, Ruler 1 of Dos Pilas apparently captured Shield Skull and may even have interred his remains at the site. This dynastic upset may have led to a short interregnum at Tikal, since Shield Skull's successor, Ruler A, did not inherit the throne until at least three years later.

One other link between Dos Pilas and Tikal is still rather enigmatic. Recent excavations by the Vanderbilt project have revealed a new panel (Panel 18, Fig. 4-4) from the central structure on the summit of Structure L5-49. Although the panel dates to the Late Classic period,

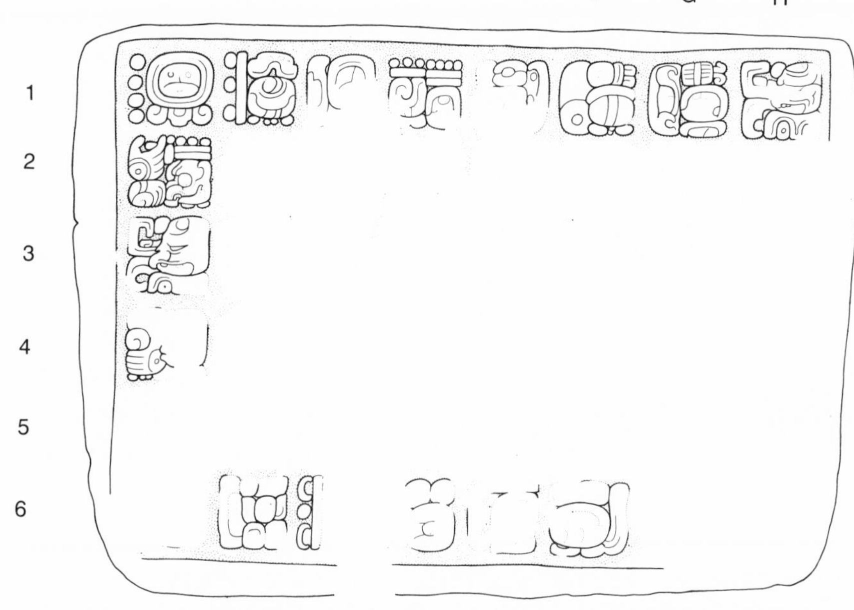

Figure 4-4. Left: Dos Pilas Panel 18. Height: 1.04 m. Drawing by David Stuart, courtesy of Petexbatun Regional Archaeological Project, Vanderbilt University.

Figure 4-5. Below: A mythological figure at Dos Pilas and Tamarindito; *a*, Dos Pilas Panel 18:A3 (after drawing by David Stuart); *b*, Tamarindito Hieroglyphic Stairway 3, Step VI:B1; *c*, Tamarindito Stela 3.

it nonetheless refers to an individual who celebrated the beginning of the era at 13.0.0.0.0. In an eroded passage, the text also records the names of this figure's parents, as well as a possible reference to the so-called Woman of Tikal ("Lady 6 Sky"; see below; David Stuart, personal communication, 1990). Nikolai Grube points out that the protagonist of the panel is the same as an individual mentioned on Tikal Stela 5 (personal communication, 1990). Presumably, then, Tikal and Dos Pilas shared not only the same Emblem, but also a connection to a poorly understood figure in mythological time.

However, Figure 4-5 illustrates one snag in this hypothesis. Virtually the same mythological name occurs on Tamarindito Hieroglyphic Stairway 3: note the snouted creature, macaw bill (at Tamarindito in fuller form), and subfixed star sign—only the skull on the example from Panel 18 fails to appear at Tamarindito, and this may result from glyphic overlapping, which occasionally obscures components of signs (cf. Fig. 4-5*a* and *b*). At Tamarindito, this entity is the founder of the dynasty; if the buccal mask is any indication, a later ruler at the site even dresses as him (Fig. 4-5*c*). Could this figure have been venerated at several sites, regardless of genealogical connections between them? The linkage with Dos Pilas and Tikal would seem not to be entirely exclusive.

A

B

C

THE ORIGINS OF THE DOS PILAS FAMILY

There exist only three hints of lords before Ruler 1, the first well-documented lord at Dos Pilas. One piece of evidence comes from Panel 6, which refers in a parentage statement to an individual who is oth-

Figure 4-6. Uacho Black on Orange vessel from the Duende cave. Glyphs may show the name of early ruler at Dos Pilas. Drawing kindly provided by James Brady, Director, Petexbatun Cave Project.

erwise unattested at Dos Pilas. This individual may well be the father of Ruler 1.

Another clue occurs on a shattered vessel recorded by James Brady from a cave near the duende pyramid (Fig. 4-6). The style of the vessel clearly identifies it as Uacho Black on Orange (R. E. W. Adams 1971 : 30, Table 26), a ceramic dating to the early years of the Late Classic period—that is, to a time *before* Ruler 1. Yet the penultimate glyph (at least on the preserved portion of the fragmented pot) is without question the Dos Pilas/Tikal Emblem Glyph. The chances are excellent that this is the name of an early ruler of Dos Pilas; regrettably, the find is unique, and the name has no parallel elsewhere.

The other evidence is more tentative. On Tamarindito Stela 4 (dating to 9.6.0.0.0) occurs a name apparently belonging to a foreign lord: the appellative differs from that of Tamarindito Ruler 2, who erected the stela, but resembles greatly the name on Dos Pilas Panel 6 (Fig. 4-7). Conceivably, Stela 4 and Panel 6 record the same individual. Another possibility—that these men come from different generations of the same family—is perhaps more reasonable, if only because Stela 4 and Panel 6 have widely divergent dates.[2] Thus, Tamarindito Stela 4 may document a member of the Dos Pilas dynasty who has no other record.

The evidence from Tamarindito is tenuous but important. It suggests that the Dos Pilas dynasty resided near Lake Petexbatun during the Hiatus. (Indeed, the bottom register of Panel 10 may represent a carving from this early phase of Dos Pilas history; see Fig. 3-1.) But it should also be noted that, despite its proximity to Dos Pilas (less than 4 kilometers), Arroyo de Piedra fails to mention its neighbor during this time. This omission suggests, perhaps, that Dos Pilas was something less than a regional power during this period. In addition, many of Dos Pilas' marriage "alliances" probably took place during the reigns of Ruler 1 and, less likely, Ruler 2. An intrusive dynasty might be expected to use such a device to consolidate its position (note that this stratagem was used by some Postclassic polities of Central Mexico [Calnek 1982 : 59]).

DOS PILAS RULERS: WORKS AND LIVES

Ruler 1

With Ruler 1, Dos Pilas moves into an era of more complete historical documentation (see Fig. 4-8 for the Dos Pilas dynastic sequence and Table 4-1 for a complete set of dates). Ruler 1 is unique at the site

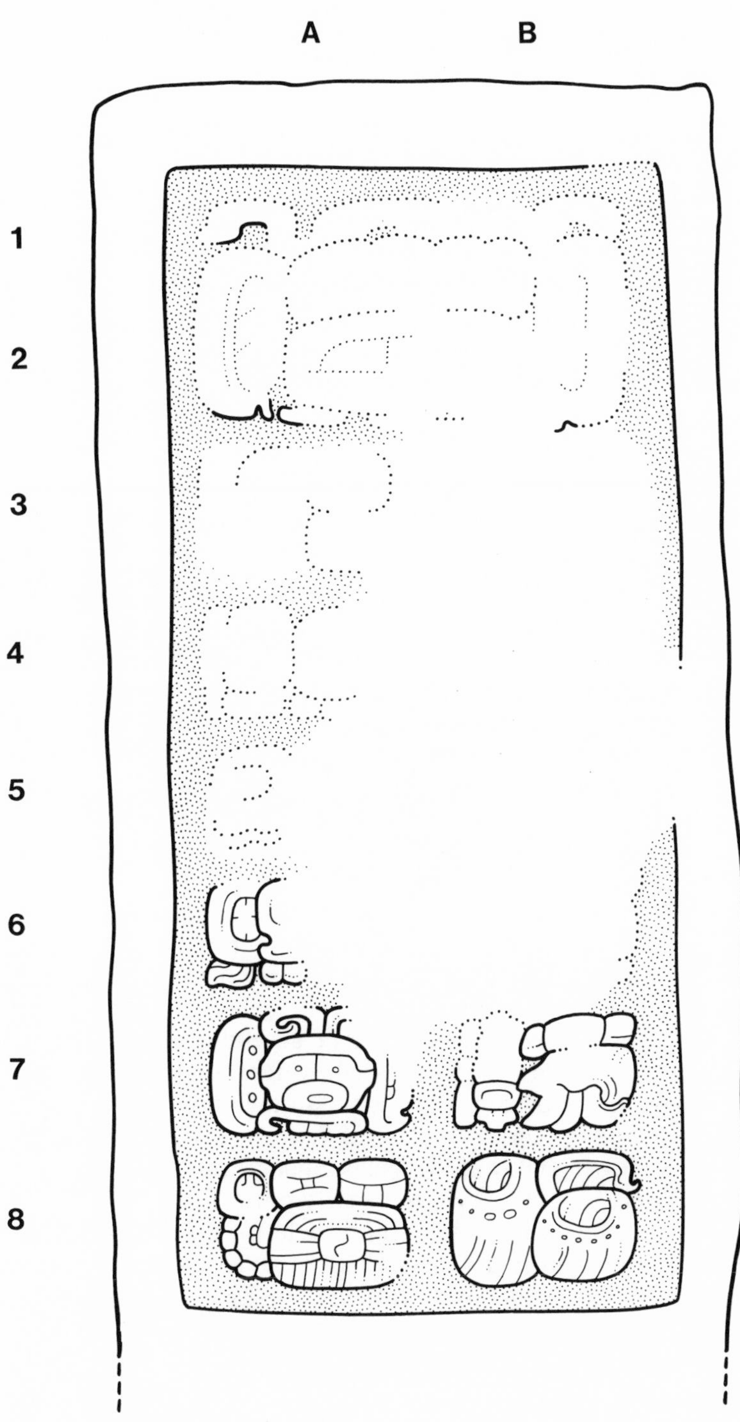

Figure 4-7. Dos Pilas Panel 6, with name of possible early ruler of the Dos Pilas dynasty at B7. Height of carving: 1.63 m.

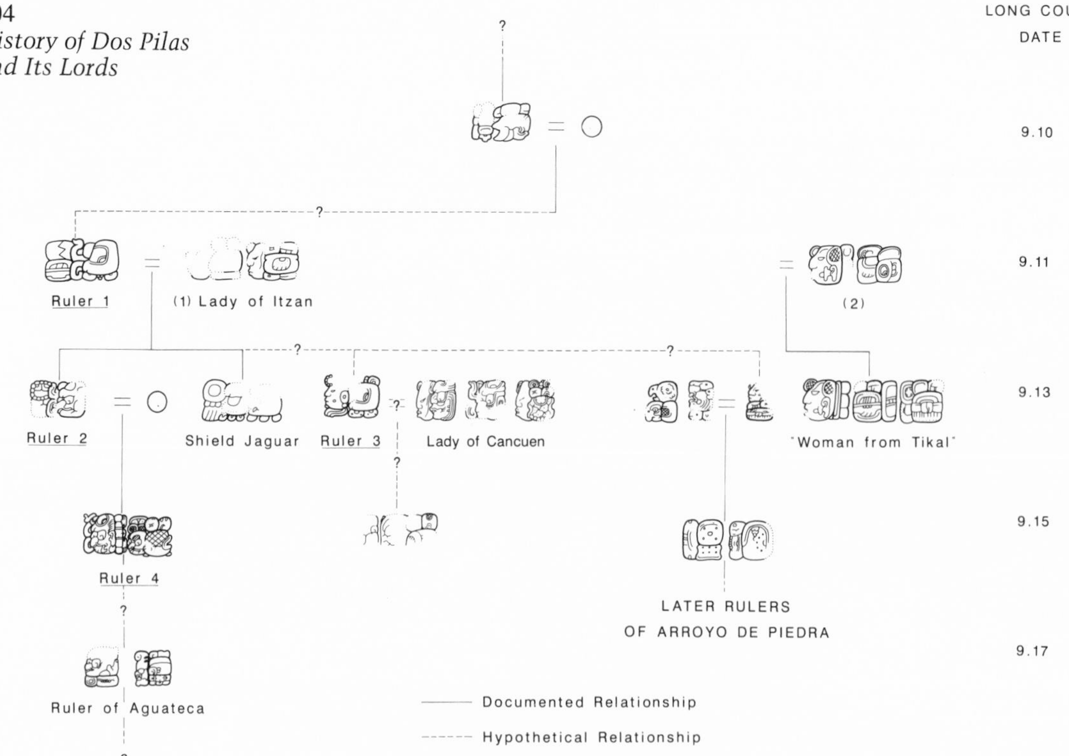

Figure 4-8. The dynastic sequence of Dos Pilas. (Birth sequence of siblings is not always certain.)

for having two variant names, which glyphic passages confirm to be equivalent (Houston and Mathews 1985:9–10, Figs. 5-6). His dates are less secure. Mathews and I have argued elsewhere (ibid.: 11) that Ruler 1 acceded at 9.10.12.11.2. We supported this argument with a supposed parallelism between anniversary phrases involving *hel* signs (ibid.: Fig. 7). The phrases purportedly read, in loose paraphrase, "The completion of the change of Ruler X's *n*th katun in office."

Additional evidence now indicates that the argument is in error. To begin with, there appears to be a genuine distinction between T573, which occurs in an explicit anniversary expression on Hieroglyphic Stairway 1 (Houston and Mathews 1985:Fig. 7c), and T676, which marks the supposed anniversary of Ruler 1's accession (ibid.: Fig. 7b). Many epigraphers believe the signs to be equivalent (Riese 1984a:266), but David Stuart suggests that T676 may simply express an ordinal construction, such as "second" in place of "two" (personal communication, 1986). A growing body of evidence supports this view. For one, the signs use different subfixes: T676 usually takes T178, probably as an ordinal construction at Palenque, *-tal* (Schele 1982:Fig. 31). For another, the signs consistently appear in distinct glyphic contexts (*pace* Riese 1984a). Scribes at Seibal uniformly employ T676 to indicate the first katun of cycle 10 (e.g., Stelae 10 and 11), and a similar practice with respect to rulers occurs at Yaxchilan (e.g., Yaxchilan Lintel 37, I. Graham 1979:83).

To return to Dos Pilas, the anniversary expression on Hieroglyphic Stairway 2 may now be read as "Completion, *third* his katun, Ruler 1"

Table 4-1. ***Dates of Dos Pilas rulers***

Date		Julian Equivalent[a]	Provenance
Earlier Dates			
13.0.0.0.0	4 Ahau 8 Cumku	−3113 Sep 11	Pan. 18
Ruler 1			
(9.9.12.11.2	8 Ik 5 Ceh)	625 Oct 15	HS 2
(9.9.12.11.2	8 Ik 5 Ceh)	625 Oct 15	HS 4
(9.)10.15.0.0	6 Ahau 13 Mac	647 Nov 7	HS 4
(9.10.15.4.9)	4 Muluc 2 Cumku	648 Feb 4	HS 4
(9.)11.0.0.0	(12 Ahau 8 Ceh)	652 Oct 11	HS 2
(9.11.4.5.14)	6 *Ix 2 Kayab	657 Jan 12	HS 2
(9.11.9.15.19)	9 Cauac 17 Yaxkin	662 Jul 10	HS 2
(9.11.)10.0.0	11 Ahau *18 Ch'en	662 Aug 20	HS 2
(9.11.)10.0.0	11 Ahau *18 Ch'en	662 Aug 20	HS 2
(9.11.11.9.17)	9 Caban 5 Pop	664 Feb 20	HS 2
(9.12.0.0.0)	10 Ahau 8 Yaxkin	672 Jun 28	HS 2
(9.12.0.8.3	4 Akbal 11 Muan)	672 Dec 8	HS 2
(9.12.0.8.3)	4 Akbal 11 Muan	672 Dec 8	HS 4
9.12.*0.*10.11	13 Chuen 19 Kayab	673 Jan 25	St. 8
(9.12.4.16.2	4 Ik) *5 Zotz'?	677 Apr 25	HS 2
(9.12.5.9.14)	*2 Ix *17 Muan	677 Dec 13	HS 2
(9.12.5.10.1)	9 Imix 4 Pax	677 Dec 20	HS 2
(9.12.5.10.1)	9 Imix 4 Pax	677 Dec 20	HS 4
(9.12.6.16.17)	11 Caban 10 Zotz'	679 Apr 30	HS 2
(9.12.6.16.17)	11 Caban 10 Zotz'	679 Apr 30	HS 4
(9.12.)7.0.0	8 Ahau 13 Tzec	679 May 26	HS 2
(9.12.)7.0.0	8 Ahau 13 Tzec	679 May 26	HS 2
(9.12.10.0.0)	9 Ahau (18 Zotz')	682 May 10	St. 9
(9.12.)10.0.0	9 Ahau 18 Zotz'	682 May 10	HS 2
9.12.10.0.0	9 Ahau 18 Zotz'	682 May 10	HS 4
(9.12.12.11.2)	2 Ik 10 Muan	684 Dec 4	HS 2
9.12.12.11.2	2 Ik 10 Muan	684 Dec 4	HS 4
(9.12.13.17.7)	6 Manik 5 Zip	686 Apr 3	Pan. 7
(9.)13.0.0.0	8 Ahau 8 Uo	692 Mar 15	AGT St. 5
Ruler 2			
9.12.*0.*10.11	13 Chuen 19 Kayab	673 Jan 25	St. 8
(9.13.6.2.0)	11 Ahau 18 Uo	698 Mar 24	St. 8
(9.13.10.11.12	5 Eb 10 Zac)	702 Sep 11	St. 8
(9.13.13.8.2)	1 Ik 5 Yaxkin	705 Jun 17	St. 1
(9.13.)15.0.0	13 Ahau 18 Pax	706 Dec 31	St. 1
9.14.0.0.0	6 Ahau 13 Muan	711 Dec 1	St. 14
(9.14.0.0.0)	6 Ahau 13 Muan	711 Dec 1	St. 8
(9.14.0.0.0	6 Ahau 13 Muan)?	711 Dec 1	ARP St. 7
(9.14.)5.0.0	*12 Ahau *8 Kankin	716 Nov 4	St. 11
(9.14.)5.0.0	12 Ahau 8 Kankin	716 Nov 4	HS 1
(9.14.5.3.14)	8 Ix 2 Cumku	717 Jan 17	St. 14

Table 4-1 ***continued***

Date		Julian Equivalent[a]	Provenance
(9.14.6.2.0)	*9 Ahau *3 Pax?	717 Dec 9	HS 1
(9.14.6.6.0)	11 Ahau 18 Pop?	718 Feb 27	St. 16
(9.14.6.10.2)	2 Ik 0 Xul	718 Feb 24	St. 16
9.14.9.10.13	1 Ben 16 Tzec	721 May 15	St. 15
(9.14.9.16.15)	6 Men 18 Zac	721 Sep 14	HS 1
(9.14.)10.0.0	5 Ahau 3 Mac	721 Oct 9	St. 15
(9.14.10.4.0)	7 Ahau 3 Kayab	721 Dec 28	St. 15
(9.14.11.4.14)	*4 Ix 12 Kayab?	723 Jan 6	HS 1
(9.14.11.4.15)	5 Men 13 Kayab	723 Jan 7	HS 1
(9.14.)13.0.0	6 Ahau 8 Ceh	724 Sep 23	HS 1
(9.14.15.1.19)	11 Cauac 17 Mac	726 Oct 22	St. 8
(9.14.15.2.3)	3 Kan *2 Kankin	726 Oct 26	St. 8
Ruler 3			
(9.14.15.5.15)	9 Men 13 Kayab	727 Jan 6	St. 8
9.15.0.0.0	4 Ahau 13 Yax	731 Aug 18	St. 5
9.15.0.0.0	4 Ahau 13 Yax	731 Aug 18	St. 5
9.15.0.0.0	4 Ahau 13 Yax	731 Aug 18	St. 5
9.15.4.6.4	8 Kan 17 Muan	735 Nov 29	St. 2
(9.15.4.6.4)	8 Kan 17 Muan	735 Nov 29	AGT St. 2
(9.15.4.6.5)	9 Chicchan 18 Muan	735 Nov 30	St. 2
(9.15.4.6.5)	9 Chicchan 18 Muan	735 Nov 30	AGT St. 2
(9.15.4.6.11)	2 Chuen 4 Pax	735 Dec 6	St. 2
(9.15.4.6.11)	2 Chuen 4 Pax	735 Dec 6	AGT St. 2
(9.15.)5.0.0	10 Ahau 8 Ch'en	736 Jul 22	AGT St. 2
(9.15.9.)9.0	5 Ahau 8 Kayab	740 Dec 28	HB 1
(9.15.9.)9.0	5 Ahau 8 Kayab	740 Dec 28	AGT St. 2
(9.15.9.16.11)	13 Chuen 14 Xul	741 May 28	AGT St. 1
(9.15.9.16.12)	1 Eb 15 Xul	741 May 29	HB 1
Ruler 4			
(9.14.9.16.15)	6 Men *18 Zac	721 Sep 14	HS 1
(9.15.9.16.15)	4 Men 18 Xul	741 Jun 1	AGT St. 1
(9.15.9.17.17)	13 Caban 20 Yaxkin	741 Jun 23	AGT St. 1
(9.15.)10.0.0	3 Ahau 3 Mol	741 Jun 26	AGT St. 1
(9.15.10.13.0)	3 Ahau 18 Uo?	742 Mar 13	St. 4
(9.15.10.17.15)	7 Men 13 Yaxkin	742 Jun 16	HB 1
(9.15.)11.0.0	(12 Ahau 18 Yaxkin)?	742 Jun 21	St. 4
9.15.13.13.0	4 Ahau (3 Uo)	744 Aug 9	SBL HS 1
(9.15).15.0.0	9 Ahau 18 Xul	746 May 31	SBL HS 1
(9.15.16.7.17)	6 Caban 10 Kankin	747 Oct 30	SBL HS 1
(9.15.16.7.17)	6 Caban 10 Kankin	747 Oct 30	SBL HS 1
9.15.16.12.1	12 *Imix 14 Cumku	748 Jan 22	AGT St. 6
(9.16.9.4.19)	13 *Cauac 7 Mol	760 Jun 25	AML HS 1
(9.16.9.15.3)	9 Akbal 11 Cumku	761 Jan 15	TAM HS 2

Date		*Julian Equivalent*[a]	*Provenance*
Later rulers			
9.15.16.12.1	12 *Imix 14 Cumku	748 Jan 22	AGT St. 6
(9.16.9.4.19)	13 *Cauac 7 Mol	760 Jun 25	AML HS 1
(9.16.18.15.11)	1 *Chuen 14 Kayab?	769 Dec 7	AGT St. 6
(9.16.19.0.14)	*5 Ix 12 *Pop?	770 Feb 8	AGT St. 6
(9.16.19.0.17)	8 *Caban (15 Pop)?	770 Feb 11	AGT St. 6
(9.16.19.10.11)	7 Chuen 9 Zac	770 Aug 24	AGT St. 6
(9.)17.0.0.0	13 *Ahau 18 Cumku	771 Jan 20	AGT St. 6
(9.17.0.0.0)	13 Ahau 18 Cumku	771 Jan 20	SBL St. 6
(9.17.0.0.0)	13 Ahau 18 Cumku	771 Jan 20	SBL St. 7
(9.17.)10.0.0	12 Ahau 8 Pax?	780 Nov 28	SBL St. 5
(9.)18.0.0.0	11 Ahau 18 Mac	790 Oct 11	AGT St. 7
(9.)18.0.0.0	11 Ahau 18 Mac	790 Oct 11	AGT St. 14
(9.18.)10.0.0	10 Ahau 8 Zac	800 Aug 15	SBL St. 7
(9.18.11.12.0)	12 Ahau 18 Zotz'	802 Apr 7	AML HS 1
(9.18.11.13.4)	10 Kan *2 Xul	802 May 1	AML HS 1
(9.18.13.17.1)	1 *Imix 9 Ch'en	804 Jul 6	AML Pan. 2
(9.18.13.17.1)	1 Imix 9 Ch'en	804 Jul 6	AML HS 1
(9.18.17.1.13)	2 Ben 6 Zac	807 Aug 12	AML Pan. 1
(9.18.17.1.13)	2 Ben 6 Zac	807 Aug 12	AML Pan. 1

[a]Julian equivalents accord with the 584285 correlation advocated by Lounsbury (1982:166).

Key: AGT = Aguateca; AML = La Amelia; ARP = Arroyo de Piedra; SBL = Seibal; TAM = Tamarindito.

Note: Parentheses enclose unattested portions of the date; asterisks denote eroded but reconstructible text. Question marks indicate uncertainty about a reconstruction. In some cases, the same date occurs more than once on a single monument.

or, in less awkward paraphrase, "Completion of Ruler 1's *third* katun" (note the corrected ordinal), an anniversary that appears in much clearer form on Dos Pilas Hieroglyphic Stairway 4. Since there are no explicit references to royal titles, the allusion may well be to Ruler 1's birth at 9.9.12.11.2 (October 15, A.D. 625) rather than to his accession. This placement accords well with data from Aguateca Stela 5, which shows that Ruler 1 was in his fourth katun at 9.13.0.0.0, thereby placing his birth sometime before 9.10.0.0.0. But there is one major problem: Ruler 1's other katun notations, particularly those at the site of Naranjo, would seem to be consistent with a later date of birth. The inscriptions of Palenque have a similar set of discrepancies in their record of royal katuns (Linda Schele, personal communication, 1983).

Parentage statements (Houston and Mathews 1985:11, 14, Fig. 8; C. Jones 1977:41; Schele, Mathews, and Lounsbury 1977) help identify Ruler 1's wives and children. One of his wives came from the site of Itzan, which has a slightly earlier historical record than Dos Pilas. Ruler 1 had two sons by this woman: Ruler 2 and Shield Jaguar, who

Figure 4-9. Dos Pilas Hieroglyphic Bench 1. Width: 2.15 m. Drawing by Stephen Houston, courtesy of Petexbatun Regional Archaeological Project, Vanderbilt University.

ruled either very briefly or not at all. There is a more distant possibility that "Shield Jaguar" is simply a preaccession name of Ruler 2. Another consort gave birth to a third child, the so-called Woman of Tikal, whom Marcus cites as an example of Tikal's widespread influence (1976: 58–60).[3] Parentage statements at Naranjo and a recently discovered fragment from Dos Pilas Hieroglyphic Bench 1 (Fig. 4-9) leave little doubt that this child came from the area of Dos Pilas. The woman, whom I prefer to call Lady 6 Sky, is important because she contributed to the revitalization of the Naranjo dynasty, which had been seriously affected by war with Caracol (Fig. 4-10; Sosa and Reents 1980). Her impact on Naranjo did not stop there: at least one later ruler of Naranjo used the name employed by her half-brother, Ruler 2, and a reference on Naranjo Stela 22 shows that during her lifetime Naranjo captured one Smoking Frog from Tikal, an event suggesting that she brought with her the traditional antagonisms of her family. That she enjoyed such influence must speak in part for the prestige and influence of her home site.[4] Recently discovered fragments from Hieroglyphic Bench 1 show that she died at about the same time as Ruler 3.

Ruler 1's relations with foreign sites extended beyond the transfer of one of his children to Naranjo. Hieroglyphic Stairway 4 (Fig. 4-11) explicitly refers to Ruler 1 as the *ahaw*—possibly "ally" in this connection—of a lord of Site Q, almost certainly Calakmul. In contrast to Tikal, which had poor relations with Calakmul, Dos Pilas seems to have had amicable ties with the site.[5] Ruler 1 not only attended the accession of Calakmul ruler Jaguar Paw Smoke, one of the most extraordinary personalities of the Classic period (Stuart and Houston 1990), but also visited Calakmul on at least one other occasion, as can be seen from a toponymic expression on Stela 9 (Fig. 4-12, F4).

Figure 4-10. Naranjo Stela 24, showing a royal lady from Dos Pilas. Height of carving: 1.92 m. Drawing by Ian Graham (1975: 63). Ian Graham and Eric von Euw, *Corpus of Maya Hieroglyphic Inscriptions, Volume 2, Part 1, Naranjo.* Peabody Museum of Archaeology and Ethnology. Copyright 1975 by the President and Fellows of Harvard College.

There is also much evidence of warfare. Hieroglyphic Stairways 2 and 4 record not only a battle against Tikal and the capture of its ruler, probably under the auspices of Calakmul (Mathews 1979b), but also the capture of Torch Macaw (most likely a title accorded to captives) and a war against the *site* (not the dynasty) of Dos Pilas. This last reference is enigmatic, since a war against the home site would seem to be extraordinary. Perhaps the best explanation for this anomaly is the pattern of Maya political rhetoric. For example, Assyrian scribes often wove "humiliating encounter(s)" into accounts of later successes so as to contrast trifling defeats with glorious victories; the latter neutralized the former (Grayson 1980: 171). Perhaps the Maya occasionally did the same, thus avoiding the necessity of omitting momentous, if embarrassing events or of recording blatant falsehoods.

Before leaving Ruler 1, it is necessary to discuss Aguateca Stela 5,

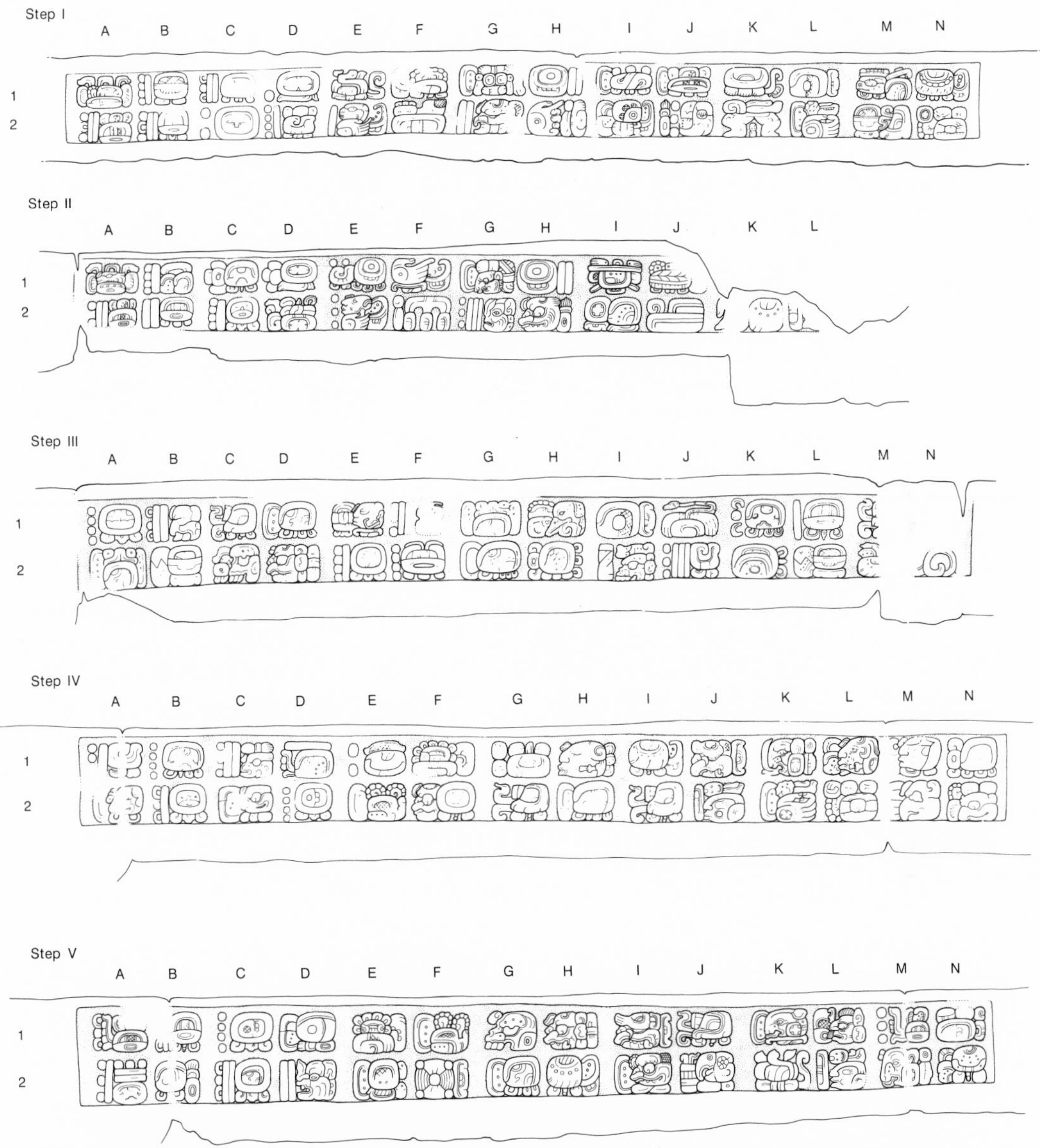

Figure 4-11. Dos Pilas Hieroglyphic Stairway 4. Height of carvings: Step I, .20 m; Step II, .22 m; Step III, .25 m; Step IV, .25 m; Step V, .28 m. Step IV:M1 indicates that Ruler 1 is the *ahaw* of a ruler of Calakmul.

which poses several historical problems (Fig. 4-13). The stela is now in many fragments, some undocumented and others still buried (Houston and Mathews 1985:Fig. 19). Nonetheless, at least one date on the monument is fairly clear. This date is 9.13.0.0.0, at which time Ruler 1 celebrated a Period Ending. The other dates on the monument are less easily deciphered. Specifically, the dedicatory date should fall in the reign of Ruler 4, whose names and titles appear on the stela; yet the date seems to fit squarely in the time of Ruler 1 (ibid.: 24). Mathews and I were perplexed by this matter, although we overlooked one possible solution: if one presumes that some of the text on Stela 5 is missing (a reasonable proposal, given the fragmentary state of the monument), the dedicatory date may simply be 9.16.5.0.0, from which is counted the only Distance Number remaining on the stela.[6] This Distance Number duly arrives at the accession date of Ruler 4; indeed, a portion of an accession verb appears just before the end of the clause. A second, hypothetical Distance Number may then have linked the accession date to 9.13.0.0.0. Obviously, Stela 5 will continue to be a problem until its fragments are assembled and the gaps in its text filled. But the solution proposed here suggests that Aguateca Stela 5 may be the final monument, not of Ruler 1's reign, but of Ruler 4's.

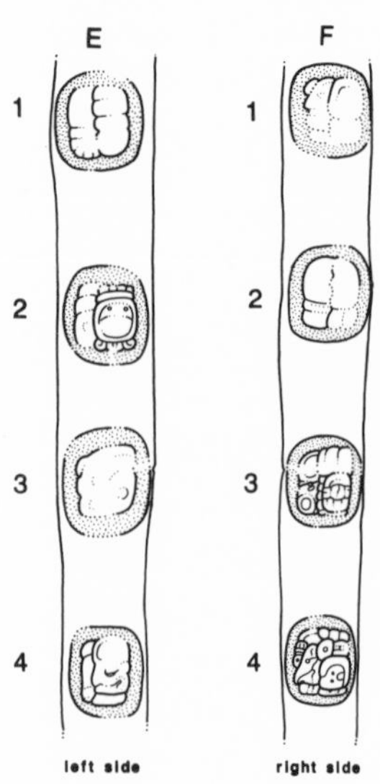

Figure 4-12. Sides of Dos Pilas Stela 9, showing probable Calakmul place name at F4. Width: .42 m.

Ruler 2

As mentioned earlier, Ruler 2 was the child of Ruler 1 and a woman from Itzan. His key dates are well documented, thanks to a superb study by Mathews of Dos Pilas Stela 8 (Fig. 4-14), which supplies much of this information (Mathews 1979a; cf. Hochleitner 1972). Of particular note is the reference to his death and probably his burial date on a bone text from Tikal, in the grave of a possible distant relative (Proskouriakoff 1973:170). The inscription of Stela 8 (H14–I15) specifies that his burial took place at Dos Pilas, perhaps in Structure L5-1 or in Structure P5-7, near which many of his stelae occur. Burial 30, discovered in Structure L5-1 during the 1991 season of the Vanderbilt project, may well be Ruler 2's tomb, although there is no explicit glyphic evidence from the burial to confirm this identification.

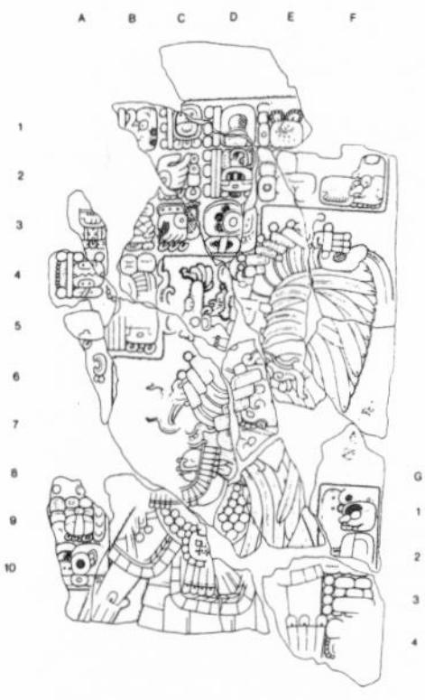

Figure 4-13. Aguateca Stela 5. Width: 1.8 m. Drawing courtesy of Ian Graham.

Ruler 2 has an unusually complete historical record. He is responsible for many of the monuments at the site and seems to have been more inclined than other rulers to erect stelae at hotun endings (at least insofar as this can be judged from extant sculptures). A good example of his monuments is Stela 15, which makes extensive use of couplet constructions, including the first known references to the sites of Seibal and Aguateca (Fig. 4-15).[7]

The longest inscription of Ruler 2's reign is Hieroglyphic Stairway 1 (Fig. 4-16), which records his parentage (Step III, M1–O1) and suggests, in an eroded section, that he fathered Ruler 4 (Step II, F2). Another expression on the stairway (Step III, A3–B3) commemorates Ruler 2's accession (Houston and Mathews 1985: 11, Fig. 7). In the bottom central riser, a subsidiary text contains an elite (but nonroyal) title (Step III, pW2) that involves the stewardship of secondary sites under the aegis of a royal dynasty (Mathews and Justeson 1984:212–213).

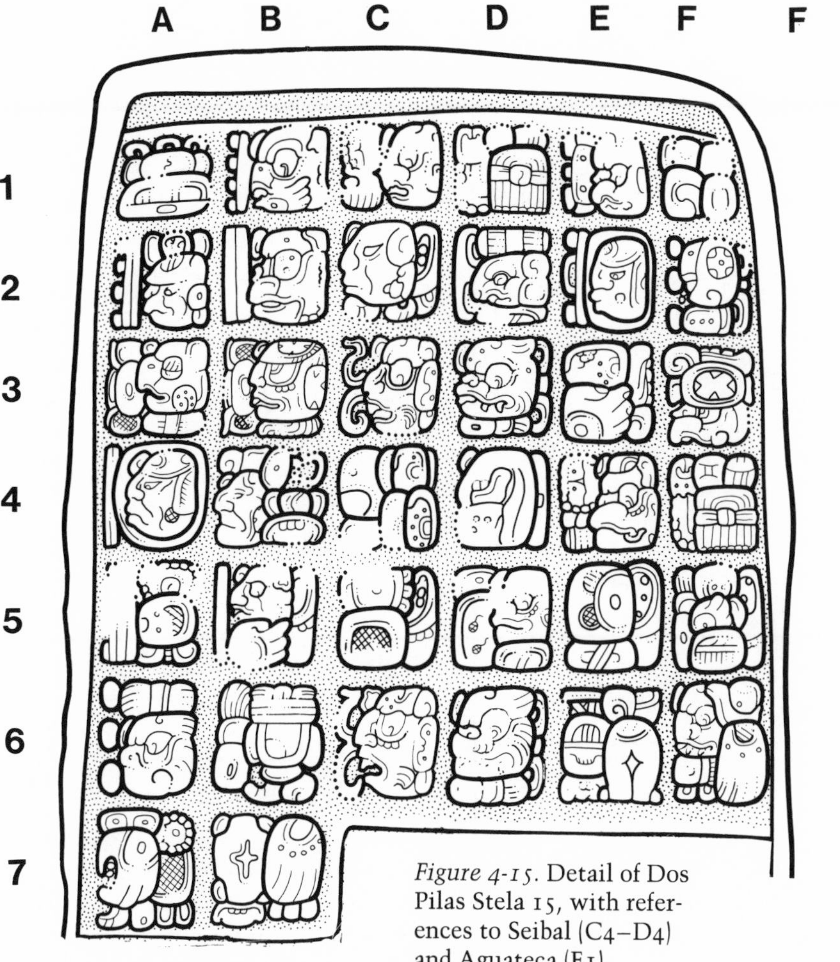

Figure 4-15. Detail of Dos Pilas Stela 15, with references to Seibal (C4–D4) and Aguateca (E1).

Figure 4-14. The back of Dos Pilas Stela 8. Height of carving: >4.95 m. Drawing courtesy of Ian Graham.

The title is also documented in association with a captive on Tamarindito Hieroglyphic Stairway 1 and a woman from the Pasión site of Akul (see below), indicating that this status is not restricted to the Usumacinta River drainage, although, to be sure, it is most common there.[8]

Three monuments—Dos Pilas Stelae 1, 14, and 15—document Ruler 2's military adventures. The first, Stela 1, shows that Dos Pilas and Tikal continued to be antagonists during Ruler 2's lifetime, for it records the defeat of a person from Tikal. Hereafter, all references to Tikal cease at Dos Pilas, as though the rulers of Dos Pilas had begun to lose their preoccupation with distant sites in the northeastern Peten, shifting more to local power struggles. Stelae 14 and 15 both record shell-star wars (see below), but against sites that cannot be securely identified. One place was apparently *NIKTE-il-na*, *Nikteilna*, "community house, house where people meet" (Barrera Vásquez 1980:570, 666), a name rather similar to that proposed for a building at Copan (Fash and Stuart 1991:171). The same name may appear in the titles of a royal spouse at Tamarindito (Fig. 4-17, Step V, A1–B1), who came from a place called Chakha, possibly equivalent to Chacrío, a stream

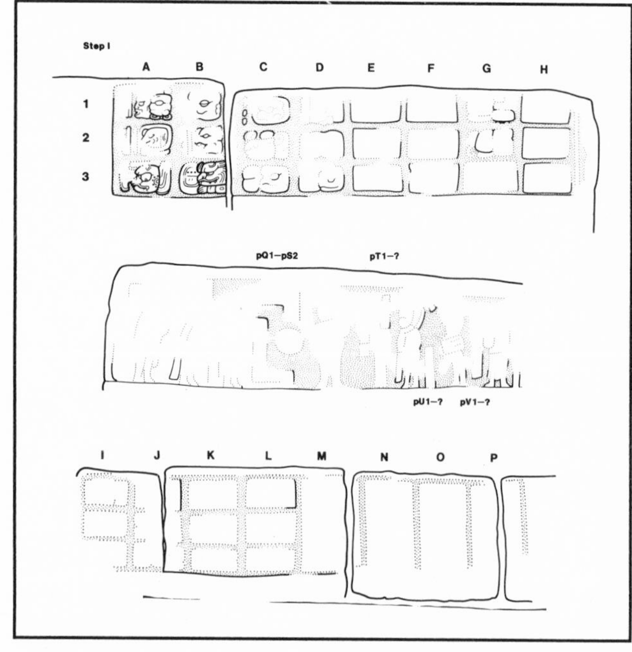

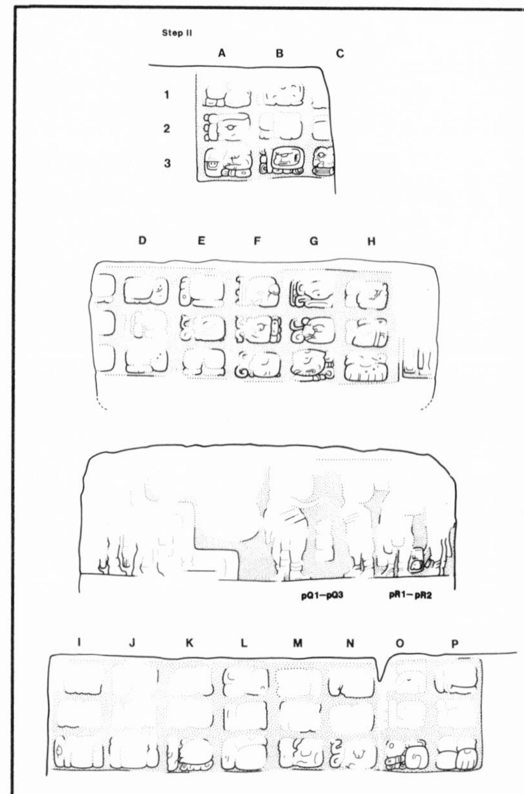

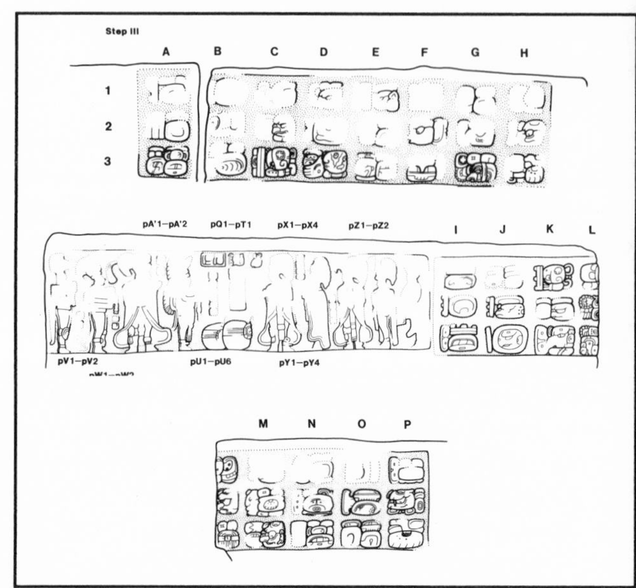

Figure 4-16. Dos Pilas Hieroglyphic Stairway 1. Height: Step I, .55 m; Step II, .50 m; Step III, .51 m.

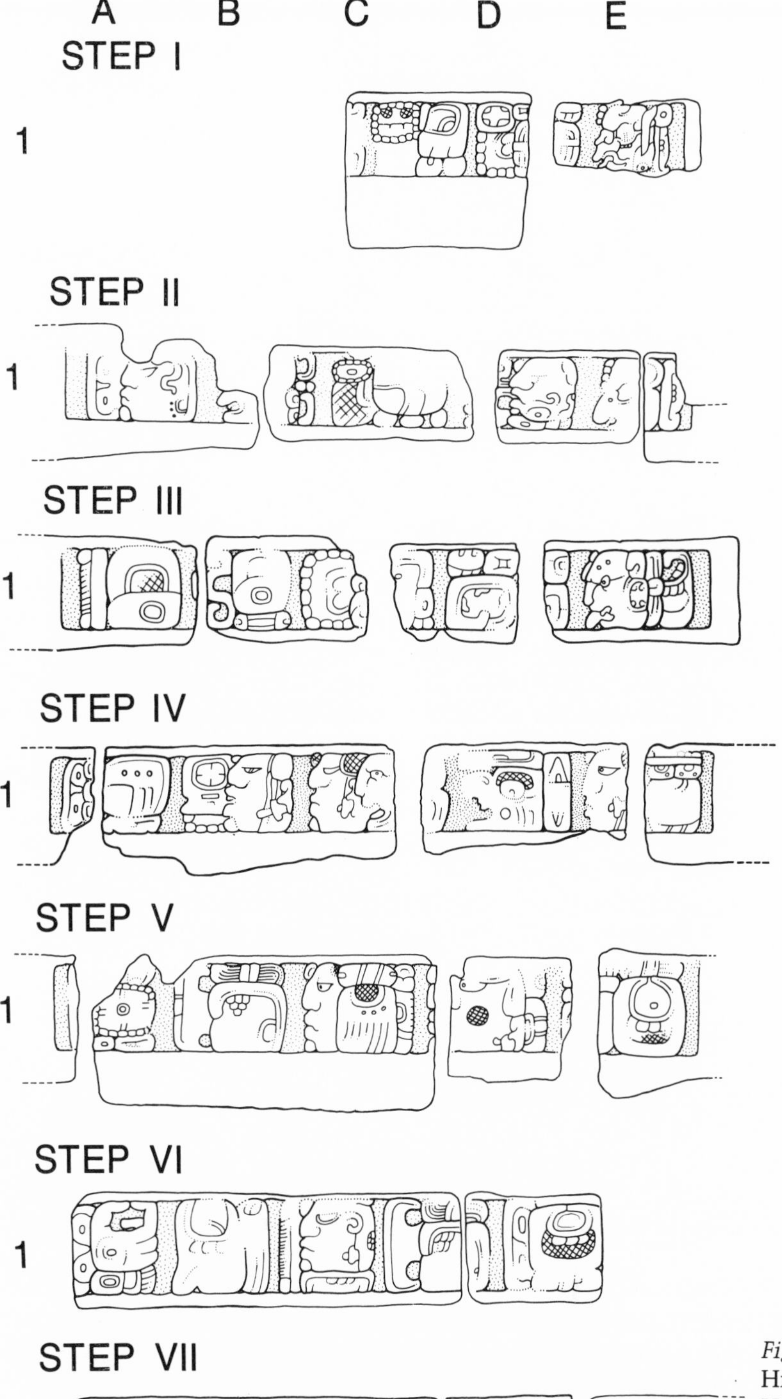

Figure 4-17. Tamarindito Hieroglyphic Stairway 3. Height of carving: Step I, .25 m; Step II, .26 m; Step III, .28 m; Step IV, .28 m; Step V, .30 m; Step VI, .32 m; Step VII, .34 m.

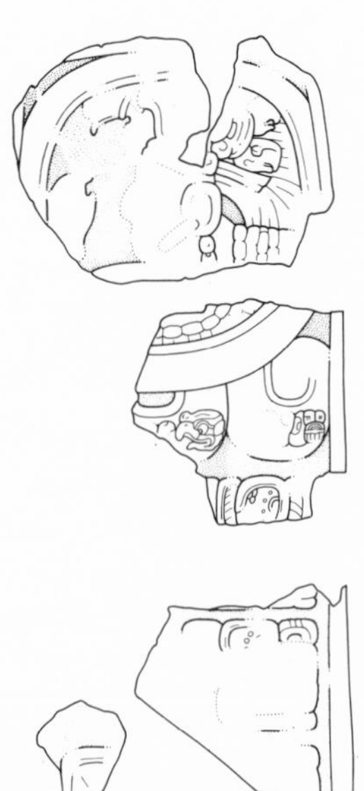

Figure 4-18. Arroyo de Piedra Stela 7. Height: >1.44 m.

northeast of Dos Pilas. Regrettably, the location mentioned on Stela 15 has no parallel in Pasión inscriptions.

References to Ruler 2 are widespread. Tamarindito Hieroglyphic Stairway 3 mentions him sometime around 9.14.0.0.0, at which time he performed an event (now eroded in the text) under the auspices of a local ruler, most likely the twenty-sixth ruler of the Tamarindito dynasty (Fig. 4-17). Another reference to Ruler 2 appears in a posthumous citation on Arroyo de Piedra Stela 2 (E3b–F3; Houston and Mathews 1985:15, 17). On this monument Ruler 2 is mentioned as an "overlord" whose name is recorded before the parents of the local ruler (ibid.:27); the mother of this ruler also comes from Dos Pilas, although the father is of the Tamarindito/Arroyo de Piedra dynasty. Finally, Ruler 2's name may appear on the shattered Stela 7 at Arroyo de Piedra, which probably dates to 9.14.0.0.0 (Fig. 4-18).[9]

Ruler 3

Two of the longest stela texts at Dos Pilas date to the reign of Ruler 3. Stela 8, for example, recounts events that occurred, for the most part, during the life of Ruler 2; yet it also mentions the accession of Ruler 3, who came to rule within days of Ruler 2's burial. Unfortunately, the text fails to explain the relationship between the dynasts. There are no surviving parentage statements in the Petexbatun region after 9.14.11.4.15, a date slightly before the reign of Ruler 3 (Houston and Mathews 1985:17). The only clue is one on Stela 11, which suggests that Ruler 3 may have been the brother of Ruler 2 (Fig. 3-27).

It is from the time of Ruler 3 that we have the best glyphic evidence of subordinate lords residing at Dos Pilas. This evidence comes from Hieroglyphic Bench 1 and Panel 19, excavated in 1990 by Joel Palka of Vanderbilt University. Both are found in groups that may have been occupied by people other than the ruler, including perhaps the spouse of a king (cf. Webster 1989). Panel 19 is of special interest for its explicit depictions of three members of the nobility, one of whom may have been the guardian of a son of the ruler (Fig. 4-19). The glyph at Q2 indicates that this same individual may have come from the site of Calakmul, with which Dos Pilas had strong connections during the reign of Ruler 1.

Much like his predecessors, Ruler 3 continued to interact aggressively with other sites in the Pasión drainage. Among his most important achievements was the capture of a Seibal lord, Yich'ak Balam (D. Stuart 1987). As a result of this action, the Dos Pilas dynasty controlled Seibal for ten years (Lounsbury 1982: 154, 165), enough time, it seems, to supervise the construction of a tomb by a local lord. A branch of the dynasty perhaps controlled Seibal for another fifty years (Houston and Mathews 1985: 17). It is also likely that Ruler 3 married a lady from Cancuen; both appear on Dos Pilas Panel 19, presiding over the bloodletting ceremony of a child, probably their offspring, possibly a youthful Ruler 4. The burial of this woman may have been found in 1990, in a cist 1 meter below Hieroglyphic Bench 1, a monument that records her death.

Ruler 3 is not the first Dos Pilas lord to erect monuments at Aguateca; that honor apparently must go to Ruler 2 or even Ruler 1 (see comments on Aguateca Stela 5). But his monuments are the first surviving records from the site. One stela (Stela 2, Fig. 4-20) duplicates

Figure 4-19. Left: Dos Pilas Panel 19, showing bloodletting of youth, with Ruler 3 and Lady of Cancuen in attendance. Height: .64 m. Drawing by David Stuart and Stephen Houston, inking by David Stuart, courtesy of Petexbatun Regional Archaeological Project, Vanderbilt University.

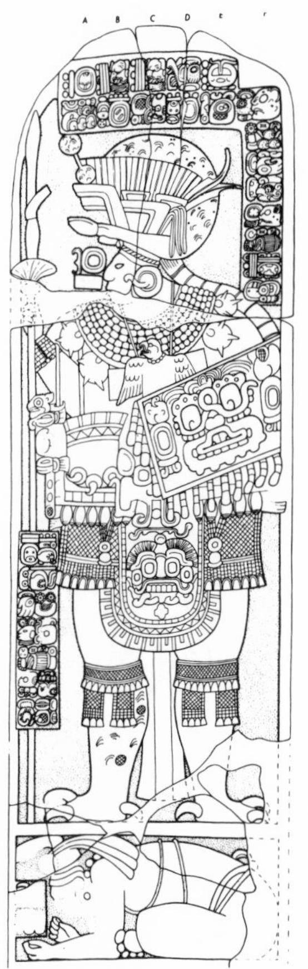

Figure 4-20. Below: Aguateca Stela 2. Height of carving: 2.90 m. Reproduced with permission from Publication 33, Middle American Research Institute, New Orleans, Louisiana (I. Graham 1967:Fig. 5).

information on Dos Pilas Stela 2, and the other (Stela 3) celebrates a hotun ending. This pattern of stela erection has other implications: it is extremely unusual for a dynasty to erect coeval monuments at two sites, particularly when there does not seem to be any evidence of a local, subordinate dynasty. Aguateca and Dos Pilas are an example, then, of a phenomenon best described as "twin capital" settlement, which may be a response to the logistical difficulties of political administration or to the limitations of transport (see below). Tamarindito and Arroyo de Piedra may be another instance of "twin capitals" in the Pasión.

Ruler 3's death is recorded in two places: Aguateca Stela 1 and Dos Pilas Hieroglyphic Bench 1. Unlike Ruler 2's burial, which is almost certainly at Dos Pilas, Ruler 3's could have been at Dos Pilas, Aguateca, or some other location. Aguateca Structure 6 is perhaps one strong candidate for his sepulcher, for Stela 1 once stood in front of it.

Ruler 4

Ruler 4 is the last member of his family to be documented at Dos Pilas. Nonetheless, most of his dates come from other sites. Aguateca Stela 1 indicates that Ruler 4 acceded to rule only days after the demise of his predecessor, Ruler 3; Tamarindito Hieroglyphic Stairway 2 has his last date, 9.16.9.15.3 (Fig. 4-21), after which he disappears from the epigraphic record. Between these dates are references from Seibal (Hieroglyphic Stairway 1) and Cancuen (Hieroglyphic Stairway 1). The former commemorates Ruler 4's last attested Period Ending rites and perhaps the carving of the monument (D. Stuart 1987:148). The stairway is also a tangible expression of Dos Pilas' continued influence over Seibal.[10]

The Cancuen monument, of which some fragments were formerly attributed to a site near Cancuen (Rafael Morales, personal communication, 1984; Houston and Mathews 1985:18; Reents and Bishop 1985: Fig. 5), contains a reference to Ruler 4, who evidently presided over an event by a local lord.[11] Mathews has suggested that Ruler 4 captured a member of the Cancuen dynasty (Houston and Mathews 1985:18). We now know that the supposed Emblem is in fact a reference to a place known as *akul*, which differs wholly from the true Cancuen Emblem.

Figure 4-22 shows the evidence for this reinterpretation. The Akul sign and Cancuen Emblem Glyph both contain representations of turtle shells (Fig. 4-22*a* and *b*). However, in the case of Akul there is neither a *ya* prefix nor a *kin* infix, both of which characterize the Cancuen sign. The spelling of Akul is made perfectly explicit in two contexts. One is the name of a royal lady at Bonampak, where the glyphs appear phonetically (Fig. 4-22*c* and *d*); the other is the title of Ruler 4's captive. Usually this title comprises a turtle shell (Fig. 4-22*e*), but in one place it clearly reads *a-ku-l(u)/AHAW* or Akul Ahaw, "Akul lord"; in another text it occurs as a logograph with phonetic complement, *AKUL-(lu)* (Fig. 4-22*f*). Akul is probably none other than San Juan Akul (often spelled Acul), 12 kilometers due north of Dos Pilas. Lacandon Maya lived in Akul during the first half of the nineteenth century

Figure 4-21. Portion of Tamarindito Hieroglyphic Stairway 2. Height of carving: .35 m.

(Thompson 1977:14), and, to judge from the glyphic reading, the place name goes back rather more than that in time—according to Kevin Johnston (personal communication, 1991) it is still possible to see Precolumbian ruins in the area. In historical terms, Akul contributed ladies, one of *ahaw* status, the other of *sahal*, to the dynasties of Machaquila and Bonampak. In contrast, Ruler 4 boasted throughout his life of taking a captive from the site.

This is not to say that Dos Pilas had little contact with Cancuen: Panel 19 proves quite the opposite. The panel also provides ambiguous evidence that Ruler 4 (or one of his siblings or first cousins) was a child of a royal woman from Cancuen. Conceivably, his status as an important "player" at Cancuen derived from this relationship.

Ruler 4 seems also to have captured a lord from the site of El Chorro, as stated on Dos Pilas Hieroglyphic Stairway 3 (Fig. 4-23; Houston and Mathews 1985:18). Another captive is from Yaxchilan; this lord may have been taken during or perhaps slightly before the interregnum between the death of Shield Jaguar and the accession of Bird Jaguar IV (Mathews and Willey 1991:62–63). Possibly, the capture occasioned the interregnum. Finally, the discovery in 1991 of another fragment of Hieroglyphic Stairway 3 shows that a lord of the "Ik Site," possibly Motul de San José, fell prey to Ruler 4 at about the same time a ruler of Machaquila captured another lord of the Ik site (I. Graham 1967:Fig. 63). (Parenthetically, Hieroglyphic Stairway 3 is remarkable for its references to captures that are closely spaced in time. In some respects the monument seems almost to be a record of a single campaign, in which a raiding party systematically worried the area north of the Pasión River.)

Ruler 4 apparently died as he lived: violently. The Tamarindito/ Arroyo de Piedra dynasty, which once gloried in its connections with Dos Pilas, may eventually have warred against Ruler 4 and perhaps killed him; at least, there are no later references to the lord (Peter Mathews, personal communication, 1983; Houston and Mathews 1985: 18). At this time, Dos Pilas' textual record falls silent, and within a few years a squatter settlement would appear in the Dos Pilas plaza.

Ruler 4 is remarkable for the number of sites at which his name appears, although whether this stems from his achievements or, more

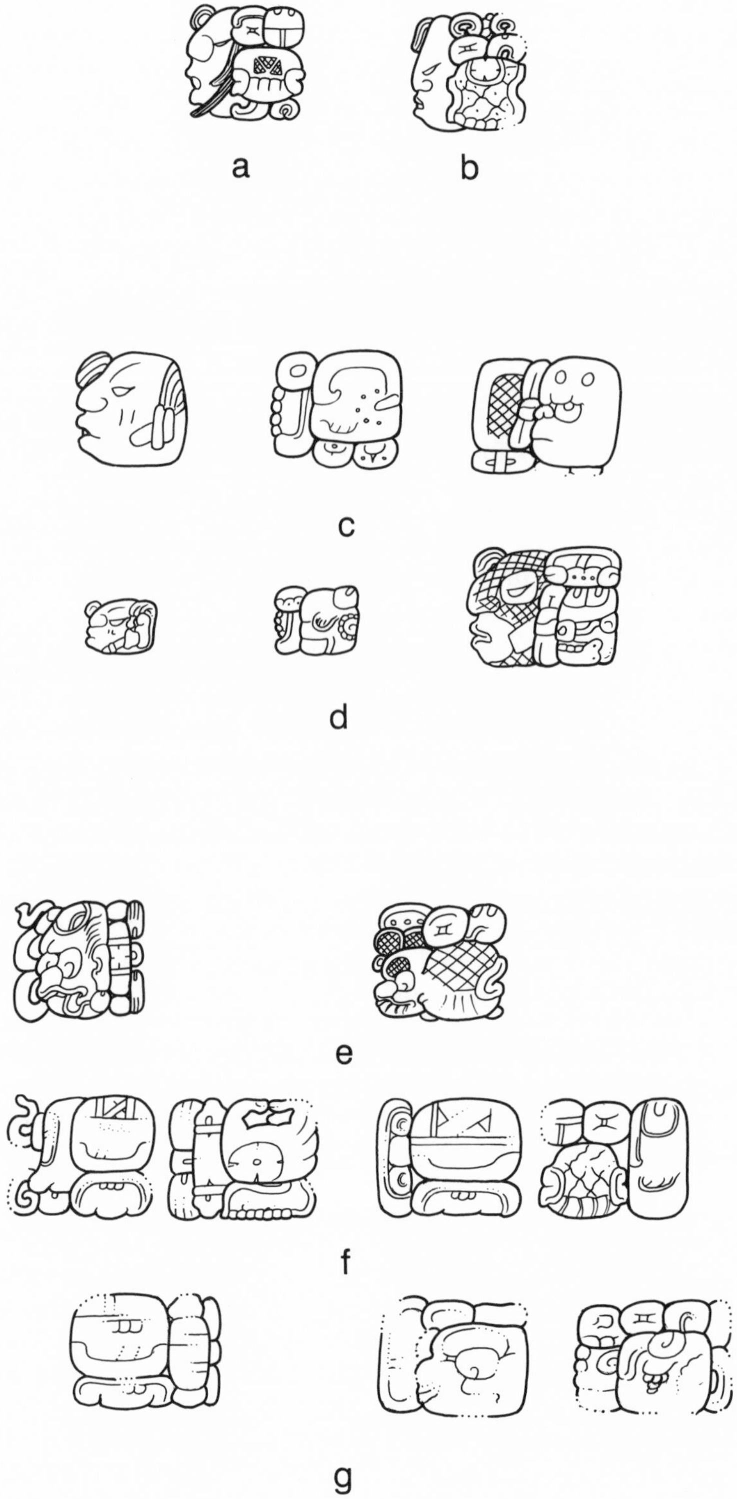

c

d

e

f

g

Figure 4-22. The Akul sign: *a*, Lady Akul Ahaw (Machaquila, stone D from Structure 4, after I. Graham 1967:Fig. 30); *b*, Lady of Cancuen (Dos Pilas Panel 19:I3, after drawing by David Stuart and Stephen Houston, courtesy of the Petexbatun Regional Archaeological Project); *c*, Lady Akul Patah (Bonampak Stela 2:E6–E7, after Mathews 1980:Fig. 2); *d*, Lady Akul Patah (Bonampak Stela 1:I1b–J1, after Mathews 1980:Fig. 3); *e*, Ruler 4, guardian of Akul Ahaw (Aguateca Stela 1:A13–B13, after I. Graham 1967:Fig. 3); *f*, Ruler 4, guardian of Akul Ahaw (Cancuen Hieroglyphic Stairway 1:A1–B2, after photograph by author); *g*, Ruler 4, guardian of Akul Ahaw (Seibal Hieroglyphic Stairway 1:W1–W2, after Maler 1908 Pl.36, no. 2).

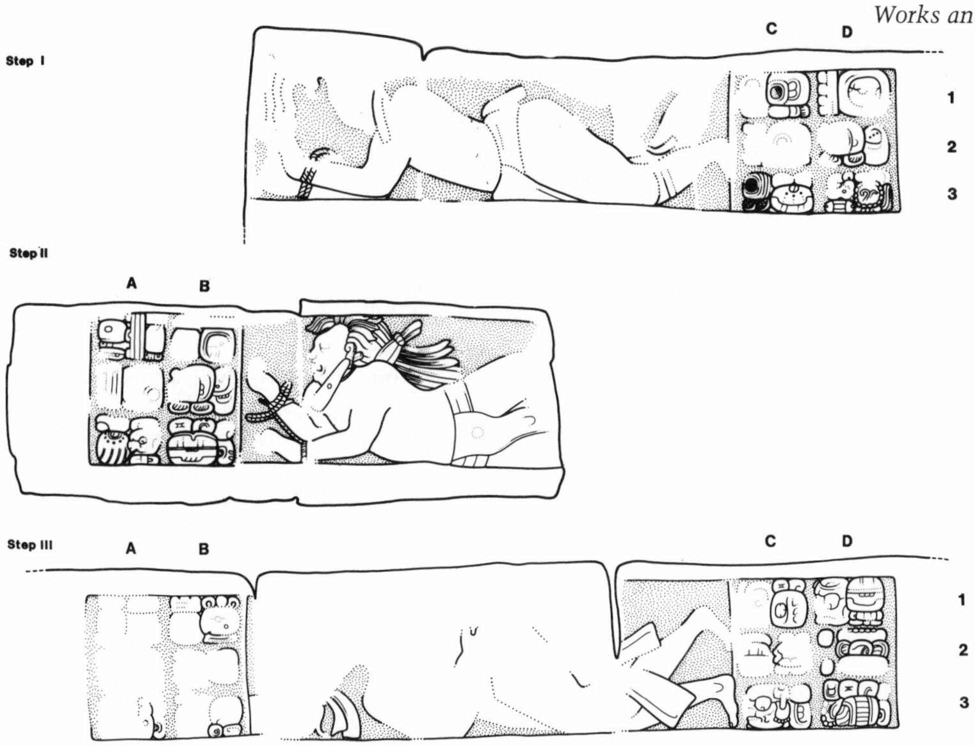

Figure 4-23. Dos Pilas Hieroglyphic Stairway 3. Height: Step I, >.48 m; Step II, .56 m; Step III, >.56 m.

likely, from those of his predecessors, is less than clear. Certainly his reign is marked by dramatic changes in foreign relations, with the dissolution of some of Dos Pilas' old alliances and the apparent weakening of Dos Pilas as a dynastic seat. In administrative terms, the important question is whether Ruler 4's successes in some manner presaged his failure. Did the long reach of the dynasty outstrip the administrative ability of this Late Classic polity (Johnston 1985:56)? Or did its initial success stem from administrative and tactical innovations?

Later Rulers

Rulers at other sites in the Pasión drainage continue to use the Dos Pilas Emblem after the apparent demise of Ruler 4, although Dos Pilas itself lacks any certain records from this period. The dominant site seems now to be Aguateca, which begins to erect stelae that are considerably more massive than earlier monuments at the center.

The first record of note is Aguateca Stela 6, which displays a weathered Initial Series date (9.15.16.12.1; I. Graham 1967:Fig. 15). This is the birth date of a ruler of the Dos Pilas dynasty who apparently acceded to the throne at 9.16.19.0.14. In a striking parallel, the span between this date and the final date of Ruler 4 corresponds closely to an unusually long interregnum at Yaxchilan (see earlier discussion). Nevertheless, an intervening ruler may yet be found between Ruler 4 and the Aguateca lord, who perhaps descends from a different branch of the family.

The Stela 6 ruler very likely appears on Aguateca Stela 7, dating to 9.18.0.0.0 (I. Graham 1967: Fig. 17), although the poor condition of Stela 6 makes comparisons difficult. The most persuasive evidence that the lords are the same is the 3-katun *ahaw* title on Stela 7; this notation, which establishes limits on the age of the ruler, is congruent with the birth date on Stela 6. According to Ixtutz Stela 4, this lord may have attended a stela erection at Ixtutz, which lies 78 kilometers from Aguateca (I. Graham 1980: 181; Escobedo 1991: 41–42). In an apparent couplet construction, Stela 4 refers both to the Emblem Glyph of Aguateca and to a title employed by at least one earlier ruler at the Dos Pilas dynasty, Ruler 3.

Earlier rulers at Dos Pilas seldom recorded the names of sculptors (D. Stuart 1986), the first examples perhaps being on Aguateca Stela 5 and Seibal Hieroglyphic Stairway 1. The clearest instance, however, exists on Aguateca Stela 7, which was probably the last stela to be erected by the Dos Pilas dynasty at its "core" sites of Dos Pilas and Aguateca (I. Graham 1967: Fig. 18). One sculptor apparently came from Tamarindito, where he enjoyed high status (note the *ahaw* title; Lounsbury 1973); the other originated at an unknown site, the Emblem of which occurs in full form on Seibal Stela 8. This sculptor was of lower rank than the other: the reference on Aguateca Stela 7 is merely to "he of X" rather than to "*ahaw* of X." The sculptor of the Seibal stairway probably came from this site, where he had a similar status.[12]

The Dos Pilas dynasty occupied other sites during the last hundred years of Cycle 9 (Houston and Mathews 1985: 18–19, 23–24). One branch of the family was responsible for the panel and staircase ensemble that constitutes La Amelia Hieroglyphic Stairway 1. The stairway dates, which Mathews has reconstructed, reveal the birth and accession dates of a La Amelia lord. He was born on 9.16.9.4.19 (just before the terminal date of Ruler 4's reign), underwent a preaccession rite some forty-two years later (cf. Houston and Mathews 1985: 15), and then acceded to rule within days of this rite. Later events on the stairway refer to ball games in which figures on the side panels participate.

The stairway at La Amelia demonstrates that La Amelia was in contact with Aguateca. At positions H1–G3 occur the name and titles of the ruler on Aguateca Stela 7, who possibly presided over a "seating" rite involving the lord of La Amelia (Fig. 4-24). The implications of this reference are the following: first, that the Dos Pilas Emblem, here in late form with appended T115 affix, was in simultaneous use in at least two sites; second, that both lords, who evidently participated in the same polity, employed the *ahaw* title; and third, that the Aguateca lord may have been the more important of the two. In short, the Dos Pilas polity still embraced a large area, although perhaps with diminished political centralization.

One of the titles of the ruler of La Amelia, T12.168: 44: 519, is also found at the sites of Seibal and Chapayal (Houston and Mathews 1985: 19, 23–24). Mathews and I proposed that this title is a personal name, probably referring to one individual (ibid.: 23). But the disparity in dates

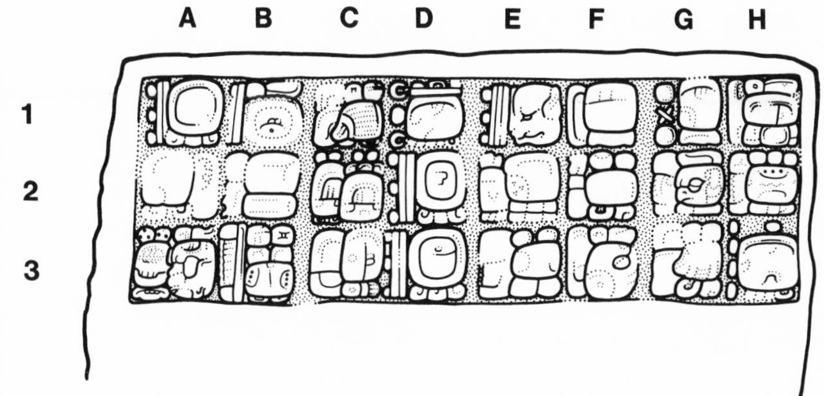

Figure 4-24. Hieroglyphic riser of La Amelia Hieroglyphic Stairway 1. Height of carving: .47 m.

and, most important, in times of accession suggests that they were different people (Peter Mathews, verbal communication; cf. Houston and Mathews 1985: Fig. 18). An important topic for future research is the subject of relations between La Amelia, Aguateca, Seibal, and Chapayal. Were they constituents of the same polity, as prior history would suggest, or did they rule independently?

DOS PILAS AND ITS NEIGHBORS

Dos Pilas is not the only site in the Pasión drainage with a rich monumental record (Table 4-2). At least twenty-four other sites possess monuments, ranging from eighty-five sculptures at Seibal to one carving at El Cedral. Twelve of these sites use Emblem Glyphs.[13] As Mathews and Justeson show (1984), Emblems refer not to sites, but rather to lordship over polities, which were largely autonomous in the conduct of foreign relations.[14] Toponyms specify sites within the polities. A review of the distance between autonomous sites, some the centers of long-lived dynasties and polities, indicates that Pasión polities may have fluctuated in size (depending on relative political success), but that most were relatively small, and nothing like the vast hierarchies proposed by Joyce Marcus (1976: 46). Itzan, for example, lies 14 kilometers from Altar de Sacrificios and approximately 10 kilometers from El Chorro. In an extraordinary case of political packing, Dos Pilas lies within 4 kilometers of Arroyo de Piedra.[15] This is not to say, however, that such sites were always free of foreign influence; the evidence from Arroyo de Piedra suggests intermittent loss of political autonomy.

It can be appreciated from various compilations that the Pasión region has a long written history, beginning before and continuing long after the dates of the Dos Pilas dynasty (Mathews and Willey 1991; Houston 1987: Table 8). What distinguishes the dynasty, however, is not the length of its written record, which is unusually brief for such an important family, but rather the extension of its influence. For example, Dos Pilas evidently engaged in sustained contact with the northern Peten, where its dynasty probably originated (see earlier discussion). The dynasty also captured lords from sites some 50 kilome-

Table 4-2. ***Other Pasión dates***

Date		*Event*	*Provenance*
8.18.0.0.0	12 Ahau 8 Zotz'		TRS St. 1
8.18.4.4.0	11 Ahau 8 Yaxkin?		TRS St. 2
8.18.18.15.0	6 Ahau 18 Kankin		TRS St. 1
8.18.18.15.0	6 Ahau 18 Kankin		TRS St. 2
8.18.19.8.7	12 Manik 20 Yaxkin	BG	SBL HS 1
8.19.0.0.0	10 Ahau 13 Kayab	C19K	SBL HS 1
8.19.0.0.0	10 Ahau 13 Kayab		TRS St. 1
8.19.0.0.0	10 Ahau 13 Kayab		TRS St. 2
9.1.0.0.0	6 Ahau 13 Yaxkin	IS	ALS St. 10
9.1.17.10.8	3 Lamat 16 Mac	B	TAM St. 5
9.2.0.0.0	4 Ahau 13 Uo		ALS St. 11
9.2.0.0.0	4 Ahau 13 Uo		TRS St. 1
9.2.0.0.0	4 Ahau 13 Uo		TRS St. 2
9.3.0.0.0	2 Ahau 18 Muan	IS	ALS St. 13
9.3.0.0.0	2 Ahau 18 Muan?		ALS Alt. 3
9.3.19.0.0	4 Ahau 3 Zac	C19T	TAM St. 5
9.4.0.0.0	13 Ahau 18 Yax	IS	ALS St. 18
9.4.10.0.0	12 Ahau 8 Mol	IS	ALS St. 12
9.5.4.5.8	12 Lamat 6 Yax		TAM St. 4
9.5.6.12.18	11 Etz'nab 6 Kayab		TAM St. 4
9.5.11.16.10	11 Oc 8 Pop		TAM St. 4
9.6.0.0.0	9 Ahau 3 Uayeb	IS	TAM St. 4
9.6.0.0.0	9 Ahau 3 Uayeb	C6K	TAM St. 4
9.7.0.0.0			ARP
9.7.15.12.9	1 Muluc 12 Zotz'		ALS St. 9
9.7.15.12.9	1 Muluc 12 Zotz'		ALS St. 18
9.7.15.12.9	1 Muluc 12 Zotz'		ALS Alt. 1
9.8.19.11.16	9 Cib 4 Pax	A	ARP St. 1
9.9.0.0.0	3 Ahau 3 Zotz'	IS	ARP St. 1
9.9.5.0.0	9 Ahau 18 Uo		ALS Alt. 2
9.9.15.0.0	8 Ahau 13 Cumku	IS	ALS St. 8
9.10.0.0.0	1 Ahau 8 Kayab	IS	ALS St. 9
9.10.0.0.0	1 Ahau 8 Kayab	IS	PAB St. 1
9.10.0.6.13	4 Ben 16 Tzec		ALS Sc. Pan. 1
9.10.3.17.0	4 Ahau 8 Muan	IS, D	ALS St. 4
9.10.3.17.0	4 Ahau 8 Muan	D	ALS Sc. Pan. 1
9.10.3.17.0	4 Ahau 8 Muan		ALS Sc. Pan. 2
9.10.4.1.3	8 Akbal 11 Kayab		ALS St. 4
9.10.4.1.3	8 Akbal 11 Kayab		ALS Sc. Pan. 2
9.10.4.1.3	8 Akbal 11 Kayab		ALS Vase
9.10.10.0.0	9 Ahau 18 Kankin		ALS St. 4
9.10.11.12.17	6 Caban 5 Ch'en?	IS	ALS St. 5
9.10.11.13.0	9 Ahau 8 Ch'en		ALS Sc. Pan. 1
9.10.11.13.0	9 Ahau 8 Ch'en		ALS Sc. Pan. 2
9.11.0.0.0	12 Ahau 8 Ceh		ITN HS 1
9.11.10.0.0	11 Ahau 18 Ch'en	IS	ALS St. 1
9.12.18.1.6	3 Cimi 4 Zotz'	B	CNC HS 1
9.13.0.0.0	8 Ahau 8 Uo	C13K	CRO St. 1
9.13.0.0.0	8 Ahau 8 Uo?		CRO Alt. 6
9.13.13.14.18	7 Etz'nab 1 Kankin		CNC HS 1
9.14.0.0.0	6 Ahau 13 Muan	C14K	ALS St. 7
9.14.0.0.0	6 Ahau 13 Muan		ARP St. 7

Date		Event	Provenance
9.14.0.0.0	6 Ahau 13 Muan		MQL St. 13
9.14.10.0.0	5 Ahau 3 Mac		ALS St. 2
9.15.0.0.0	4 Ahau 13 Yax	IS, C15K	ARP St. 2
9.15.4.15.3	5 Akbal 11 Xul	IS, B	ITN St. 17
9.15.10.0.0	3 Ahau 3 Mol	IS	MQL St. 11
9.15.10.11.5	7 Chicchan 3 Pop?		ITN HS 2
9.15.11.15.15	2 Men 8 Tzec		ITN St. 17
9.15.11.16.15	9 Men 8 Xul		ITN St. 17
9.15.14.13.17	4 Caban 15 Uo		ITN St. 17
9.15.15.0.0	9 Ahau 18 Xul?		CRO Alt. 3
9.15.17.8.17	9 Caban 5 Muan		ITN St. 17
9.16.0.0.0	2 Ahau 13 Tzec	C16K	CRO Alt. 2
9.16.9.8.11	7 Chuen 19 Zac	A	TAM HS 2
9.16.9.14.3	2 Akbal 11 Kayab		TAM HS 2
9.16.9.15.9	2 Muluc 17 Cumku		TAM HS 2
9.16.9.15.10	3 Oc 18 Cumku		TAM HS 2
9.16.9.17.14	8 Ix 17 Uo		TAM HS 2
9.16.10.0.0	1 Ahau 3 Zip	CHP	MQL St. 12
9.16.10.0.0	1 Ahau 3 Zip	CHP	TAM HS 2
9.16.11.7.13	7 Ben 11 Yax		TAM HS 2
9.16.15.4.8	4 Lamat 6 Xul		CNH St. 1
9.16.16.11.5	7 Chicchan 18 Ceh		ITN St. 17
9.16.17.4.18	6 Akbal 6 Xul		ITN St. 17
9.16.18.5.1	5 Imix 4 Xul		ALS St. 15
9.16.19.10.19	2 Cauac 17 Zac	B	MQL St. 2
9.17.0.0.0	13 Ahau 18 Cumku		ALS St. 15
9.17.0.0.0	13 Ahau 18 Cumku		CRO Alt. 4
9.17.0.0.0	13 Ahau 18 Cumku		ITN St. 13
9.17.5.0.0	6 Ahau 13 Kayab		ITN St. 17
9.17.7.6.3	4 Akbal 1 Tzec		ITN St. 17
9.17.10.4.14	2 Ix 17 Uo		ITN St. 17
9.17.10.4.15	3 Men 18 Uo		ITN St. 17
9.17.10.6.5	7 Chicchan 8 Zotz'		ITN St. 17
9.17.10.6.17	6 Caban 0 Tzec		ITN St. 17
9.17.16.6.1	5 Imix 14 Uo		AGC St. 1
9.17.19.7.4	3 Kan 2 Zip		AGC St. 1
9.18.0.0.0	11 Ahau 18 Mac	C18K	AGC St. 1
9.18.0.0.0	11 Ahau 18 Mac		CNC St. 2
9.18.0.13.18	3 Etz'nab 11 Ch'en		AGC St. 1
9.18.5.0.0	4 Ahau 13 Ceh?		CNC Alt. 1
9.18.8.1.5	4 Chicchan 3 Mac		MQL St. 2
9.18.9.1.3	11 Akbal 12 Ceh?		MQL St. 2
9.18.9.15.10	12 Oc 18 Mol	A	MQL St. 2
9.18.9.16.3	12 Akbal 11 Ch'en		MQL St. 2
9.18.10.0.0	10 Ahau 8 Zac	CHP	CNC St. 1
9.18.10.0.0	10 Ahau 8 Zac	CHP	MQL St. 2
9.18.10.0.0	10 Ahau 8 Zac	CHP	MQL St. 2
9.18.10.7.4	11 Kan 12 Cumku		MQL St. 2
9.18.10.7.5	12 Chicchan 13 Cumku		MQL St. 2
9.19.0.0.0	9 Ahau 18 Mol		MQL St. 2
9.19.4.15.1	8 Imix 14 Zotz'		MQL St. 3
9.19.5.0.0	2 Ahau 13 Yaxkin		MQL St. 3

Table 4-2 *(continued)*

Date		*Event*	*Provenance*
9.19.5.11.0	1 Ahau 13 Cumku		MQL St. 3
9.19.10.0.0	8 Ahau 8 Xul		MQL St. 4
9.19.10.12.0	1 Ahau 8 Cumku		MQL St. 4
9.19.12.8.18	9 Etz'nab 16 Kankin	IS	ITN St. 6
9.19.15.0.0	1 Ahau 3 Tzec	C15T	MQL St. 8
9.19.15.13.0	1 Ahau 3 Cumku		MQL St. 8
9.19.17.13.10	3 Oc 3 Cumku		ITN St. 6
9.19.19.16.0	6 Ahau 18 Pop		ITN St. 6
9.19.19.17.19	6 Cauac 17 Zip		SBL St. 11
10.0.0.0.0	7 Ahau 18 Zip		MQL St. 7
10.0.0.0.0	7 Ahau 18 Zip	C10Bk	SBL St. 11
10.0.0.0.0	7 Ahau 18 Zip		SBL Str. A-3
10.0.0.13.0	7 Ahau 18 Pax		MQL St. 7
10.0.0.14.15	3 Men 13 Cumku		MQL St. 7
10.0.5.0.0	13 Ahau 13 Uo		MQL St. 6
10.0.5.16.0	8 Ahau 13 Cumku		MQL St. 6
10.0.10.0.0	6 Ahau 8 Pop		MQL St. 5
10.0.10.17.5	13 Chicchan 13 Cumku		MQL St. 5
10.1.0.0.0	5 Ahau 3 Kayab		SBL St. 8
10.1.0.0.0	5 Ahau 3 Kayab		SBL St. 9
10.1.0.0.0	5 Ahau 3 Kayab		SBL St. 10
10.1.0.0.0	5 Ahau 3 Kayab	C1K	SBL St. 11
10.1.0.0.0	5 Ahau 3 Kayab		SBL St. 21
10.2.0.0.0	3 Ahau 3 Ceh		SBL St. 1
10.2.0.0.0	3 Ahau 3 Ceh?		SBL St. 17
10.3.0.0.0	1 Ahau 3 Yaxkin?		SBL St. 18
10.3.0.0.0	1 Ahau 3 Yaxkin		SBL St. 20

Source: Taken with modifications and additions from Mathews and Willey 1991: Appendix 7; many decipherments deduced independently; site codes from I. Graham 1975: Appendix A.

Key to events: A = accession; B = birth; BG = ballgame; Bk = baktun; C = completion; D = death; HP = half period; IS = Initial Series; K = katun; S = sacrifice; T = tun.

Note: To simplify this list, I have omitted parentheses and asterisks; only question marks remain so as to indicate uncertainty.

ters distant, including individuals from Yaxchilan and possibly from Motul de San José. And, most important, the dynasty waged wars resulting in what appears to be indirect control of vanquished centers. Dos Pilas lords either presided over or enacted rites at conquered sites, perhaps with the collusion of rulers from local dynasties (Houston 1987:294). How such control was maintained and enforced is still a mystery, as, indeed, is the strength of this influence. In the case of Ruler 4, he may have been a close relative of his apparent subordinate at Cancuen.

Yet part of Dos Pilas' success may be attributed to diplomacy. During or perhaps slightly before the reigns of Rulers 1 and 2, the dynasty intermarried with foreign royalty. A woman from Dos Pilas figures in an inscription at Arroyo de Piedra; Ruler 1, in turn, married a lady of Itzan. In the case of Arroyo de Piedra, the marriage coincides with a time in which Ruler 2 of Dos Pilas was the overlord of Arroyo de Piedra (Houston and Mathews 1985: Fig. 12). Indeed, the marriage may express this relation, since such ties help preserve the loyalty of subordinates (see Calnek 1982: 59; Carrasco 1984: 45, for comparative evidence on hypogamous unions from the Postclassic Valley of Mexico).

The relationship with Arroyo de Piedra was apparently short-lived, as were many such alliances (Houston and Mathews 1985: 18). Nevertheless, it set a pattern that runs through much of Dos Pilas' history. Smaller sites under the control of Dos Pilas seem to have been ruled by separate families, some perhaps the junior branches of the Dos Pilas dynasty. This pattern became particularly pronounced after the probable capture and execution of Ruler 4. The principal seat of the dynasty then moved to Aguateca, and several smaller sites began to erect their own dynastic memorials. Presumably, the events were related: a signal disruption in the dynasty may have led to more autonomy for subordinate families.

Of greater interest is the impact of Ruler 4's defeat, which resulted, it seems, in the decline of Dos Pilas. The nature of this dynastic crisis is problematical, since it may involve a number of events, including struggles over the succession and the occupation or desolation of Dos Pilas by Tamarindito. But, whatever the result, the aftermath of Ruler 4's defeat apparently led to a restructuring of dynastic control, with the devolution of some power to smaller sites. This process may reflect the importance of Classic rulers and the political centrality of their persons: a strong ruler may have ensured a strong polity; an ineffectual or defeated ruler, a weak one (Demarest 1986: 185; 1990).

POLITICAL GEOGRAPHY IN THE PASIÓN

Several conclusions may be drawn from Pasión history. The first is that the region constitutes a well-defined political zone, since interactions occured largely between sites in the drainage. (Similar interaction zones, also embracing distinct watersheds or contiguous sites, are found around Yaxchilan, Lake Peten Itza, and Tikal.) The second is that the polities fluctuated in influence, but that most were relatively small in size, with few being more than an approximate day's walk in radius (Brush and Bracey 1955; R. E. W. Adams 1978: 27). Conceivably, this pattern resulted from fundamental constraints imposed by the inefficient transportation of goods (Sanders and Webster 1988: 541). A third conclusion is that the polities included smaller sites ruled by dependent lords, whose autonomy seems to have grown through time. The Dos Pilas polity exemplifies this pattern. Fourth, some polities embraced several major centers. The "twin capitals" of Dos Pilas/Aguateca and Arroyo de Piedra/Tamarindito are especially good examples of coeval occupation by a single dynasty. Fifth, relations between polities alternated between war, a policy endorsed enthusiastically by Dos Pilas, and diplomacy, which took the form of marriage and attendance at important functions. One relation did not necessarily preclude the other. Sixth, the recorded history of Dos Pilas is comparatively brief, and certainly far shorter than the span of occupation implied by material remains at the site (Chapter 2; Houston 1987: Fig. 72). Last, Pasión history may now be seen as immensely complicated, with rapid shifts in the political fortunes of key players. Each site has its own story, which must be evaluated in full before writing in broad stroke the dynastic history of the Pasión.

5. The Composition and Interaction of Late Classic Polities

CLASSIC INSCRIPTIONS allude to a range of matters, including astronomical events and the actions of mythological creatures. But for our purposes the texts are most important for the light they shed on politics, particularly the composition and interaction of polities. Some of the debates concerning Classic Maya politics were mentioned in Chapter 1, which also sketched the problems inherent in archaeological and epigraphic approaches. Chapters 2 and 3 focused on a site and a region—Dos Pilas and the Pasión—where some of these problems can be addressed. Chapter 4 extracted a historical narrative from these inscriptions and made the point that regional perspectives are by far the most appropriate for studies of Classic Maya politics.

Still untouched are other vexing questions: Can we be certain that the Pasión and its key site of Dos Pilas are consistent with other areas? That is, do royal and nonroyal titles and internal organization vary from area to area? And how may we reconstruct general processes from such a welter of sites and periods? It is to these problems that we turn now.

INTERNAL COMPOSITION

At any one time Maya inscriptions refer to relatively few people: rulers, their immediate families, some subordinates (both as warriors and as courtiers), sculptors (some of high rank), and important captives. Not a single, clear reference exists to the commoners who presumably supported the elite. The fact that the record is so limited raises the fundamental problem of determining whether elite life reflected that of other sectors in Classic society.

There are two, opposed perspectives to the debate, with other views in between. One extreme holds that the elite were central to the maintenance of Maya society and religion; as a result, students of the Maya are entirely justified in concentrating on the elite, for it is the elite and their actions, ways of life, beliefs, and rituals that inform the rest of society, or at least give voice to the predominant concerns of other, subordinate groups (Schele and Miller 1988; Schele and Freidel 1990: Chap. 2, passim). Starting with Robert Redfield (1941), other scholars point to the internal variety of Maya society, based on differences of class, economic function, and "folk" versus "urban" traditions (e.g., Borhegyi 1956); the logical extreme of this view is that data from Maya script may be not only esoteric, but irrelevant to broader studies of the past.

Both perspectives tend toward polar opposites. My view (or bias, to state it correctly) inclines to the former—that the elite world documented in script and art reflects larger patterns and events that affected all members of society. At the same time, elite customs by definition exclude other groups within society, making it difficult to insist that the elite represent exemplars of ancient Maya life. Fortunately, this intractable problem does not affect our interest in regional political organization, which operates at the highest levels of governance and which is mediated by the elite. The glyphic record is well suited to this level of study.

What is crucial in studying the elite is the nature of the relations within this group, since these bring into sharper focus the nuances of elite status. Parentage statements, which specify the parentage of particular individuals, are a case in point. They allow the partial reconstruction of genealogies, including data on the wives, children, and siblings of specific rulers. Such statements are by now well documented in Maya epigraphy (C. Jones 1977; Schele, Mathews, and Lounsbury 1977; Mathews 1980:61; D. Stuart 1985a; 1989), although some scholars have adduced unconvincing evidence suggesting that certain compounds refer instead to uncles and aunts (J. A. Fox and Justeson 1986; disputed in Hopkins 1988; 1991:259–260). Another relationship glyph identifies the consorts of rulers (Berlin 1977:Fig. 8, no. 31; see also T1.526:599, on Yaxchilan Lintel 25:V1, I. Graham and Von Euw 1977:56); other signs, their brothers, sisters, and uncles (D. Stuart 1989).

Such glyphs illuminate relationships within Classic dynasties. At top presided the ruler, the *ch'ul ahaw*, "divine lord" (Ringle 1988), who was sometimes joined in royal rituals by his heir apparent (sometimes termed a *ch'ok ahaw* or "unripe, young lord," David Stuart, personal communication, 1987), spouse, or members of the nobility (Fig. 5-1; Miller 1986:94; Schele 1982:296). Evidently, both ruler and heir (and perhaps a very few others) used the native Emblem, although joint use is rare—mostly this was the exclusive privilege of the ruler (Miller 1986:43, 54). This pattern does not seem to have occurred in Yucatan, particularly in Chichen Itza, where joint rule by brothers appears to have been the pattern (Tozzer 1941:19, 177; Schele and Freidel 1990:346–376). In general, Yucatan and other areas outside the southern Lowlands probably differed greatly from the central Maya Lowlands. An intense concern with lineal descent, from ruler to ruler, over many generations, is not clearly attested in northern inscriptions, aside, possibly, from Coba, where texts are badly eroded.

Provincial Rulers

Relationships outside the immediate family (but within a particular polity) are more difficult to reconstruct. One set of glyphs, still of uncertain reading but possibly *sahal*, characterizes a relationship between rulers and subordinates in the western portion of the Maya Low-

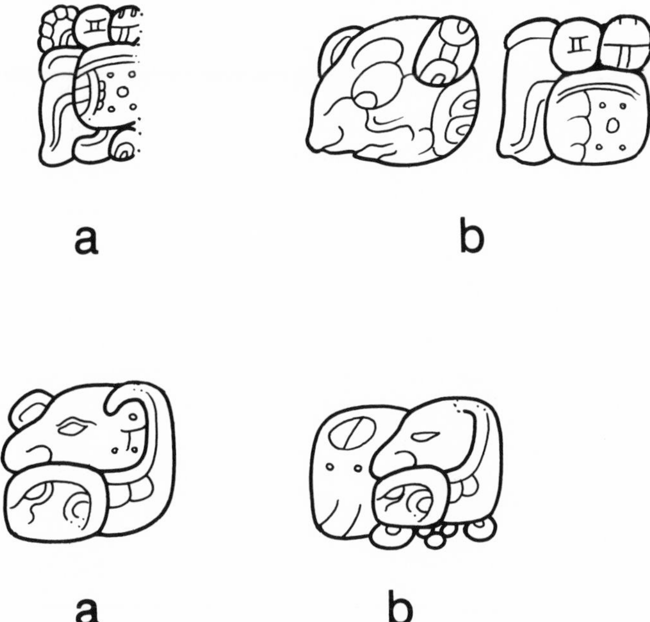

Figure 5-1. Top: Royal titles of the Classic Maya: *a, ch'ul ahaw,* Dumbarton Oaks "El Cayo" panel; *b, ch'ok ahaw,* Piedras Negras "Lintel" 3.

Figure 5-2. Bottom: Secondary titles of the Classic Maya: *a, sahal; b, ba sahal.* Both from Piedras Negras "Lintel" 3.

lands (Fig. 5-2; Mathews and Justeson 1984; D. Stuart 1984a; personal communication, 1989). Many other parts of the Lowlands do not mention the title, suggesting that, if such individuals existed, they were not sufficiently important to be mentioned in inscriptions. These subordinates evidently ruled or, more likely, administered smaller sites under the supervision of a suzerain. The clearest evidence of this practice comes from the polities near the Usumacinta River, where subordinates not only resided at peripheral centers but occasionally served as court officials at the sites of their overlords (Miller 1986:45). This honor was often reciprocated, when the overlords visited minor sites to participate in dances and other elite rituals. Apparently, some of these provincial rulers were ranked, so that a few used the title *ba sahal,* or "first 'provincial lord'" (D. Stuart, personal communication, 1989). Such ranking, found also among sculptors and siblings (D. Stuart 1989), may have been conditioned by genealogical distance from the lord or perhaps by order of appointment by the ruler.

Without exception, records at subordinate sites document only very brief spans of history, rarely of more than twenty years' duration. Another peculiarity of subordinate sites is the imitative nature of their behavior. At the center of Laxtunich, for example, a subordinate acceded to rule on a Period Ending date, and within a few years of an episode of warfare (illustrations in Lamb and Lamb 1951; Mayer 1984:Pls. 203-204; Schele and Miller 1986:86).[1] This pattern duplicates the events leading up to Bird Jaguar II's reign at Yaxchilan, which is the site that exercised control over Laxtunich.

We know that subordinate lords often inherited their rank, since at least one monument from Lacanha shows that both mother and father could hold this title (D. Stuart 1984a: Fig. 10). Yet there could also be an explicit genealogical link between provincial lords and the ruler. A panel looted from the region of Piedras Negras shows that a *sahal* was the brother of the ruler of Piedras Negras, and another person holding this title was the maternal uncle of one of the later rulers of Yaxchilan (M. D. Coe and Benson 1966; D. Stuart 1989). At Palenque, a later ruling dynasty issued from ancestors of this status (D. Stuart, personal communication, 1986; Schele 1991: 7, 10). The accession suggests strongly that in times of dynastic crisis the *sahal*s represented a pool of eligible candidates for the highest office in the polity.

But the reverse was also true. Subordinates represented natural sources of rebellion, as did the junior or cadet branches of chiefly families in Polynesian "conical clans" (Kirch 1984: 34–35). The Polynesian parallel is suggestive. Often, political rivals went into voluntary or involuntary exile, both to reduce conflict with the throne and to provide a means of extending a ruler's influence over poorly consolidated territory at the margins of a polity (ibid.: 235–237). The only real danger of political instability lay in the distance of provincial centers from court, for exiled rivals might find it easier to break away from a remote overlord. I suspect that similar processes operated among the Classic Maya: monuments at subsidiary sites show frequent visits by the paramount ruler, intent, perhaps, on suppressing the ritual and political independence of subordinates.[2]

The God C Title

Other titles of subordinates have recently come to light, including one that is far more widespread than the *sahal* title.[3] This is a set of signs consisting of the following elements (Fig. 5-3): an initial *ah* or *a*, the head of God C, read *ch'u* or *ch'ul* (or, in Yucatecan languages, *k'u* and *k'ul*), and a phonetic sign for *na* or *nV* (where *V* is an undetermined vowel; Barthel 1952; Ringle 1988). To date, the sign is undeciphered. One possible reading, *ah ch'ul na*, "he of the divine house or temple" (Ringle 1988: 9–11), remains one of several possibilities. The problem is that this reading fails to account for the salient feature of the title, which, without exception, refers to subordinate figures at Maya courts.[4] A more compelling decipherment is one based on a Yucatec root *k'ul* or its Cholan equivalent *ch'ul* (D. Stuart 1990b), as in Yucatecan *k'ul*, "a certain official of government . . . a lawyer-mediator and third person between others . . . overseer, a master of chambers in the house of the *batab*" (Barrera Vásquez 1980: 420–421; my translations).

Holders of the title are often depicted as courtiers, attending respectfully on their lord. A few play ball with the ruler, serve as court sculptors (as attested on Bonampak "Lintel" 4), or appear in cameo portraits in tombs (as on the sarcophagus at Palenque). Virtually all such references date to the Late Classic period, with a peak in the middle of this phase. The chronological distribution accords closely with use of the *sahal* title. There are relatively few references at the beginning of the Late Classic era, growing to a larger number in the middle years, falling off by the inception of the Terminal Classic period

a

b

c

Figure 5-3. The *ah ch'ul na* (God C) title: *a* and *b*, after unpublished drawing by Ian Graham; *c*, after Robertson 1983:Fig. 153.

(Fig. 5-4). In fact, as David Stuart points out to me, there is no overlap between the *sahal* and the God C title, suggesting that they refer to mutually exclusive offices or positions.

In a few cases the title appears in the names of royal spouses. However, the pattern is unusual, for the *ah* of the God C title appears *beneath* the *na* sign that marks female names. Interestingly, at least two of these women also use Emblem Glyphs (of Calakmul and an unidentified site), indicating that the title applied to nonruling members of the royal family as well as to courtiers. Texts from Tonina lend support to this inference by showing that some holders of the title were brothers of rulers.

The title raises useful questions about the internal organization of Classic polities. At one place—Copan—the God C title appears in texts recovered from residential compounds well away from the ritual center of the site. At present, two such compounds are known, from Groups 9N-8 and 9M-18 (Willey, Leventhal, and Fash 1978; Webster 1989). Both appear on hieroglyphic benches, albeit in an unusual form. Here the title is a possessed noun designating a local figure as the *ah ch'ul na* of a particular ruler (Fig. 5-5). The spelling of the noun has led some scholars to interpret it as a "house offering" or a dedication verb (Schele and Freidel 1990: Fig. 8:16). This is almost certainly incorrect. Rather, the expression serves as a statement of relationship between

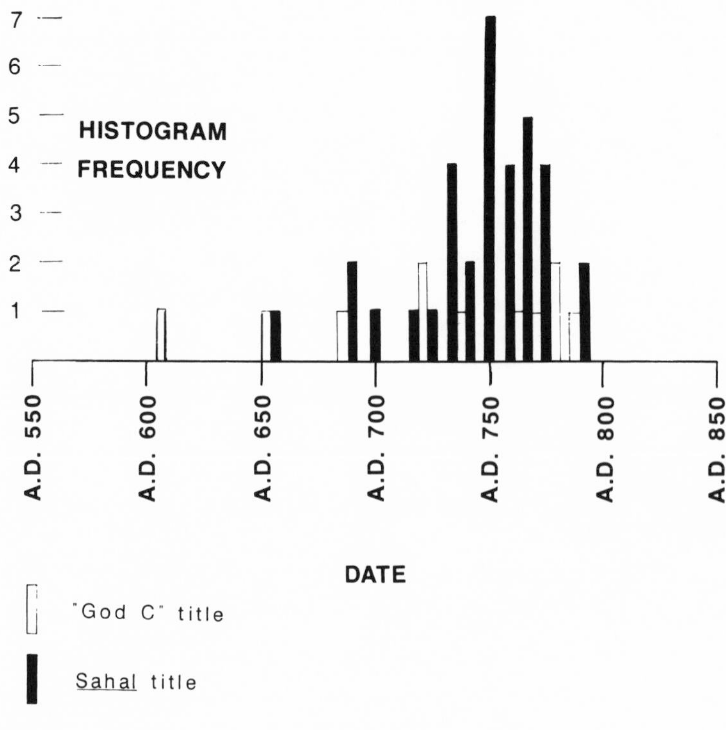

Figure 5-4. Top: Distribution through time of the *sahal* and *ah ch'ul na* titles. Data on *sahal* titles courtesy of David Stuart.

Figure 5-6. Below: Relationship glyph (including God C title) from sculptured bench in Copan Structure 9N-82. After drawing by Anne Dowd, Schele and Freidel 1990:Fig. 8:16.

Figure 5-5. Bottom: Glyphs spelling *ya-ba-ki* (*a*, after unpublished drawing by David Stuart) and *ya-tz'i-bi* (*b*, after M. D. Coe 1973:103).

the person named *before* the possessed noun and the person named after. In both cases, the second person is a ruler of Copan.

Glyphic decipherment supports this interpretation. The expression at Copan reads *ya-CH'UL-na,* in which the *ya* sign combines the prevocalic ergative pronoun—indicating possession—and *a* or *ah*—the first letter of the God C title (D. Stuart 1985b; Bricker 1986:Chap. 4); transcribed differently, the expression might read *u(y)-a-CH'UL-na.* Since Mayan syntax places the possessed noun before the possessor, the name that follows *ya-CH'UL-na* belongs to the possessor of the holder of the God C title. Put more simply, "Person X is the (God C title) of Person Y, the Copan ruler."

Similar patterns occur elsewhere, including a number of examples pointing to a reading of *ah* rather than *a* for the first glyph in the title. *Ah-* is a well-known agentive prefix documented glyphically in *ah bak*

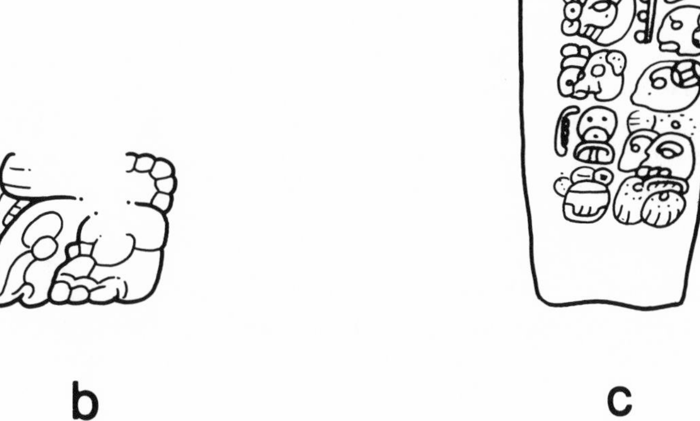

Figure 5-7. Comparison of names and titles on objects reputed to be from Jaina, Mexico: *a*, after Kubler 1977:Fig. 3; *b*, after ibid.:Fig. 4; *c*, after Spinden 1913:Fig. 196*b*.

and *ah tz'ib*, which refer to holders of captives and to scribes, respectively (D. Stuart 1985a; 1987). Both are attested in possessed forms, *ya-ba-ki* and *ya-tz'i-bi*, which render *u(y)-ah-bak* and *u(y)-ah-tz'ib*, "his holder of captives" and "his scribe" (Fig. 5-6). Parallel expressions exist in Chontal, among other languages: *yak'inob*, "su sacerdotes" (his priests) (Smailus 1975:69).

On a bowl from the region of Jaina, Campeche, the God C title is spelled with a unique phonetic twist (Fig. 5-7*a*). First appears the name of Ah ch'ul na/Yiban, who is pictured on the bowl. Then comes a statement expressing his relationship to a lord mentioned on another object from Jaina (Fig. 5-7*b, c*). (Note that both objects may have come originally from Xcalumkin, if Peter Mathews is correct in his identification of the Emblem; personal communication, 1984.) The relationship

Figure 5-8. Relationship glyphs from a looted sculpture, Piedras Negras area. After photographs courtesy of Linda Schele.

is spelled *ya-h(a)-ch'ul-na*, or *u(y)-ah-ch'ul-na*, or "his *ah ch'ul na*"—precisely the title used by Yiban! Yet another possessed God C title can be found on a looted panel from the region of Piedras Negras; it denotes the relationship between a person and Ruler 4 of Piedras Negras (Fig. 5-8). In sum, the possessed title at Copan has many parallels. And it seems also to have begun with *ah-* rather than *a-*.[5]

The decipherment has important implications for Copan. It gives us the probable term for the leading resident of compounds such as Group 9N-8. Beyond this, it hints that members of the Copan elite resembled courtiers at other sites. Whether the actual roles of the courtiers were the same is difficult to prove. To my mind the title suggests rather closer and more subordinate ties to Copanec royalty than other authors have argued (e.g., Fash 1988). At the same time, the evidence from Copan may support another interpretation, that a single title of broad distribution could enjoy widely different meanings—at Copan a powerful noble competing with royal authority, at other sites a deferential servant. Here as elsewhere, we should be careful to avoid a confusion of title and function.

What is noteworthy about the God C title at Copan is that the person mentioned in Group 9M-18 is the subordinate of a *deceased* lord, even though the bench was erected during the reign of a later ruler. David Stuart and I believe that this reference underscores the personal nature of titles invested in subordinates, betokening an intimate relationship with a particular king, dead or alive. Another relationship of an intimate and sustained nature appears to have existed between people of *ch'ul ahaw* status, so that a subordinate ruler might mention his relationship to a certain overlord even after the death of the latter (Houston and Mathews 1985).

In sum, the God C title is relatively common at Maya courts. The glosses from Yucatec suggest that holders of the title served as intermediaries between the ruler and the people. Petitions may have been directed to such figures, who would then intervene on behalf of the supplicant. More direct contact with the sovereign might have been prohibited.

Other Subordinates

At other centers, such as the eastern Peten site of La Rejolla (northeast of Dos Pilas, near the border with Belize), superordinate lords do not specify their status. Rather, local rites seem to have been

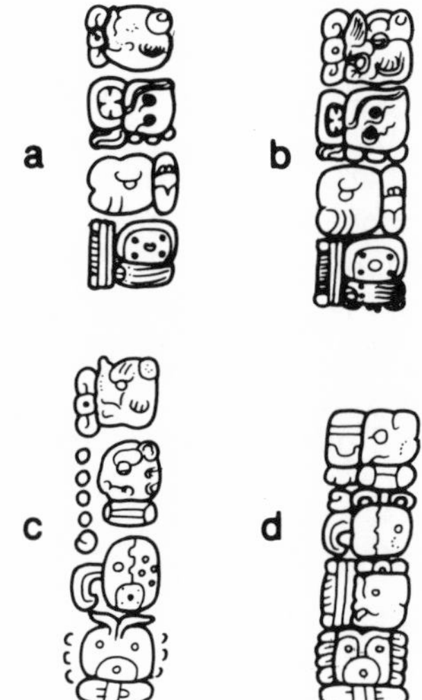

Figure 5-9. Sculptors' signatures from the Piedras Negras area: *a,* Piedras Negras Throne 1, author drawing; *b,* looted panel in the Cleveland Museum of Art, after Schele and Miller 1986:Pl. 1; *c,* Piedras Negras Stela 15, author drawing; *d,* looted panel in the New Orleans Museum of Art, Accession No. 67.31, author drawing.

performed under the supervision of a foreign lord, in this instance from the large site of Caracol. Presumably, then, the lords of La Rejolla were at least informally under the control of Caracol. La Rejolla is equally interesting for the changing complexion of its relationship with Caracol. One monument, Stela 1, records both a local lord and Caracol Ruler V. A later carving, Stela 3, apparently records only Caracol Ruler VI, without reference to a local ruler. Perhaps La Rejolla's autonomy diminished through time, shifting from partial independence to a status considerably less than that.

The specific means by which subordinate centers were integrated to larger centers are still uncertain. Evidence from Palenque and Yaxchilan demonstrates that major rulers occasionally took wives from such centers (D. Stuart 1984a), perhaps as spoils of war and certainly as instruments to bind minor families to major dynasties (Marcus 1976:159). A separate set of evidence suggests that sculptors employed at major sites, such as Piedras Negras (D. Stuart 1986), also carved monuments at sites known or suspected to have been under their sway (Fig. 5-9). Conceivably, the transmission of scribal art to subsidiary centers both expresses a close relationship between sites and constitutes a reward to obedient lords, since the gift bestows on subordinates the opportunity to erect self-glorifying monuments.[6] (This reasoning presumes, of course, that the full array of scribal skills was generally restricted to major centers, as seems likely given the highly arcane and specialized nature of hieroglyphic writing.)

An analogous process, involving gifts of elite goods such as polychromes with historical texts, probably took place between major sites and subordinate centers[7] as well as between families of roughly equivalent status. George Dalton describes such gifts as "primitive valuables," which are intimately connected to "ceremonial exchange . . .

and alliance formation" (Dalton 1977:198). These valuables were exchanged during most political and social transactions, often serving as tokens of alliance within "alliance blocks, social fields, or interaction spheres" (ibid.:191, 201).

But such means are noncoercive, integrating by marriage alliance and material enticement rather than force. There is a large body of evidence that the Classic Maya placed heavy emphasis on armed conflict (Webster 1977:363), so that at least some of the skirmishes celebrated in Maya art may have been against rebellious subordinates as well as foreign foes; the appearance on Tamarindito Hieroglyphic Stairway 1 of a captive with a *sahal* title suggests as much (although to be sure the *sahal* may have been the subordinate of a foreign ruler). At the least, the brief and changing glyphic record at subsidiary sites suggests that structures of local control may not have been of great constancy or resilience.

INTERACTION BETWEEN POLITIES

Late Classic polities are identified by their Emblems (Mathews 1985), of which more than forty are known. Despite Marcus' assertions (1976:11, passim), such polities seem generally to have been the largest political groupings of the Classic: only rarely did they operate under the direction of foreign dynasties, and even then intrusive control was likely to be ephemeral. The problem remains, however, of discerning patterns in the relations between polities. For this, we must review broad categories of polity interactions.

Warfare during the Classic Period

Relations between polities may be grouped into several classes: warfare, alliance, overlordship, and a miscellaneous category of uncertain references. Of the four classes, warfare has received perhaps the most attention, both in a series of studies by archaeologists (Demarest 1978; Webster 1976; 1977; 1978; 1979; 1980; Freidel 1986a) and in epigraphic research (Proskouriakoff 1963; Marcus 1976; Sosa and Reents 1980; Lounsbury 1982; Houston 1983; Riese 1984b; Schele and Miller 1986; Schele and Freidel 1990).

David Webster in particular has argued not only that warfare was endemic to Classic society, but also that it played a crucial role in societal development through the operation of intense and constant competition between opposing groups. He believes that the Late Classic Maya institutionalized warfare, which became both a symptom and a cause of stress in their society (Webster 1976:113). Nonetheless, because his interpretations predate much relevant epigraphic work, Webster fails to illustrate his arguments with concrete historical evidence. More historical treatments come from Arthur Demarest (1978) and David Freidel (1986a), who posit the existence of restraining forces on warfare: i.e., that warfare (which represents but one expression of conflict) was devoted principally to the enterprise of taking captives rather

Figure 5-10. Glyphs for "war" (*a*, after I. Graham 1979:91), "arrive" (*b*, after Beetz and Satterthwaite 1981:Fig. 4, C11*b*), and "see" (*c*, after ibid.:Fig. 4, C12*a*).

than the conquest of territory, and that for all the resulting short-term instability the net effect was long-term political equilibrium. More intensive struggles did exist, but between distinct ethnic or linguistic groups.

A potential problem with these ideas, which recall arguments made by J. Eric S. Thompson (1950:7), is that they run counter to some recent interpretations of "war" verbs, in particular the "shell-star" events (Fig. 5-10*a*) elucidated by Berthold Riese (1984b) and Floyd Lounsbury (1982). Such events evidently involved major battles, at times resulting in the conquest of territory. The best examples of this are the war by Caracol against Naranjo (Sosa and Reents 1980, following a suggestion by Peter Mathews), and the battle by Caracol against Tikal, after which Tikal's monumental record falls silent until the middle of the Late Classic (Houston 1987). The evidence would seem, then, to refute the arguments made by Demarest and Freidel: warfare did on occasion result in substantial increments to territory or at least in enhanced control over neighboring polities.

Yet, in some respects the shell-star events are the exceptions that prove the rule. They are relatively rare, and the events at Caracol do not clearly implicate war as the main cause of change; it is equally possible that the battles followed other events, which went unmentioned in glyphic texts. Another point is that shell-star events do not seem always to have led to substantial increases in territory. Dos Pilas, for example, has been characterized as a "conquest state" (Houston and Mathews 1985), and assuredly it relied heavily on conflict with its neighbors as a means of consolidating its position. Nonetheless, the amount of land and the number of people under its direct control may have been relatively small. The impressive archaeological signs of warfare in the Pasión area—the apparent fortifications at Dos Pilas, Santo Tomás, Aguateca, and Punta de Chimino (Chapter 2)—seem to *postdate* the peak of these sites as centers of Classic dynasties, suggesting that war had changed considerably by the end of the Classic period, when new measures were needed to thwart enemies.

We should also view shell-star events in long-term perspective. Even if they did seize territory, Classic polities were apparently incapable of controlling it. This is perhaps borne out by the consistent distance between autonomous centers: 41 kilometers at 8.18.0.0.0 (n = 6; s = 13.73); 66.43 kilometers at 9.3.0.0.0 (n = 7; s = 25.74);

59.72 kilometers at 9.8.0.0.0 (n = 18; s = 24.35); 57.5 kilometers at 9.13.0.0.0 (n = 22; s = 22.85); and 52.18 kilometers at 9.18.0.0.0 (n = 32; s = 22.33; data based on distribution of sites with Emblems, from Mathews 1985: Figs. 10-14). Thus, there is little evidence of progressive political expansion. Similarly, the mean distance between subordinate and superordinate centers is 11.36 kilometers, the maximum distance 25 kilometers (here excepting the shell-star conquests). There is little, then, to indicate that conquests led in the long term to political unification and to polities of great size. As on the northwest coast of North America, "victory in a raid did not entail political incorporation or permanent subjection of the defeated, although it did sometimes entail extermination of lineages, capturing women (did some dynastic marriages have this origin?) . . . and . . . capturing men as slaves" (Dalton 1977:201). Demarest and Freidel would seem to be correct, then, in viewing war during the Late Classic period as being dedicated to something other than territorial aggrandizement.

The distance between autonomous centers has another implication. The midway point between many of these sites approximates the distance an individual can travel in a day "at a good clip" across the Peten landscape, with somewhat greater ranges by river travel (R. E. W. Adams 1978:27; Sanders and Webster 1988:541). The correspondence may be fortuitous, but it is tempting to argue that distance, and by extension the spatial limitations of direct administrative supervision, figured importantly in restricting the size of Classic polities (R. E. W. Adams 1978:35). Beyond this distance subordinate centers—which demonstrably possessed their own elite lineages (see preceding discussion)—may have found it easier to exercise independent action.

We can speculate that the internal structure of Maya polities may have had a direct impact on the outcome of shell-star events. Conceivably, a blow to a ruling lineage encouraged revolt by, and independence in, subordinate families.[8] As a result, the defeat of a ruling family perhaps undermined the personal ties on which their control was based. It would be far from easy for a conqueror to reassemble these ties, particularly if his dynasty had its seat at a remote center.

In sum, glyphic records do not support the notion that wars and other forms of armed conflict played a large role in the expansion of polities, although they may have been useful in subduing rebellious nobility. Strangely, virtually all such records are restricted to the Late Classic period, as are the terms relating to categories of subordinates; the iconography of the Early Classic period, however, is replete with martial imagery (Schele and Freidel 1990: Fig. 4:15). It is still unclear what these patterns mean: does negative evidence indicate the absence of such wars and of such subordinates? Or did decorum prevent such matters from being mentioned glyphically?

Alliance

Warfare is only one category of interpolity interaction. Another is alliance, usually by the expedient of royal marriages. Joyce Marcus discusses this kind of interaction (1976), but perhaps overstresses the long-term impact of such unions.[9] Generally speaking, hypogamous, hypergamous, and isogamous marriages express close ties between two polities, although their motivation may differ dramatically. Nevertheless, available evidence indicates that such ties are just as likely to rupture in succeeding generations, as happened at Dos Pilas. As Dalton observes of many stateless societies, antagonism and dependence are closely intertwined, in a pattern that is "the opposite of isolation and self-sufficiency" (Dalton 1977:200).

Other forms of alliance are less readily characterized. For example, the Bonampak murals make it clear that high-ranking lords from foreign sites officiated at the presentation of an heir and the display of captives (Miller 1986:passim). Presumably the attendance of lords at the heir-designation conferred legitimacy on the selection.

Epigraphers have recently recognized the existence of glyphs referring to such royal visits. One is a sign reading *hul*, "to arrive (at)" (Fig. 5-10*b*; MacLeod 1990; Nikolai Grube, personal communication, 1990). This glyph usually precedes a place name, thus recording that "person X arrived at place Y."[10] Another way of describing visits is through use of the *il-* glyph, based on a root meaning "to see" (Fig. 5-10*c*; D. Stuart 1987; Stuart and Houston 1990).[11] In several texts, including Stela 1 and Panel 7 from Dos Pilas (Fig. 5-11), the sign indicates that certain guests witnessed dynastic events at foreign sites. Most likely, the guests would have been on relatively good terms with the local dynasty. This appears to have been the case with the lords of Dos Pilas and Calakmul, although not at other sites (Chapter 4).[12] At the same time, we should not assume too quickly that the "visitors" were actually present, for proxies might have attended.[13]

Other Relations

In addition to interaction by alliance, there also exists a small set of "overlord" statements, which identify particular lords as suzerains of other rulers (Houston and Mathews 1985:Fig. 12; cf. Becquelin and Baudez 1982:Figs. 160-161). The statements are noteworthy for two reasons. First, they show shadowy evidence of higher-order political organization, in which "holy lords" could be subordinate to others of the same rank. These are the only glimmerings in Maya epigraphy of the panregional organization posited by Marcus. The fact that such references are rare suggests that these arrangements were not common in the Classic period.[14] Second, the overlord statements compel us to reconsider the implications of glyphic titles. If two individuals carried the same title, they probably held roughly the same rank. But the rulers did not necessarily have the same degree of influence or polities of the same size and population. Literal interpretation of titles should be avoided when comparing Maya rulers, who, despite similar titles, may have had real differences in power and importance.

A final category of interactions is that of "miscellaneous" contacts. In most cases the contexts of these references are poorly understood, although in the cave at Naj Tunich these interactions may simply have taken place at a pilgrimage center, which records the names

Figure 5-11. Dos Pilas Panel 7.

and arrivals of individuals from Ixlu, Ixtutz, and Sacul (G. E. Stuart 1981). Other examples are much less well understood, particularly the many instances of intersite contact along the Usumacinta River (Schele and Mathews 1991). Some may have been visits; others are not so readily interpreted.

Our review of evidence for political organization and interaction outside the Pasión drainage has pointed to the following conclusions, which amplify observations made at Dos Pilas and neighboring sites. First, glyphs reveal both specific features of internal organization and the means by which ostensibly independent polities dealt with one another. Second, these patterns show considerable geographic diversity. Some offices are of limited distribution. A few areas, such as the Pasión, avoid subordinate titles that are common elsewhere. And the northern parts of the Yucatan peninsula exhibit collective rule that contrasts with patterns to the south (Freidel 1983:375). Such divergences strongly suggest that societal disintegration during the Terminal Classic period varied greatly: each area probably had a different pathology, molded to a large extent by regional peculiarities of political organization. Third, interaction both within and between polities may have changed over the course of the Classic period and often within spans much shorter than that; the Late Classic period displays a much greater degree of elaboration of titles, possibly because new roles and offices were being developed as polities grew in population (Culbert 1988a:Table 4.2). This apparent volatility in political organization is reflected in the unstable position of the *sahal*. Finally, the fact that rulers or subordinates used particular titles does not prove that they held precisely the same status. Comparable diversity of meaning characterizes the use of titles in the ancient Near East, where *ensí* might signify "ruler" in one period, "provincial governor" in another, or *lú* might mean both "man" and "leader" (Cooper 1983b). Such variety compels us to wonder whether the "holy lord of Tikal," with its population of fifty thousand or more, enjoyed quite the same status or prestige as the "holy lord of Dos Pilas and Aguateca," with a combined population in the neighborhood of ten thousand or so.

The one pattern that most areas share results from geography. Many interactions during the Late Classic (the Early Classic is poorly documented in this respect) were conditioned by waterways, which partly determined the directionality and range of political dialogues. Consequently, the interaction zones alluded to in Chapters 2 and 4 may have been determined largely by the disposition of rivers, streams, and lakes. This does not explain, however, regions such as southern Belize, which is abundantly endowed with streams but which includes sites with few references to foreign centers.

LATE CLASSIC POLITIES: A MODEL

Information presented in Chapters 1 and 4 underlines the principal deficiency in Marcus' 1976 model of Classic Maya political organization. The elaborate and large-scale hierarchies she proposed cannot be substantiated by available evidence, which points instead to a fragmentary and unstable political landscape. But what is to replace her model?

In the last decade Mayanists have discussed a number of alternatives. One is the "feudal society" proposed by Richard E. W. Adams and Woodruff Smith (1981). If "feudalism" is taken to mean that subordinates acknowledged an overlord yet also enjoyed a measure of autonomy (Mabbett 1985:14), then few would dispute the applicability of the term. Yet the definition is so broad as to describe many different kinds of political organization. A more specific use of the term, which Adams and Smith seem to advocate, stresses parallels with feudal Europe, particularly the emphasis on landholdings and rights to serf labor. It is fair to say that there is no explicit evidence for such emphases in Classic Maya society.

Another term, distilled from a variety of sources (e.g., H. T. Wright and Johnson 1975), is the "archaic state" (Marcus 1990). As interpreted by Marcus (1990:4), this polity consists of hierarchies of decision-makers disposed into a four-tiered hierarchy of settlement. If so defined, the archaic state fails to describe much of the Maya Lowlands during the Classic period, although it may apply to larger sites, such as Tikal or Calakmul. Moreover, it is unclear how archaeologists are expected to study "hierarchic decision-making," other than by comparing site size. For reasons outlined in Chapter 1, size is not a convincing basis for discussing political organization.

Segmentary States and Galactic Polities

In a symposium presented in 1989, most participants agreed that the Late Classic Maya lived, not in feudal or archaic polities, but in "segmentary states" (e.g., Ball and Taschek 1989:13; Bey and Ringle 1989; see J. W. Fox 1987:3–6 and 1989 for applications to Postclassic Highland Guatemala) and "galactic polities" (Demarest 1990). The following sections explore what these terms mean, how the concepts developed, how archaeologists have applied them, and why these models are convincing for the Classic Maya.

The segmentary state was first defined by Aidan Southall (1956; 1965), who detected this form of polity in the Precolonial societies of Africa and Southeast Asia (1988; see also Stein 1977). The segmentary state is a fragile political structure of great instability (Southall 1956:260). Among its most important features are (1) its basis in ritual, personal, and charismatic authority rather than in the effective coercion of reluctant vassals; (2) the limited and relative nature of its territorial sovereignty, which dissipates with increasing distance from the capital (this is aggravated by the limitations of foot transportation in many segmentary states; Southall 1988:63); and (3) the duplication of administrative structures at provincial sites.

Other work in Africa supports and extends the notion of a segmentary state. Lucy Mair, for example, emphasizes the importance of clientage in the operation of segmentary states, which are predicated on an intimate bond between a political superior and those to whom the superior has delegated some authority (1962:141, 146). She also notes the duplication of elements in the state, so that "a minor chief was a replica in miniature of his superiors" (ibid.:147), even down to patterns of succession and the style of his house (ibid.: 120, 148). Other scholars point to the inherent weakness of rule on the periphery of a polity (Southwold 1961: 2–3; Lloyd 1965: 67; Vansina 1968: 246–247), the structural parallels between the administrations of overlords and subordinates (Bradbury 1969: 32), and, most important, the personal effectiveness of a ruler in maintaining and extending the control of a segmentary state (Lloyd 1965: 70; Vansina 1968: 245). This is not to say that such research ignores the great variety in such states (Stevenson 1968: 232); some polities are manifestly stronger than others, although episodes of strength tend soon to be followed by periods of weakness and decentralization (Feeley-Harnik 1985: 276). In short, without the development of effective administration, segmentary states grow only as large as the ruler's personal influence.

In recent years Arthur Demarest has suggested that a related model, that of the "galactic polity" first proposed for Southeast Asia by Stanley J. Tambiah (1976; 1977), be applied to the Maya (Demarest 1984: 146; 1986: 182–183, 185; 1990). Briefly, a galactic polity consists of the following structural elements: (1) organization along both cosmological and topographical lines (Tambiah 1976: 102); (2) the replication in peripheral units of the larger whole, or, phrased differently, the symmetrical duplication of units and the parallelism of functions (ibid.: 112–113); (3) the signal absence of a "performance oriented bureaucracy" marked by universalistic recruitment, pyramidal chain of command, and continuous communication between superiors and inferiors (ibid.: 123); (4) extreme fluidity of polity boundaries, principally as a result of diminished or augmented power at a capital (ibid.); (5) generally abortive attempts to enhance centralization (Hall 1976: 7); (6) perennial struggles between overlord and subordinates; (7) attempts to control subordinates by marriage alliances and by the suppression of hereditary succession among provincial rulers (Tambiah 1976: 127; Hall 1976: 5); and (8) the dual role of a ruler as an exemplar of order and stability and as an instigator of change through the conduct of warfare, the objectives of which were the capture of prisoners and booty (Tambiah 1976: 118, 120).

In essence, then, the galactic polity is based on the person of the ruler and on the ruler's obsessive concern with legitimation, rather than on institutions and bureaucracy (Mabbett 1985: 4). Subordinates have ties directly to the ruler, either through marriage or through appointive position (see discussion above). If the ruler is strong, the polity "irradiates" political influence over its subordinates, allies, and adversaries; if the ruler is weak, the polity disintegrates (Bentley 1986: 280). To a large extent, "elite domination depended . . . on symbolic resources, on demonstrable claims to spiritual potency" (ibid.: 285).

It may seem at first that the Demarest/Tambiah model is overly parochial, with strong roots in the particulars of Southeast Asian history. But the emphasis throughout is not on cultural detail, but on political structure and its basis in symbolic structures, for thirty years the focus of research on traditional politics in Southeast Asia (Benda 1962). Moreover, the model finds ample precedent in the sociological, anthropological, and archaeological literature, which provides many examples of polities operating according to the same principles underlying the galactic polity. For example, if reduced to its essentials, the galactic polity is difficult to distinguish from Southall's segmentary state, since both emphasize similar features, including the ritual privileges and supremacy of the ruler (Southall 1988:60, 61). That these features appear in many societies does not necessarily signify historical contact between such groups or a "stage" of political development, for they encompass societies of considerable difference in size and influence. What they do indicate, however, is the presence of a cluster of functionally related features: governance based primarily on personal ties to the ruler, and the concomitant absence of an effective and spatially dispersed bureaucracy.

In the main, details of these features are taken from historically documented societies. Archaeology can never hope to match such detail, but if used with due caution it can extend the range of galactic polities into pre- and proto-history. The sections that follow outline the intellectual background and structural parallels of the galactic polity model. The first section discusses the sociological and anthropological literature, which is especially rich in parallels; the second explores supporting evidence from archaeological research. Both sections should be read with the understanding that the model merely sketches a form of political organization, from which, in actual practice, there have been many deviations, depending on the historical development of particular polities. Often, there is an enormous range of variation in such polities, and within some segmentary states/galactic polities, there are also clear signs of structural change, from the immense kingdom of Vijayanagara (Fritz 1986) to the debilitated kingdom of late Mughal Delhi (Mabbett 1985:16) and the "theater states" of Bali (Geertz 1980).

The Segmentary State and Galactic Polity: Intellectual Antecedents

The most important antecedent of the segmentary state/galactic polity models is Max Weber's theory of the "patrimonial state," which involves a form of domination derived from "strictly personal" ties to a ruler (Weber 1968:1006). Weber noted that patrimonial kings attempt by various means to control provincial rulers, but that their efforts are largely fruitless, particularly in regions remote from the overlord's capital (ibid.:1051). The polity he described is also somewhat stronger than the segmentary state/galactic polity, which operates without benefit of an effective bureaucracy (see Feeley-Harnik 1985:305 in regard to the transformation of galactic polities into "radial" polities with effective provincial administration).

In another parallel, the segmentary state/galactic polity model expresses Emile Durkheim's distinction between mechanical solidarity (the solidarity of likeness) and organic solidarity (integration through functional complementarity) (Durkheim 1960). The segmentary state/galactic polity is integrated by mechanical solidarity, with little real functional differentiation between the elements of the polity. A similar point has been made by Michael Coe, who outlined key similarities between the Khmer of Southeast Asia, a state functioning through mechanical solidarity, and the ancient Maya (1961:65).

Archaeology, Segmentary States, and Galactic Polities

Several archaeologists have discussed their finds in terms of the segmentary state and galactic polity. For example, the royal center at Vijayanagara in India has been interpreted variously as the seat of a galactic polity (Fritz, Michell, and Rao 1984:148) and as the focus of a segmentary state, which consisted in this instance of relatively autonomous provincial polities and little or no permanent bureaucratic organization (Fritz 1986:46). The city itself functioned as an elaborate stage for the "theater" of state; by its monumental architecture and the rituals enacted therein, the center affirmed the prestige and legitimacy of the ruler (ibid.) and perpetuated the loyalty of vassals by enlisting them in costly dynastic rituals (Geertz 1980:131–132). Archaic Greece has also been characterized as a congeries of segmentary states (Runciman 1982:353), although it exhibited a vastly different scale from the sprawling polity centered on Vijayanagara.

Other archaeologists do not explicitly invoke the galactic polity and segmentary state models, but they do allude to similar political structures in which internal linkages are weak and easily fissionable. In connection with ancient Mesopotamia, Robert Adams suggests that the "lowermost, rural echelons . . . of strong urban organization" may also assume an "oppositional role when conditions for this are more favorable" (1981:250). Thus, the most "common condition throughout most of antiquity [was] a shifting mosaic of hierarchical, stabilizing tendencies associated with the ascendancy of one or another city, and leveling, fragmenting ones that extruded deep into the countryside when its powers were seen to diminish" (ibid.). Although his view provides little direct support for segmentary states or galactic polities in Mesopotamia, it does attest to tensions between competing polities, usually centered on cities, and between center and periphery.[15] At least some of the "shifting mosaic" noted by Adams perhaps stemmed from the varying effectiveness of rulers (Diakonoff 1969).

An archaeological construct currently in vogue may also parallel the galactic polity and segmentary state. This construct is the "early state module," which has been presented in a number of works by Colin Renfrew (1982; 1984). The early state module is a recurrent autonomous unit, regularly spaced, and of fairly uniform size (ca. 20–30 kilometers in diameter [Renfrew 1982:282] or ca. 1,500 square kilometers in area). It is thus an intangible concept inferred from tangible and empirically verifiable patterns in material remains. According to Renfrew, the early state module tends to be focused on "central persons," presumably the rulers of the module qua polity (1984:105). Such modules develop not so much from territorial aggrandizement as from "internal reorganization," apparently under stimulus from roughly equal-sized modules nearby (Renfrew 1982:283; Price 1977). These neighbors are termed "peer polities" (Renfrew 1982:286), since they are generally of equivalent size and development.

A number of criticisms have been leveled against the notion of early state modules: that it is descriptive rather than explanatory; that the equivalent and empirically based units it describes may be of statistically random origin (Fisher 1985:3; and, in another context, Koenig and Williams 1985:259); and that the peer polity and early state module concepts are fundamentally tautologous, in that, having been inferred from the spacing of centers, they are then held to account for such patterns (Renfrew 1986:7). Nevertheless, the spacing of many ancient centers in the Old World does seem to be regular and small-scale (Friedman and Rowlands 1978:220; G. Johnson 1982:415), and the early state module/peer polity concepts are as useful as any in conceptualizing the spatial dimensions of prehistoric political organization. The irony is that the most successful applications are those with corroborative historical information (Cherry and Renfrew 1986:150).

In his exposition of the early state module/peer polity models, Renfrew consistently stresses that the limitations of ancient transport and communication determined the size of early state modules (1984:101; see also Brush and Bracey 1955; Southall 1988:63). This point has also been made by Gregory Johnson, who believes that administrative control within an early state module was effectively restricted to a radius of about 20 kilometers, or a one-day round-trip distance from a given high-order center. Johnson feels that this distance relates to the cost of rural participation in center economies (1982:415), rather than to problems in the direct supervision of outliers (cf. Tambiah 1976:127). To facilitate administration, ancient rulers in Mesopotamia may have placed additional centers at less than one-day round-trip intervals across the landscape (Johnson 1982:415; 1987:115–116). It is probably no coincidence that the distance between the capitals of Aguateca and Dos Pilas corresponds closely to this figure. I suspect strongly that administrative needs lay behind the pattern of twin capitals near Lake Petexbatun (Chapter 4).[16]

The archaeological literature in Mesoamerica has developed similar, but not identical, themes. Charles Spencer, for example, suggests that cyclical growth and decline in the polities of Precolumbian Oaxaca signals the absence of effective administration (1982:259), a conclusion that invites comparison with the structural limitations of galactic polities and segmentary states. Similarly, an argument has been made that the Classic Maya suffered from cyclical instability because of the "conditional" nature of their states (Webb 1975:163–164): that is, rulers relied on the conditional obedience of their subordinates, which could be withdrawn when a ruler died or was shown to be weak or incompetent (see Vansina 1968:246, 248, for African analogies). The political fragmentation that attends such crises has also been documented in Postclassic Yucatan (Freidel 1983:385) and Early Classic Belize (ibid.:380), where subsidiary centers appear to have asserted themselves after the collapse of a regional center. Others have commented on the restricted size and replicative quality of Classic architecture and political organization (Willey 1986:190) and explained it in terms of the difficulties of travel (R. E. W. Adams 1978:35), which involves distances remarkably like those adduced for Mesopotamia (see preceding discussion).

SEGMENTARY STATES AND GALACTIC POLITIES OF THE MAYA

Evidently, the Late Classic Maya lived within small polities organized along the lines of a galactic polity or segmentary state. Much depended on the efficacy of particular rulers, whose kingdoms fluctuated in size and material prosperity according to their success; even Dos Pilas, so successful in other respects, suffered catastrophically from the forced removal of its ruler (Chapter 4). As Malcolm Webb remarks, the ruler's success resulted in large measure from luck and personal attributes rather than from an impersonal administration with coercive fiat (Webb 1975:163–164). It is probably for this reason that Maya rulers stressed their roles as shamans, with control over invisible but potent forces (Freidel and Schele 1988; Houston and Stuart 1989b; Schele and Freidel 1990:86–87). Even today, in the most developed country in the world, Japanese emperors preserve similar shamanic functions, albeit in vestigial form (Bolitho 1985:28).

Marriages linked dynasties, both subordinate and sovereign,[17] but in alliances that tended to instability (Spores 1974:306). There is also evidence of the centrifugal tendencies of peripheral sites, ruled by hereditary provincial lords, and the centripetal impulses of the overlords, who invested much energy in involving subordinates in dynastic rituals and in demonstrating their legitimacy and competence by grandiose construction projects and the acquisition of captives. The administrative and material duplication of elements during the Classic period is well attested in the archaeology and epigraphy (e.g., Willey 1986:190), which support the view that Classic society consisted of successive orderings of like rather than complementary units. Less well documented is the fluidity of political boundaries during the Classic, or the shifting allegiances of subordinates. These features will require investigation at epigraphically attested subsidiary sites, which to date have received little archaeological attention. A final feature, the small size of Classic polities, very likely derived from a combination of the limited distance a Maya could travel in a day and the difficulties of supervising directly a group of recalcitrant provincial nobility. In other words, the fidelity of subordinate lords was never to be assumed, but rather to be won by sundry enticements and grandiloquent displays.

Thus, the Classic and particularly the Late Classic political landscape was a shifting and uneven patchwork in which the structural limitations of Maya polities precluded unification and empire. The polities were flexible, but also eminently fissionable, with a crippling dependence on direct lines of authority (Spores 1974:302, 307). Whether Dos Pilas overcame some, but not all, of these limitations is still unclear: did it thrive, however briefly, because its dynasty was intrusive and unsettling, or because it manipulated adversaries and allies to good effect? Or did Dos Pilas flourish because it was but one capital of several in a polity capable of dispersed administration?

A more difficult though pressing problem is moving beyond a description of the structure of Late Classic polities to a discussion of how they began, developed, and disappeared. We have already examined their variety, partly concealed and distorted by the widespread use of similar titles, regardless of the actual influence of a polity. Nonetheless, despite the variability, most polities in the southern Lowlands can be accommodated within models of the segmentary state and galactic polity, where size is less a consideration than structural segmentation.

We have also seen evidence of political fragmentation and the arrogation of titles by subordinate lords. The latter deeply affected the Dos Pilas dynasty, which was both a beneficiary and a victim of this process; it began by assuming a title used by others and ended by passing it on to lesser figures (see Chapter 4). What we have not done, however, is examine Maya segmentary state/galactic polities in terms of their creation and disappearance, in terms of the structural shifts attested in the kingdoms of Southeast Asia, where incipient bureaucracies might develop and the need for charismatic control diminish (Tambiah 1976). Answers will lie not so much in the Late Classic period, our focus in this book, but in the Formative, Early Classic, and Terminal Classic periods, when, regrettably, inscriptions have less to say about political interaction. But of one thing we can be relatively sure: that the Late Classic Maya took their polities to the limits of segmentary structure, to the very boundaries of "primitive" society itself (Kirch 1984:262; Sahlins 1972:148). Future work will explain why these boundaries were never broached, why Late Classic society of the southern Lowlands remained weak and unstable until the nighttime of the collapse.

Notes

2. Dos Pilas and Its Archaeological Setting

1. The maps employ conventions introduced by Teobert Maler in the nineteenth century but first applied in a sophisticated and comprehensive manner by the Piedras Negras survey, mapped between 1932 and 1939 (Parris and Proskouriakoff, in Satterthwaite 1943).

2. This estimate includes contiguous patio groups and other monumental constructions, as well as the areas lying in between. It excludes swampy terrain devoid of mounds. Of course, 71+ hectares is a static estimate of Dos Pilas' size. Much of the site may not have been occupied at the same time, and the true limits of the site, as these were conceived anciently, would be extremely difficult to reconstruct.

3. Another influence on settlement is the height of the water table. All construction at Dos Pilas lies above the 144.50-meter contour, below which the ground tends to be swampy. A cursory survey of mounds north of the ruins shows a similar preference for high ground. Only one group, lying 1.5 kilometer north of the site of Arroyo de Piedra, occurs much below 144.50 meters. More work needs to be done to determine if it appears alone.

4. Structural descriptions in this chapter follow those outlined in *A Lexicon for Maya Architecture* (Loten and Pendergast 1984). Terms for other units, such as "patio groups," accord with suggestions by Wendy Ashmore (1981b: 43–58). The following patio groups were noted but left unmapped, as they lay outside the boundaries of the Dos Pilas plan: (1) 35 meters south of Structure M5-34; (2) 90 meters south of Structure N5-35; (3) 150 meters north of Structure N4-1; (4, 5, 6) 2 groups 20 meters south of Structures L5-20 and -21, respectively, with a third group some 50 meters farther; (7) 179 meters north of Structure P4-11, including an eastern mound with looted crypt; (8) 200 meters at 320° from Structure P4-1; (9) 70 meters north of Structure O4-32; (10, 11) two patio groups immediately adjacent to Structure O5-7, incorporating entrance to substantial cave with probable Late Classic midden; (12) 50 meters south of Structure O5-14. Also, there exists a substantial structure connected with a wall 10 meters south of Structure P5-5 (partly illustrated in Houston and Mathews 1985: Fig. 2).

5. This molding is identical to a fragment recovered near a "palace" at Anonal (Tourtellot 1983a: 1256) and is similar to fragments from Seibal Structure A-14. Structure A-14 resembles Dos Pilas Structure N5-21 in its eastern location and decorated stairway (ibid.). See section on construction for further remarks.

6. The Dos Pilas plaza has some of the characteristics of the Plaza plan 2, if only because of the presence of Structure L5-1. From its eastern location Structure L5-1 would seem to be a burial mound, and indeed the monument associated with the structure refers to the death and burial of Ruler 2 (Mathews

1979a). The difficulty with this interpretation is that a far stronger association exists between Ruler 2 and Structure P5-7, which is of suitable size to house the burial of an important ruler.

7. Another interpretation is that such tripartite arrangements result from purely aesthetic decisions, as exemplified by the House of the Governor at Uxmal (Kowalski 1986:152–153).

8. Well-preserved masonry is visible on only a few structures at Dos Pilas. The lower building platform of Structure L5-49 provides the best example, particularly on its back side, which preserves sections of finely dressed veneer masonry. The east structure on the summit of Structure L5-49 also displays this kind of stonework. Only three other groups show comparable preservation. The first is Group M4-1, and especially Structure M4-3, which includes fine block facings in its lower courses. The second is Group N5-6, of which Structure N5-23 is particularly well preserved, with its continuous coursing of slab facing stones. The third is the Dos Pilas ballcourt (Structures L4-16 and L4-17); the lower batter on its playing surface consists of rectangular slabs a meter in height. The masonry from these groups is exceptionally hard, in no small part the reason for its preservation.

9. Other architectural features express contact between the Peten and the Puuc. At Machaquila there is evidence for stone reproductions of thatching, also seen at Puuc sites like Labna (I. Graham 1967:Fig. 36; Pollock 1980:Fig. 83; although see this feature on the relatively early and possibly anomalous House E at Palenque, personal observation, 1983). In addition, Machaquila contains protruding "cordholders" of a sort well documented in the Puuc (I. Graham 1967:41; Pollock 1980:Figs. 50, 56), as well as standing masonry resembling Puuc veneer stones (I. Graham 1967:Fig. 35; see also Tikal Structures 5C-47 and 5E-58; Orrego Corzo and Larios Villalta 1983:7, 179–180). Puuc influence may correspond to the first of two proposed "intrusions" from the north (Sabloff 1973:131), although note that the sporadic nature of archaeological evidence lends itself to notions of intermittent rather than continuous and evolving contact.

10. One piece lies on the frontal platform of Structure L4-35. It is dressed on one side and tenoned on the other. Scorings on the tenoned side appear to be symmetrical, suggesting a zoomorphic face. Like sculptures have been discovered near Hieroglyphic Stairway 4.

11. A structure has two orientations. Here we emphasize the most important one: the direction a building faces along its primary axis.

12. Antonia Foias of Vanderbilt University believes that there is relatively little in the way of Terminal Classic remains at the site. According to her research, most objects associated with disruptive features are fully Late Classic in date. She bases her conclusion on a negative trait: the apparent absence of finewares, recovered in such abundance at Altar de Sacrificios. Nonetheless, in 1989 Joel Palka and Kevin Johnston excavated unusual ceramics from the excavations in the Dos Pilas plaza, including sherds with late designs, grey finish, and volcanic temper that I identified in the field; other sherds corresponded to the type Zopilote Smudged, a supposed marker of the Terminal Classic period at Altar de Sacrificios (Karl Taube, personal communication, 1989; Demarest and Houston 1989). I suspect that we will eventually define a ceramic phase at Dos Pilas dating to the final years of the Late Classic period, but after the Late Classic florescence of the site.

13. Investigations at Altar de Sacrificios yielded only "40 or so" house mounds (Willey and Smith 1969:33), a figure that invites some skepticism. Altar is a large site, and the covering vegetation dense (ibid.: 16): could mounds have been missed?

14. It is not clear how Mathews and Willey calculate their figure of 20.25 hectares for the area of Tamarindito (1991: Fig. 5), unless it is to include empty terrain. Kevin Johnston informs me of several outliers to the north of Itzan (Johnston 1989), and Tamarindito includes several groups to the southwest, to the south, and in a curving band to the east (personal observation, 1990).

15. Aguateca's walls define this area.

16. Plans for other sites in the lower Pasión, including El Caribe, La Amelia, El Pabellón, and Aguas Calientes, are published in Morley 1937–1938: 2: Figs. 41, 45; ibid.: 5, part 2: Pl. 200). Visits to La Amelia and El Caribe in 1984 showed that these plans are incomplete. El Caribe is at least twice as large as rendered on the Carnegie map and includes several patio groups to the southeast. The Carnegie plan of La Amelia also excludes several looted mound groups situated 200 meters to the southwest. Unfortunately, all of these sites have been damaged by looting. El Caribe Structure VII, for example, has been thoroughly gutted by thieves from the hamlets of El Tumbo and Canaan. This is equally true of most mounds at La Amelia.

17. These structure counts are doubtless affected by severe sampling problems. Punta de Chimino, for instance, is smaller than Tamarindito, but happens to have been mapped thoroughly by Takeshi Inomata of Vanderbilt University.

18. Natural bridges reinforced by masonry cross the fissure in three places near the plaza (I. Graham 1967: 3). Note that the orientation of mounds at Aguateca accords with the bearing of the fissure.

19. Ian Graham first numbered the mounds at Aguateca (1967: Fig. 1), but the number of structures discovered since then makes his scheme unwieldy. The "palace" corresponds to his Structure 19. Takeshi Inomata, who is in charge of Vanderbilt research at Aguateca, will soon replace my scheme with a more complete one.

3. The Monumental Sculpture of Dos Pilas: A Summary

1. The mean thickness for stelae is .38 meter, for altars .37 meter, and for panels .25 meter.

2. The practice of erecting such stairways perhaps passed to Dos Pilas at the time of Ruler 1's marriage to a lady of Itzan (Houston and Mathews 1985: 11).

3. Another problem is that the later stelae are arranged by style dates, which, at Dos Pilas, show either late medians or "flat curves" in the terminology of Tatiana Proskouriakoff (1950).

4. This activity probably took place during the final years of the Late Classic period, when vandals most likely effaced the eyes of figures on Dos Pilas monuments.

5. The reasons for including Tikal are explained more fully in Chapter 4. Suffice it here to say that Tikal had strong historical links with Dos Pilas; indeed, Tikal may even have been the place of origin for the royal family of Dos Pilas.

4. The History of Dos Pilas and Its Lords

1. Dos Pilas Hieroglyphic Stairway 4 follows an analogous pattern in regard to Tikal rulers: Shield Skull is simply referred to as a "native" of the "Tikal place," rather than as a holy lord. Evidently, the rulers of Dos Pilas and Tikal did not acknowledge each other's right to use of the Emblem Glyph.

2. The repeated use of royal names is attested in the inscriptions of Tamarindito, Piedras Negras, Tikal, Yaxchilan, and Palenque.

3. Note that the existence of a second wife does not necessarily indicate polygamy, although such surely existed among the Classic Maya. The second wife may simply have replaced the first.

4. Such influence may have been widespread, indeed. Eric Thompson noted long ago that Naranjo shared a Long Count date with the remote site of Coba in Quintana Roo (Thompson, Pollock, and Charlot 1932:138). This date—9.12.10.5.12 4 Eb 10 Yax, which appears on Coba Stela 1:G7–H13—is the same as that of Lady 6 Sky's arrival at Naranjo (see below). Shared dates of this sort, without clear reference to period endings or astronomical events, are quite rare in Maya epigraphy; presumably, then, a historical link existed between Naranjo, Coba, and, ultimately, Dos Pilas. Unfortunately, Stela 1 is highly weathered: only the date is legible, making it impossible to confirm any connection between Coba and the Dos Pilas dynasty.

5. In an earlier study, Mathews and I suggested that a woman from Dos Pilas had married into the dynasty of El Chorro, producing an heir for that family (Houston and Mathews 1985:14). Joel Palka later demonstrated that we were wrong (personal communication, 1990). The main sign of the woman's title refers not to Dos Pilas or Tikal, but to a location on or near the Usumacinta River. Texts at Bonampak and Lacanha also record the place name.

6. I thank David Stuart for urging me to reevaluate the implications of the Distance Number on Stela 5.

7. Seibal Hieroglyphic Stairway has dates going back to 8.18.19.8.7, but these do not represent contemporary references.

8. Of course, it is also possible that the captive was taken from a site in the Usumacinta drainage.

9. Another interpretation is that this name belongs to a sculptor, since it occurs within a subsidiary text rather than in the main body of the inscription.

10. Some scholars assert that Dos Pilas' victory and continued influence over Seibal were of negligible significance, since Seibal was little more than a village throughout much of the Late Classic period (Norman Hammond, personal communication, 1989). In my judgment, this assertion is premature. Published reports of investigations at Seibal make it clear that relatively little of the site has been excavated (A. L. Smith 1982). Accordingly, we can hardly be certain of Seibal's status at the time of the war with Dos Pilas.

11. In 1990, I visited Cancuen in the company of Stacey Symonds of Vanderbilt University. The site had been looted recently, and we documented gaping holes in the following structures (see Tourtellot, Sabloff, and Sharick 1978: Fig. 5, for reference map): C-6c, C-9, C-15, C-22, as well as several trenches in mounds outside the Peabody Museum map. A number of the mounds went unreported by the Peabody team, and at least one structure still has standing architecture. Aside from glyphic fragments on sawn blocks of Hieroglyphic Stairway 1, there are at present no carved monuments visible at the site. Nonetheless, looting at Cancuen was not as serious as we had feared, and the site would well repay further study, particularly in areas to the south and north of the "acropolis" and ballcourt.

12. There is another possible interpretation of this compound (T12.854). A similar compound occurs with scribal titles at Xcalumkin (Glyph 20–22, Glyphic Group, North Building, inner doorway, David Stuart, personal communication, 1987). Perhaps the title is simply another belonging to scribes.

13. For the identification of particular Emblems, see Berlin (1958:112, 118); I. Graham 1967:51–99; Riese 1975:55–56; Houston and Mathews 1985: Fig. 3; and Houston 1987:Figs. 54, 55. The putative Emblem of Anonal may simply be a title.

14. I assume the existence of political autonomy when the following conditions are met: (1) that a site contain its own dynasty; (2) that a site not mention "overlords"; (3) that a site not record the performance or supervision of rites

by foreign lords in an independent manner. Nonetheless, "autonomy" is a term used advisedly. A site may have an "overlord" who is little more than a nominal suzerain. Or conversely, a site may be nominally autonomous, yet operate under the political or economic supervision of a foreign dynasty. The conclusions drawn here are based solely on explicit glyphic evidence.

15. Dos Pilas Structure P5-7 occurs about 3 kilometers from Arroyo de Piedra and may have been constructed at the time of Dos Pilas' superordinate relation to its neighbor. Thus, packing between centers may have been encouraged by unusually close political ties or, in the case of Dos Pilas Structure P5-7, may have been an assertion of territorial dominion.

5. The Composition and Interaction of Late Classic Polities

1. The history of the Postclassic Basin of Mexico indicates that, in a fraternal system of succession (for which there is also much evidence among the Classic Maya), questionable "blood" or junior status could be nullified by military success. By this means, a wider group of individuals, some of greater competence than senior siblings, could be available for elevation to the throne (Rounds 1982:83).

2. The most persuasive evidence of this comes from a series of lintels looted from sites near Yaxchilan. Many of these lintels have only just appeared on the international art market (Linda Schele, personal communication, 1990).

3. Discussion of the God C title has been shaped through collaborative work with David Stuart.

4. The reading has other problems as well. The final sign does not always have a *na* reading. Sometimes it is T60v, which, to judge from substitution patterns elsewhere, may be *hu* or *nu* (Houston and Stuart n.d.).

5. *A-* is a variant of *ah-* in colonial Chontal (Smailus 1975:126). Glyphic orthography would appear to reflect the same free variation.

6. The movement of sculptors, as from Tamarindito to Aguateca (see Chapter 4), suggests that such practice may also have consolidated links between sovereign polities.

7. The presence of vessels recording Naranjo lords at Río Azul (personal observation, 1986) and Tikal (W. R. Coe 1967:103) may represent the passage of elite goods along such channels. The existence of such networks suggests that mechanisms other than trade may account for the movement of "prestige" items. Note especially the distribution of incensarios in the region of Palenque (Rands and Bishop 1980:44) and fine ceramics near Naranjo (Joseph Ball and Jennifer Taschek, personal communications, 1989).

8. The reduction of a polity to its constituent units is probably attested at Tikal during the Terminal Classic, when small outliers (some at considerable distance from epicentral Tikal) began to erect monuments. Since these sites have different rulers but use the Tikal Emblem, presumably they enjoyed increased and perhaps total autonomy after the apparent collapse of epicentral Tikal as a regional power.

9. Similar marriage alliances were common in the Aztec empire (Michael E. Smith 1986:72–73) and in the Mixtec cacicazgos (Spores 1974:306). Other interdynastic marriages may be added to Marcus' list: Yaxchilan and Site Q; Dos Pilas and Itzan; Dos Pilas and Naranjo; Dos Pilas and Arroyo de Piedra; Tonina and Pomona; El Peru and Zapote Bobal; El Peru and Site Q; Yaxchilan and Bonampak; and Machaquila and Cancuen (information from unpublished data in the CMHI archives). Also noteworthy is the fact that the longest-lived alliances, such as that between Dos Pilas and Calakmul, were more likely to exist between distant polities, where, in a remarkable expression of affinity, roughly coeval rulers might even have the same name, as did Ruler 3 and his contemporary at Calakmul. Could the former have been named for the latter?

10. The best examples of this pattern appear on Caracol Stela 3 and Quirigua Altar L. Moreover, according to Nikolai Grube (personal communication, 1990), stelae at Naranjo may refer to the arrival of a bride from Dos Pilas.

11. Stuart and I deciphered the *il-* glyph independently. However, it was Stuart who suggested that the event corresponded to acts of dynastic witness (personal communication, 1986).

12. The assembly of lords on the so-called "Altar vase" is sometimes presented as a good example of foreign attendance at local rites (R. E. W. Adams 1977b). *Pace* Adams, the "lords" are without question supernaturals, and not historical personages (Houston and Stuart 1989b). If the vase is to be explained, it must rather be in the context of Classic Maya myth and belief. Joyce Marcus, too, has adduced a monument with foreign references (Seibal Stela 10) as an illustration of panregional political and cosmological organization (1976:17). In point of fact these references follow an *ilah* expression, thus indicating attendance by foreign lords and perhaps little else.

13. References to witnessing ceremonies at Dos Pilas, particularly those recorded on Stela 8 and Panel 19, hint that such rituals were also important means by which a ruler validated or "notarized" events *within* his polity.

14. The list of overlord statements can be extended if we include the *yahaw te* expression (Mathews 1988). In the area of Yaxchilan this title is used by subordinates of *ahaw* status.

15. Henry Wright contends that such formations are "pre-state" societies, from which may spring a limited number of true states (1986:357–358). "Pre-state" societies, which resemble the majority of Late Classic Maya polities, are thought by Wright to exemplify the Early Uruk period in Mesopotamia (ibid.:329, 331).

16. Multiple capitals also existed among the Mixtec, who found such centers useful for purposes of administration (Spores 1984:70–71). I am indebted to Antonia Foias for bringing this information to my attention.

17. Nonetheless, it is for precisely this reason that we should be wary of overstressing the shamanic roles of Maya rulers or of identifying them as shamans per se. By any conservative definition of the term, Maya kings cannot be shamans, although they may possess some of the charismatic and mantic qualities of these healers and oracles, who typically are at once part of, and apart from society (Halifax 1982; Pasztory 1982:7–9). Similarly, some beliefs and practices with shamanic overtones may date to an earlier time in Maya history, so that by the Late Classic period they are less an expression of the ruler qua shaman than a reflection of ancient tradition. Not all religious practices can be, or should be, explained in purely functional terms.

Bibliography

Abrams, Elliot M.

1987 Economic Specialization and Construction Personnel in Classic Period Copan, Honduras. *American Antiquity* 52(3):485–499.

Adams, Richard E. W.

1971 *The Ceramics of Altar de Sacrificios.* Papers of the Peabody Museum of Archaeology and Ethnology, Harvard University, 63(1). Cambridge, Mass.

1977a (ed.) *The Origins of Maya Civilization.* School of American Research Advanced Seminar Series. Albuquerque: University of New Mexico Press.

1977b Comments on the Glyphic Texts of the "Altar Vase." In *Social Process in Maya Prehistory: Studies in Honour of Sir Eric Thompson,* edited by Norman Hammond, pp. 409–420. London: Academic Press.

1978 Routes of Communication in Mesoamerica: The Northern Guatemalan Highlands and the Peten. In *Mesoamerican Routes and Cultural Contacts,* edited by Thomas A. Lee, Jr., and Carlos Navarrete, pp. 27–35. Papers of the New World Archaeological Foundation, Brigham Young University, 40. Provo, Utah.

1980 Swamps, Canals and the Locations of Ancient Maya Cities. *Antiquity* 54(212):206–214.

1983 Ancient Land Use and Culture History in the Pasión River Region. In *Prehistoric Settlement Patterns: Essays in Honor of Gordon R. Willey,* edited by Evon Z. Vogt and Richard M. Leventhal, pp. 319–335. Albuquerque: University of New Mexico Press.

1984 Central Maya Lowland Settlement Patterns: A Trial Formulation. In *Rio Azul Project Reports, Number 1 / Proyecto Río Azul, Informe Uno: 1983,* edited by R. E. W. Adams, pp. 64–75. San Antonio: Center for Archaeological Research, University of Texas at San Antonio.

Adams, R. E. W., W. E. Brown, Jr., and T. P. Culbert

1981 Radar Mapping, Archaeology, and Ancient Maya Land Use. *Science* 213:1457–1463.

Adams, Richard E. W., and R. C. Jones

1981 Spatial Patterns and Regional Growth among Maya Cities. *American Antiquity* 46(2):301–322.

Adams, Richard E. W., and Woodruff Smith

1981 Feudal Models for Classic Maya Civilization. In *Lowland Maya Settlement Patterns,* edited by Wendy Ashmore, pp. 335–350. School of American Research Advanced Seminar Series. Albuquerque: University of New Mexico Press.

Adams, Robert McC.

1981 *Heartland of Cities: Survey of Ancient Settlement and Land Use on the Central Floodplain of the Euphrates*. Chicago: University of Chicago Press.

Altheide, David, and John Johnson
1980 *Bureaucratic Propaganda*. Boston: Allyn and Bacon.

Andrews, E. Wyllys, IV, and Anthony P. Andrews
1975 *A Preliminary Study of the Ruins of Xcaret, Quintana Roo, Mexico, with Notes on Other Archaeological Remains on the Central East Coast of the Yucatan Peninsula*. Middle American Research Institute, Tulane University, Publication 40. New Orleans.

Armillas, Pedro
1951 Mesoamerican Fortifications. *Antiquity* 25:77–86.

Ashmore, Wendy
1981a (ed.) *Lowland Maya Settlement Patterns*. School of American Research Advanced Seminar Series. Albuquerque: University of New Mexico Press.
1981b Some Issues of Method and Theory in Lowland Maya Settlement Archaeology. In *Lowland Maya Settlement Patterns*, edited by Wendy Ashmore, pp. 37–69. School of American Research Advanced Seminar Series. Albuquerque: University of New Mexico Press.

Aveni, Anthony F.
1977 Concepts of Positional Astronomy Employed in Ancient Mesoamerican Architecture. In *Native American Astronomy*, edited by Anthony F. Aveni, pp. 3–19. Austin: University of Texas Press.

Baines, John
1983 Literacy and Ancient Egyptian Society. *Man* 18:572–599.

Ball, Joseph W., and Jennifer T. Taschek
1989 Small Center Archaeology and Classic Maya Political Organization: The Mopan-Macal Triangle Project. Paper presented at 54th annual meeting of the Society for American Archaeology, Atlanta.

Barrera Vásquez, Alfredo
1980 (ed.) *Diccionario Maya Cordemex: Maya-Español / Español-Maya*. Mérida: Ediciones Cordemex.

Barthel, Thomas
1952 Der Morgensternkult in den Darstellungen der Dresdener Mayahandschrift. *Ethnos* 17:73–112.
1968 El complejo "emblema." *Estudios de Cultura Maya* 7:159–193.

Baudez, Claude F., and Pierre Becquelin
1973 *Archéologie de Los Naranjos, Honduras*. Etudes Mésoaméricaines 2. Mexico City: Mission Archéologique et Ethnologique Française au Mexique.

Becker, Marshall J.
1971 *The Identification of a Second Plaza Plan at Tikal, Guatemala, and Its Implications for Ancient Maya Social Complexity*. Ph.D. dissertation, Department of Anthropology, University of Pennsylvania. Ann Arbor: University Microfilms.

Becquelin, Pierre, and Claude F. Baudez
1982 *Tonina, Une Cité Maya du Chiapas*, vol. 3. Mission Archéologique et Ethnologique Française au Mexique, Collection Etudes Mésoaméricaines 6(3). Paris: Editions Recherche sur les Civilisations.

Beetz, Carl P., and Linton Satterthwaite
1981 *The Monuments and Inscriptions of Caracol, Belize*. University Museum Monographs, University of Pennsylvania, 45. Philadelphia.

Benda, Harry J.
1962 The Structure of Southeast Asian History: Some Preliminary Observations. *Journal of Southeast Asian History* 3:103–138.

Bentley, G. Carter
1986 Indigenous States of Southeast Asia. *Annual Review of Anthropology* 15:275–305.

Berlin, Heinrich
1958 El glifo "emblema" en las inscripciones mayas. *Journal de la Société des Américanistes* 47:111–119.
1960 Mas casos del glifo lunar en números de distancia. *Antropología e Historia de Guatemala* 12(2):25–27. Guatemala City: Instituto de Antropología e Historia.
1970 Miscelánea palencano. *Journal de la Société des Américanistes* 59:107–135.
1973 Beiträge zum Verständnis des Inschriften von Naranjo. *Bulletin de la Société Suisse des Américanistes* 37:7–14.
1977 *Signos y significados en las inscripciones mayas.* Guatemala City: Instituto Nacional del Patrimonio Cultural de Guatemala.
1987 Vericuetos mayas. In *Homenaje jubilar a José Mata Gavidia*, edited by Rigoberto Juárez-Paz, pp. 9–24. Guatemala City: Facultad de Humanidades, Universidad de San Carlos de Guatemala.

Berlo, Janet Catherine
1984 *Teotihuacan Art Abroad: A Study of Metropolitan Style and Provincial Transformation in Incensario Worship.* British Archaeological Reports International Series, 199. Oxford.

Bey, George J., and William M. Ringle
1989 The Myth of the Center: Political Integration at Ek Balam, Yucatan, Mexico. Paper presented at 54th annual meeting of the Society for American Archaeology, Atlanta.

Bolitho, Harold
1985 Japanese Kingship. In *Patterns of Kingship and Authority in Traditional Asia*, edited by Ian W. Mabbett, pp. 24–43. London: Croom Helm.

Borhegyi, S. F. de
1956 The Development of Folk and Complex Cultures in the Southern Maya Area. *American Antiquity* 21(4):343–356.

Bradbury, R. E.
1969 Patrimonialism and Gerontocracy in Benin Political Culture. In *Man in Africa*, edited by Mary Douglas and Phyllis M. Kaberry, pp. 17–36. London: Tavistock Publications.

Bricker, Victoria R.
1986 *A Grammar of Mayan Hieroglyphs.* Middle American Research Institute, Tulane University, Publication 56. New Orleans.

Brush, John E., and Howard E. Bracey
1955 Rural Service Centers in Southwestern Wisconsin and Southern England. *Geographical Review* 45:559–569.

Bullard, William R., Jr.
1952 Residential Property Walls at Mayapan. *Current Reports* 1(3):36–44. Washington, D.C.: Carnegie Institution of Washington, Division of Historical Research.
1965 Ruinas ceremoniales mayas en el curso inferior del río Lacantun, México. *Estudios de Cultura Maya* 5:41–51.

Caldwell, Joseph
1964 Interaction Spheres in Prehistory. In *Hopewellian Studies*, edited by Joseph R. Caldwell and Robert L. Hall, pp. 133–143. Illinois State Museum Scientific Papers 12(6). Springfield.

Calnek, Edward E.
1982 Patterns of Empire Formation in the Valley of Mexico, Late Postclas-

sic Period, 1200–1521. In *The Inca and Aztec States, 1400–1800: Archaeology and History*, edited by George A. Collier, Renato I. Rosaldo, and John D. Wirth, pp. 43–62. New York: Academic Press.

Carr, Robert F., and James E. Hazard
1961 *Tikal Report No. 11: Map of the Ruins of Tikal, El Peten, Guatemala*. Museum Monographs, University Museum. Philadelphia: University of Pennsylvania.

Carrasco, Pedro
1984 Royal Marriages in Ancient Mexico. In *Explorations in Ethnohistory: Indians of Central Mexico in the Sixteenth Century*, edited by H. R. Harvey and Hanns J. Prem, pp. 41–81. Albuquerque: University of New Mexico Press.

Chase, Arlen F., and Diane Z. Chase
1987 *Investigations at the Classic Maya City of Caracol, Belize: 1985–1987*. Pre-Columbian Art Research Institute, Monograph 3. San Francisco.

Cherry, John F., and Colin Renfrew
1986 Epilogue and Prospect. In *Peer Polity Interaction and Socio-political Change*, edited by Colin Renfrew and John F. Cherry, pp. 149–158. New Directions in Archaeology. Cambridge: Cambridge University Press.

Closs, Michael P.
1985 The Dynastic History of Naranjo: The Middle Period. In *Fifth Palenque Round Table, 1983*, edited by Virginia M. Fields, pp. 65–77. San Francisco: Pre-Columbian Art Research Institute.

CMHI (Corpus of Maya Hieroglyphic Inscriptions)
See I. Graham 1975; 1978; 1979; 1980; 1982; Graham and Von Euw 1977; Von Euw 1978; Von Euw and Graham 1984

Coe, Michael D.
1961 Social Typology and the Tropical Forest Civilizations. *Comparative Studies in Society and History* 4(1):65–85.
1973 *The Maya Scribe and His World*. New York: Grolier Club.

Coe, Michael D., and Elizabeth P. Benson
1966 *Three Maya Reliefs at Dumbarton Oaks*. Studies in Pre-Columbian Art and Archaeology 2. Washington, D.C.: Dumbarton Oaks.

Coe, William R.
1967 *Tikal: A Handbook of the Ancient Maya Ruins*. Philadelphia: University Museum, University of Pennsylvania.

Coggins, Clemency C.
1975 *Painting and Drawing Styles at Tikal: An Historical and Iconographic Reconstruction*. Ph.D. dissertation, Department of Art History, Harvard University. Ann Arbor: University Microfilms.

Cooper, Jerrold S.
1983a *The Curse of Agade*. Baltimore: Johns Hopkins University Press.
1983b *Reconstructing History from Ancient Inscriptions: The Lagash-Umma Border Conflict*. Sources from the Ancient Near East 2(1). Malibu, Calif.: Undena.

Culbert, T. Patrick
1973 (ed.) *The Classic Maya Collapse*. School of American Research Advanced Seminar Series. Albuquerque: University of New Mexico Press.
1988a The Collapse of Classic Maya Civilization. In *The Collapse of Ancient States and Civilizations*, edited by Norman Yoffee and George L. Cowgill, pp. 69–101. Tucson: University of Arizona Press.

1988b Political History and the Decipherment of Maya Glyphs. *Antiquity* 62:135–152.

Dalton, George

1977 Aboriginal Economies in Stateless Societies. In *Exchange Systems in Prehistory*, edited by Timothy K. Earle and Jonathon E. Ericson, pp. 191–212. New York: Academic Press.

Demarest, Arthur A.

1978 Interregional Conflict and "Situational Ethics" in Classic Maya Warfare. In *Codex Wauchope: A Tribute Roll*, edited by M. Giardino, B. Edmonson, and V. Creamer, pp. 101–111. Human Mosaic, Tulane University. New Orleans.

1984 Conclusiones y especulaciones. In Proyecto El Mirador de la Harvard University, 1982–1983. *Mesoamérica* 7:138–150. Antigua, Guatemala: Centro de Investigaciones Regionales de Mesoamérica.

1986 *The Archaeology of Santa Leticia and the Rise of Maya Civilization.* Middle American Research Institute, Tulane University, Publication 52. New Orleans.

1990 Ideology in Ancient Maya Cultural Evolution: The Dynamics of Galactic Polities. MS on file, Department of Anthropology, Vanderbilt University, Nashville.

Demarest, Arthur A., and Stephen D. Houston

1989 (eds.) Proyecto Arqueológico Regional Petexbatun, Informe Preliminar No. 1, Primera Temporada, 1989. MS on file, Department of Anthropology, Vanderbilt University, Nashville.

1990 (eds.) Proyecto Arqueológico Regional Petexbatun, Informe Preliminar No. 2, Segunda Temporada, 1990. MS on file, Department of Anthropology, Vanderbilt University, Nashville.

de Montmollin, Olivier

1988 Tenam Rosario: A Political Microcosm. *American Antiquity* 53(2): 351–370.

1989 *The Archaeology of Political Structure: Settlement Analysis in a Classic Maya Polity*. Cambridge: Cambridge University Press.

Diakonoff, I. M.

1969 The Rise of the Despotic State in Ancient Mesopotamia. In *Ancient Mesopotamia,* edited by I. M. Diakonoff, pp. 173–203. Moscow: Nauka Publishing House.

Dunham, Peter S.

1989 Maya Balkanization in the Early Classic: Expansion and the "Hiatus." Paper presented at the Archaeological Congress, Baltimore.

Durán, Fray Diego

1971 *Book of the Gods and Rites and The Ancient Calendar*. Translated and edited by Fernando Horcasitas and Doris Heyden. Norman: University of Oklahoma Press.

Durkheim, Emile

1960 *The Division of Labor in Society*. Glencoe, Ill.: Free Press.

Emmerich, André

1984 *Masterpieces of Pre-Columbian Art from the Collection of Mr. and Mrs. Peter G. Wray*. New York: André Emmerich Gallery and Perls Galleries.

Escobedo Ayala, Hector Leonel

1991 Epigrafía e historia política de los sitios del noroeste de las montañas mayas durante el clásico tardío. Licenciatura thesis, Escuela de Historia, Area de Arqueología, Universidad de San Carlos de Guatemala.

Fash, William L., Jr.
1988 A New Look at Maya Statecraft from Copan, Honduras. *Antiquity* 62:157–169.

Fash, William L., and David S. Stuart
1991 Dynastic History and Cultural Evolution at Copan, Honduras. In *Classic Maya Political History: Hieroglyphic and Archaeological Evidence*, pp. 147–179. A School of American Research Book. Cambridge: Cambridge University Press.

Feeley-Harnik, Gillian
1985 Issues in Divine Kingship. *Annual Review of Anthropology* 14: 273–313.

Fisher, A. R.
1985 The Early State Module: A Critical Assessment. *Oxford Journal of Archaeology* 4(1):1–8.

Flannery, Kent V.
1972 The Cultural Evolution of Civilizations. *Annual Review of Ecology and Systematics* 3:399–426.
1977 Review: *Mesoamerican Archaeology: New Approaches*, edited by Norman Hammond. *American Antiquity* 42(4):659–661.

Folan, William J., Ellen R. Kintz, and Loraine A. Fletcher
1983 *Coba: A Classic Maya Metropolis*. New York: Academic Press.

Förstemann, Ernst
1904 *Commentary on the Maya Manuscript in the Royal Public Library of Dresden*. Papers of the Peabody Museum of Archaeology and Ethnology, Harvard University, 4(2). Cambridge, Mass.

Forsyth, Donald W.
1980 Report on Some Ceramics from the Peten, Guatemala. In *El Mirador, Peten, Guatemala: An Interim Report*, edited by Ray T. Matheny, pp. 59–82. Papers of the New World Archaeological Foundation, Brigham Young University, 45. Provo, Utah.

Fox, James A., and John S. Justeson
1986 Classic Maya Dynastic Alliance and Succession. In *Supplement to the Handbook of Middle American Indians*, vol. 4, *Ethnohistory*, edited by Victoria R. Bricker and Ronald Spores, pp. 7–34. Austin: University of Texas Press.

Fox, John W.
1987 *Maya Postclassic State Formation: Segmentary Lineage Migration in Advancing Frontiers*. Cambridge: Cambridge University Press.
1989 On the Rise and Fall of *Tuláns* and Maya Segmentary States. *American Anthropologist* 91(3):656–681.

Freidel, David A.
1983 Political Systems in Lowland Yucatan: Dynamics and Structure in Maya Settlement. In *Prehistoric Settlement Patterns: Essays in Honor of Gordon R. Willey*, edited by Evon Z. Vogt and Richard M. Leventhal, pp. 375–386. Albuquerque: University of New Mexico Press.
1986a Maya Warfare: An Example of Peer Polity Interaction. In *Peer Polity Interaction and Socio-political Change*, edited by Colin Renfrew and John F. Cherry, pp. 93–108. New Directions in Archaeology. Cambridge: Cambridge University Press.
1986b *Yaxuna Archaeological Survey: A Report of the 1986 Field Season, Yaxuna, Yucatan, Mexico*. Dallas: Southern Methodist University.

Freidel, David A., and Jeremy A. Sabloff
1984 *Cozumel: Late Maya Settlement Patterns*. Orlando: Academic Press.

Freidel, David A., and Linda Schele
1988 Kingship in the Late Preclassic Lowlands: The Instruments and Places of Ritual Power. *American Anthropologist* 90(3): 547–567.
1989 Tlaloc-Venus Warfare and the Triumph of the Confederacy at Chichén Itzá. Paper presented at the 54th annual meeting of the Society for American Archaeology, Atlanta.
Friedman, J., and M. J. Rowlands
1978 Notes towards an Epigenetic Model of the Evolution of Civilizations. In *The Evolution of Social Systems*, edited by J. Friedman and M. J. Rowlands, pp. 201–276. London: Duckworth.
Fritz, John M.
1986 Vijayanagara: Authority and Meaning of a South Indian Imperial Capital. *American Anthropologist* 88(1): 44–55.
Fritz, John M., George Michell, and M. S. Nagaraja Rao
1984 *Where Kings and Gods Meet: The Royal Centre at Vijayanagara, India*. Tucson: University of Arizona Press.
Galindo, Juan
1833 Description of the River Usumacinta, in Guatemala. *Journal of the Royal Geographical Society of London* 3: 59–64.
Garza Tarazona de González, Silvia, and Edward B. Kurjack
1980 *Atlas Arqueológico del Estado de Yucatan*. 2 vols. Mexico City: Instituto Nacional de Antropología e Historia.
Geertz, Clifford
1980 *Negara: The Theatre State in Nineteenth-Century Bali*. Princeton: Princeton University Press.
Gillespie, Susan D.
1989 *The Aztec Kings: The Construction of Rulership in Mexico City*. Tucson: University of Arizona Press.
Gottschalk, Louis
1958 *Understanding History: A Primer of Historical Method*. New York: Alfred A. Knopf.
Graham, Ian
1961 A Newly Discovered Maya Site. *Illustrated London News* 238(6351): 665–667.
1963 Across the Peten to the Ruins of Machaquila. *Expedition* 5(4): 2–10.
1967 *Archaeological Explorations in El Peten, Guatemala*. Middle American Research Institute, Tulane University, Publication 33. New Orleans.
1970 The Ruins of La Florida, Peten, Guatemala. In *Monographs and Papers in Maya Archaeology*, edited by William R. Bullard, Jr., pp. 427–455. Papers of the Peabody Museum of Archaeology and Ethnology, Harvard University, 61. Cambridge, Mass.
1971 *The Art of Maya Hieroglyphic Writing*. New York: Center for Inter-American Relations. Cambridge, Mass.: Peabody Museum of Archaeology and Ethnology. Harvard University.
1975 *Introduction*. Corpus of Maya Hieroglyphic Inscriptions 2. Cambridge, Mass.: Peabody Museum of Archaeology and Ethnology, Harvard University.
1978 *Naranjo, Chunhuitz, Xunantunich*. Corpus of Maya Hieroglyphic Inscriptions 2(2). Cambridge, Mass.: Peabody Museum of Archaeology and Ethnology, Harvard University.
1979 *Yaxchilan*. Corpus of Maya Hieroglyphic Inscriptions 3(2). Cambridge, Mass.: Peabody Museum of Archaeology and Ethnology, Harvard University.

1980 *Ixkun, Ucanal, Ixtutz, Naranjo.* Corpus of Maya Hieroglyphic Inscriptions 2(3). Cambridge, Mass.: Peabody Museum of Archaeology and Ethnology, Harvard University.

1982 *Yaxchilan.* Corpus of Maya Hieroglyphic Inscriptions 3(3). Cambridge, Mass.: Peabody Museum of Archaeology and Ethnology, Harvard University.

Graham, Ian, and Eric Von Euw

1972 *Naranjo.* Corpus of Maya Hieroglyphic Inscriptions 2(1). Cambridge, Mass.: Peabody Museum of Archaeology and Ethnology, Harvard University.

1977 *Yaxchilan.* Corpus of Maya Hieroglyphic Inscriptions 3(1). Cambridge, Mass.: Peabody Museum of Archaeology and Ethnology, Harvard University.

Graham, John

1972 *The Hieroglyphic Inscriptions and Monumental Art of Altar de Sacrificios.* Papers of the Peabody Museum of Archaeology and Ethnology, Harvard University, 64(2). Cambridge, Mass.

1973 Aspects of Non-Classic Presences in the Inscriptions and Monumental Art of Seibal. In *The Classic Maya Collapse,* edited by T. Patrick Culbert, pp. 207–219. School of American Research Advanced Seminar Series. Albuquerque: University of New Mexico Press.

1989 Olmec Diffusion: A Sculptural View from Pacific Guatemala. In *Regional Perspectives on the Olmec,* edited by Robert J. Sharer and David C. Grove, pp. 227–246. School of American Research Advanced Seminar Series. Cambridge: Cambridge University Press.

Grayson, A. K.

1980 Assyria and Babylonia. *Orientalia* 49(2): 140–194.

Green, E. L.

1973 Location Analysis of Prehistoric Maya Sites in Northern British Honduras. *American Antiquity* 38(3): 279–293.

Greene, Merle, Robert L. Rands, and John A. Graham

1972 *Maya Sculpture from the Southern Lowlands, the Highlands and Pacific Piedmont.* Berkeley: Lederer, Street, and Zeus.

Greene Robertson, Merle

1983 *The Sculpture of Palenque,* vol. 1, *The Temple of the Inscriptions.* Princeton: Princeton University Press.

Grieder, Terence

1960 Manifestaciones de arte maya en la región de Petexbatun. *Antropología e Historia de Guatemala,* 12(2): 10–24.

Grube, Nikolai, and David Stuart

1987 *Observations on T110 as the Syllable* ***ko***. Research Reports on Ancient Maya Writing 8. Washington, D.C.: Center for Maya Research.

Haggett, P.

1965 *Locational Analysis in Human Geography.* London: Arnold.

Halifax, Joan

1982 *Shaman: The Wounded Healer.* London: Thames and Hudson.

Hall, Kenneth R.

1976 An Introductory Essay on Southeast Asian Statecraft in the Classical Period. In *Explorations in Early Southeast Asian History: The Origins of Southeast Asian Statecraft,* edited by Kenneth R. Hall and John K. Whitmore, pp. 1–24. Michigan Papers on South and Southeast Asia 11. Ann Arbor: Center for South and Southeast Asian Studies, University of Michigan.

Hammond, Norman

1974 The Distribution of Late Classic Maya Major Ceremonial Centres in the Central Area. In *Mesoamerican Archaeology: New Approaches*, edited by Norman Hammond, pp. 313–334. Austin: University of Texas Press.

1975 *Lubaantun: A Classic Maya Realm*. Monographs of the Peabody Museum of Archaeology and Ethnology, Harvard University, 2. Cambridge, Mass.

Hammond, Norman, and Wendy Ashmore

1981 Lowland Maya Settlement: Geographical and Chronological Frameworks. In *Lowland Maya Settlement Patterns*, edited by Wendy Ashmore, pp. 19–36. School of American Research Advanced Seminar Series. Albuquerque: University of New Mexico Press.

Harrison, Peter D.

1981 Some Aspects of Preconquest Settlement in Southern Quintana Roo, Mexico. In *Lowland Maya Settlement Patterns*, edited by Wendy Ashmore, pp. 259–286. Albuquerque: University of New Mexico Press.

Hartshorn, G. S.

1983 Plants: Introduction. In *Costa Rican Natural History*, edited by Daniel H. Janzen, pp. 118–159. Chicago: University of Chicago Press.

Haviland, William A.

1974 Occupational Specialization at Tikal, Guatemala: Stoneworking-Monument Carving. *American Antiquity* 39(3):494–496.

Hellmuth, Nicholas M.

1972 Excavations Begin at Maya Site in Guatemala. *Archaeology* 25(2): 148–149.

Hochleitner, Franz Joseph

1972 A inscriçao hieroglífica maia de Dos Pilas. *Atti del XL Congresso Internazionale degli Americanisti, Roma-Genova, 1972* 1:203–212. Genoa: Casa Editrice Tilgher.

Holdrige, L. R.

1947 Determination of World Plant Formation from Simple Climatic Data. *Science* 105:367–368.

Hopkins, Nicholas A.

1988 Classic Mayan Kinship Systems: Epigraphic and Ethnographic Evidence for Patrilineality. *Estudios de Cultura Maya* 17:87–121.

1991 Classic and Modern Relationship Terms and the 'Child of Mother' Glyph (T I:606.23). In *Sixth Palenque Round Table, 1986*, edited by Virginia M. Fields (Merle Greene Robertson, general editor), pp. 255–265. Norman: University of Oklahoma Press.

Houston, Stephen D.

1983 A Reading for the "Flint-Shield" Glyph. In *Contributions to Maya Hieroglyphic Decipherment I*, edited by Stephen D. Houston, pp. 13–25. New Haven: HRAFlex Books.

1985 A Feather Dance at Bonampak, Chiapas, Mexico. *Journal du Société des Américanistes* 70:127–138. Paris.

1986 *Problematic Emblem Glyphs: Examples from Altar de Sacrificios, El Chorro, Rio Azul, and Xultun*. Research Reports on Ancient Maya Writing 3. Washington, D.C.: Center for Maya Research.

1987 *The Inscriptions and Monumental Art of Dos Pilas, Guatemala: A Study of Classic Maya History and Politics*. Ph.D. dissertation, Department of Anthropology, Yale University. Ann Arbor: University Microfilms (AAC88–10625).

1989 Archaeology and Maya Writing. *Journal of World Prehistory* 3(1):1–32.

1991 Classic Maya History in the Petexbatun Region: Topics in Biography and Politics. Paper presented at 56th annual meeting of the Society for American Archaeology, New Orleans.

In press Classic Maya History and Politics at Dos Pilas, Guatemala. In *Supplement to the Handbook of Middle American Indians*, vol. 5, *Epigraphy*, edited by Victoria Reifler Bricker. Austin: University of Texas Press.

Houston, Stephen D., and Kevin Johnston

1987 Classic Maya Political Organization. Paper presented at the 86th annual meeting of the American Anthropological Association, Chicago.

Houston, Stephen D., and Peter Mathews

1985 *The Dynastic Sequence of Dos Pilas, Guatemala*. Pre-Columbian Art Research Institute, Monograph 1. San Francisco.

Houston, Stephen D., and David S. Stuart

1989a Placenames and Rituals of the Late Classic Maya. Paper presented at the annual meeting of the Society for Ethnohistory, Chicago.

1989b *The* Way *Glyph: Evidence for "Co-Essences" among the Classic Maya*. Research Reports on Ancient Maya Writing 30. Washington, D.C.: Center for Maya Research.

n.d. Ancient Maya Writing. In preparation.

Istituto Italo-latinamericano

1969 *Arte maya del Guatemala: 3 ottobre–30 dicembre*. Milan.

Ivanoff, Pierre

1968 *Découvertes chez les Mayas*. Paris: Robert Laffont.

Janzen, Daniel H.

1983 (ed.) *Costa Rican Natural History*. Chicago: University of Chicago Press.

Johnson, Gregory A.

1982 Organizational Structure and Scalar Stress. In *Theory and Explanation in Archaeology: The Southhampton Conference*, edited by Colin Renfrew, Michael J. Rowlands, and Barbara Abbott Seagraves, pp. 389–421. New York: Academic Press.

1987 The Changing Organization of Uruk Administration on the Susiana Plain. In *The Archaeology of Western Iran: Settlement and Society from Prehistory to the Islamic Conquest*, edited by Frank Hole, pp. 107–156. Smithsonian Series in Archaeological Inquiry. Washington, D.C.: Smithsonian Institution Press.

Johnson, Jay K.

1985 Postclassic Maya Site Structure at Topoxte, El Peten, Guatemala. In *The Lowland Maya Postclassic*, edited by Arlen F. Chase and Prudence M. Rice, pp. 151–165. Austin: University of Texas Press.

Johnston, Kevin

1985 Maya Dynastic Territorial Expansion: Glyphic Evidence from Classic Centers of the Pasión River, Guatemala. In *Fifth Palenque Round Table, 1983*, edited by Virginia M. Fields, pp. 49–56. San Francisco: Pre-Columbian Art Research Institute.

1989 Cartographic, Epigraphic, and Archaeological Investigations at the Ruins of Itzan, Petén, Guatemala. *Yale Graduate Journal of Anthropology* 2:43–57.

Jones, Christopher

1977 Inauguration Dates of Three Late Classic Rulers of Tikal, Guatemala. *American Antiquity* 42:28–60.

Jones, Christopher, and Linton Satterthwaite

1982 *Tikal Report No. 33, Part A: The Monuments and Inscriptions of Tikal: The Carved Monuments*. Museum Monograph 44, University Museum. Philadelphia: University of Pennsylvania.

Jones, Grant D.
1986 The Southern Maya Lowlands during Spanish Colonial Times. In *Supplement to the Handbook of Middle American Indians*, vol. 4, *Ethnohistory*, edited by Victoria R. Bricker and Ronald Spores, pp. 71–87. Austin: University of Texas Press.
1989 *Maya Resistance to Spanish Rule: Time and History on a Colonial Frontier*. Albuquerque: University of New Mexico Press.

Jones, Julie
1969 *Precolumbian Art in New York: Selections from Private Collections*. New York: Museum of Primitive Art.

Jones, Morris
1952 *Map of the Ruins of Mayapan, Yucatan, Mexico*. Carnegie Institution of Washington, Current Reports 1. Washington, D.C.

Josserand, J. Kathryn, Linda D. Schele, and Nicholas A. Hopkins
1985 Linguistic Data on Mayan Inscriptions: The *ti* Constructions. In *Fourth Palenque Round Table, 1980*, edited by Elizabeth P. Benson (Merle Greene Robertson, general editor), pp. 87–102. San Francisco: Pre-Columbian Art Research Institute.

Justeson, John S., and Peter Mathews
1983 The Seating of the Tun: Further Evidence Concerning a Late Preclassic Lowland Maya Stela Cult. *American Antiquity* 48(3):586–593.

Kelley, David H.
1962 Glyphic Evidence for a Dynastic Sequence at Quirigua, Guatemala. *American Antiquity* 27(3):323–335.

Kirch, Patrick Vinton
1984 *The Evolution of the Polynesian Chiefdoms*. Cambridge: Cambridge University Press.

Koenig, Seymour H., and George O. Williams
1985 Modeling Lowland Maya Settlement Patterns. In *Fifth Palenque Round Table, 1983*, edited by Virginia M. Fields, pp. 255–259. San Francisco: Pre-Columbian Art Research Institute.

Kowalski, Jeff Karl
1986 Uxmal: A Terminal Classic Maya Capital in Northern Yucatan. In *City-States of the Maya: Art and Architecture*, edited by Elizabeth P. Benson, pp. 138–171. Denver: Rocky Mountain Institute for Pre-Columbian Studies.

Krochock, Ruth
1989 *Hieroglyphic Inscriptions at Chichén Itzá, Yucatán, México: The Temples of the Initial Series, the One Lintel, the Three Lintels, and the Four Lintels*. Research Reports on Ancient Maya Writing 23. Washington, D.C.: Center for Maya Research.

Kubler, George
1975 *The Art and Architecture of Ancient America: The Mexican, Maya, and Andean Peoples*. Harmondsworth, England: Penguin Books.
1977 *Aspects of Classic Maya Rulership on Two Inscribed Vessels*. Studies in Pre-Columbian Art and Archaeology 18. Washington, D.C.: Dumbarton Oaks.

Kurjack, Edward B., and E. Wyllys Andrews V
1976 Early Boundary Maintenance in Northwest Yucatan, Mexico. *American Antiquity* 41(3):318–325.

Lamb, Dana, and Ginger Lamb
1951 *Quest for the Lost City*. New York: Harper and Brothers.

Lloyd, Peter
1965 The Political Structure of African Kingdoms: An Explanatory Model.

In *Political Systems and the Distribution of Power*, edited by M. Banton, pp. 63–112. London: Tavistock.

Loten, H. Stanley, and David M. Pendergast

1984 *A Lexicon for Maya Architecture*. Archaeology Monograph 8. Toronto: Royal Ontario Museum.

Lounsbury, Floyd G.

1973 On the Derivation and Reading of the "Ben-Ich" Prefix. In *Mesoamerican Writing Systems*, edited by Elizabeth P. Benson, pp. 99–143. Washington, D.C.: Dumbarton Oaks.

1982 Astronomical Knowledge and Its Uses at Bonampak, Mexico. In *Archaeoastronomy in the New World: American Primitive Astronomy*, edited by Anthony F. Aveni, pp. 143–168. Cambridge: Cambridge University Press.

Mabbett, Ian W.

1985 Introduction: The Comparative Study of Traditional Asian Political Institutions. In *Patterns of Kingship and Authority in Traditional Asia*, edited by Ian Mabbett, pp. 1–23. London: Croom Helm.

MacLeod, Barbara

1990 The God N/Step Set in the Primary Standard Sequence. In *The Maya Vase Book: A Corpus of Rollout Photographs of Maya Vases*, vol. 2, edited by Justin Kerr, pp. 331–347. New York: Kerr Associates.

Mair, Lucy

1962 *Primitive Government: A Study of Traditional Political Systems in Eastern Africa*. Bloomington: Indiana University Press.

Maler, Teobert

1908 *Explorations of the Upper Usumacintla and Adjacent Regions*. Memoirs of the Peabody Museum of Archaeology and Ethnology, Harvard University, 4(1). Cambridge, Mass.

Mapa Geológico de Guatemala

n.d. Hoja Usumacinta. Guatemala City: Instituto Geográfico Nacional.

Marcus, Joyce

1973 Territorial Organization of the Lowland Classic Maya. *Science* 180: 911–916.

1976 *Emblem and State in the Classic Maya Lowlands: An Epigraphic Approach to Territorial Organization*. Washington, D.C.: Dumbarton Oaks.

1983 Lowland Maya Archaeology at the Crossroads. *American Antiquity* 48(3):454–488.

1984 Mesoamerican Territorial Boundaries: Reconstructions from Archaeology and Hieroglyphic Writing. *Archaeological Review from Cambridge* 3(2):48–62.

1990 Ancient Maya Political Organization. Revised version of paper presented at the 1989 Dumbarton Oaks Symposium, "On the Eve of the Collapse," Washington, D.C.

Matheny, Ray

1970 *The Ceramics of Aguacatal, Campeche, Mexico*. Papers of the New World Archaeological Foundation, Brigham Young University, 27. Provo, Utah.

Mathews, Peter

1979a The Inscription on the Back of Stela 8, Dos Pilas, Guatemala. MS on file, Department of Archaeology, University of Calgary, Alberta.

1979b Notes on the Inscriptions of "Site Q." MS on file, Department of Archaeology, University of Calgary, Alberta.

1980 Notes on the Dynastic Sequence of Bonampak, Part 1. In *Third Pal-*

enque Round Table, 1978, Part 2*, edited by Merle Greene Robertson, pp. 60–73. Austin: University of Texas Press.

1984 Emblem Glyphs in Classic Maya Inscriptions. Paper presented at the 83rd annual meeting of the American Anthropological Association, Denver.

1985 Maya Early Classic Monuments and Inscriptions. In *A Consideration of the Early Classic Period in the Maya Lowlands*, edited by Gordon R. Willey and Peter Mathews, pp. 5–54. Institute for Mesoamerican Studies, State University of New York at Albany, Publication 10. Albany.

1988 *The Sculptures of Yaxchilán*. Ph.D. dissertation, Department of Anthropology, Yale University. Ann Arbor: University Microfilms (AAC90–11374).

Mathews, Peter, and John S. Justeson

1984 Patterns of Sign Substitution in Maya Hieroglyphic Writing: "The Affix Cluster." In *Phoneticism in Mayan Hieroglyphic Writing*, edited by John S. Justeson and Lyle Campbell, pp. 185–231. Institute for Mesoamerican Studies, State University of New York at Albany, Publication 9. Albany.

Mathews, Peter, and Linda Schele

1974 Lords of Palenque—The Glyphic Evidence. In *Primera Mesa Redonda de Palenque, Part I*, edited by Merle Greene Robertson, pp. 63–75. Pebble Beach, Calif.: Robert Louis Stevenson School.

Mathews, Peter, and Gordon R. Willey

1991 Prehistoric Politics of the Pasión Region: Hieroglyphic Texts and Their Archaeological Settings. In *Classic Political History: Hieroglyphic and Archeological Evidence*, edited by T. Patrick Culbert, pp. 30–71. A School of American Research Book. Cambridge: Cambridge University Press.

Mayer, Karl Herbert

1984 *Maya Monuments: Sculptures of Unknown Provenance in Middle America*. Berlin: Verlag Karl-Friedrich von Flemming.

Miller, Mary Ellen

1986 *The Murals of Bonampak*. Princeton: Princeton University Press.

Miller, Mary Ellen, and Stephen D. Houston

1987 The Classic Maya Ballgame and Its Architectural Setting: A Study in Relations between Text and Image. *RES* 14:47–66.

Millon, Ray

1973 *Urbanization at Teotihuacan, Mexico*, vol. 1, *The Teotihuacan Map, Part One: Text*. Austin: University of Texas Press.

Monaghan, John

1990 Performance and the Structure of the Mixtec Codices. *Ancient Mesoamerica* 1(1):133–140.

Morley, Sylvanus G.

1911 The Historical Value of the Books of Chilam Balam. *American Journal of Archaeology*, ser. 2, 15:195–214.

1915 *An Introduction to the Study of the Maya Hieroglyphs*. Bureau of American Ethnology, Smithsonian Institution, Bulletin 57. Washington, D.C.

1937–1938 *The Inscriptions of Peten*. 5 vols. Carnegie Institution of Washington, Publication 437. Washington, D.C.

1946 *The Ancient Maya*. Stanford: Stanford University Press.

Museo Chileno de Arte Precolombino

1983 *Museo Chileno de Arte Precolombino*. Santiago de Chile.

Navarrete, Carlos, and Luis Luján Muñoz
1963 *Reconocimiento arqueológico del sitio de "Dos Pilas," Petexbatún, Guatemala*. Cuadernos de Antropología 2. Guatemala City: Facultad de Humanidades, Universidad de San Carlos de Guatemala.
Nicholson, H. B.
1971 Pre-Hispanic Central Mexican Historiography. In *Investigaciones contemporáneas sobre historia de México: Memorias de la tercera reunión de historiadores mexicanos y norteamericanos*, pp. 38–81. Mexico City: Universidad Nacional Autónoma de México.
Orrego C., Miguel
1981 Delimitación de los parques arqueológicos de Dos Pilas y Aguateca. *Antropología e Historia* 3(2).
Orrego Corzo, Miguel, and Rudy Larios Villalta
1983 *Reporte de las investigaciones arqueológicas en el Grupo 5E-11*. Guatemala City: Parque Nacional Tikal, Instituto de Antropología e Historia de Guatemala, Ministerio de Educación.
Pasztory, Esther
1982 Shamanism and North American Art. In *Native North American Art History: Selected Readings*, edited by Zena Pearlstone Mathews and Aldona Jonaitis, pp. 7–30. Palo Alto, Calif.: Peek Publications.
Pendergast, David M.
1989 The Products of Their Times: Iconography in Social Context. In *Cultures in Conflict: Current Archaeological Perspectives*, edited by Diana Claire Tkaczuk and Brian C. Vivian, pp. 69–72. Proceedings of the Twentieth Annual Chacmool Conference. Calgary: Archaeological Association of the University of Calgary.
Pohl, John M. D., and Bruce E. Byland
1990 Mixtec Landscape Perception and Archaeological Settlement Patterns. *Ancient Mesoamerica* 1(1):113–131.
Pollock, H. E. D.
1965 Architecture of the Maya Lowlands. In *Handbook of Middle American Indians*, vol. 2, *Archaeology of Southern Mesoamerica, Part One*, edited by Robert Wauchope and Gordon R. Willey, pp. 378–440. Austin: University of Texas Press.
1980 *The Puuc: An Architectural Survey of the Hill Country of Yucatan and Northern Campeche, Mexico*. Memoirs of the Peabody Museum of Archaeology and Ethnology, Harvard University, 19. Cambridge, Mass.
Pollock, H. E. D., and Gustav Strömsvik
1953 Chacchob, Yucatan. *Current Reports* 6(1):82–101. Washington, D.C.: Carnegie Institution of Washington, Division of Historical Research.
Price, Barbara J.
1977 Shifts in Production and Organization: A Cluster-Interaction Model. *Current Anthropology* 18:209–233.
Proskouriakoff, Tatiana
1950 *A Study of Classic Maya Sculpture*. Carnegie Institution of Washington, Publication 593. Washington, D.C.
1960 Historical Implications of a Pattern of Dates at Piedras Negras, Guatemala. *American Antiquity* 25:454–475.
1963 Historical Data in the Inscriptions of Yaxchilan, Part I. *Estudios de Cultura Maya* 3:149–167.
1964 Historical Data in the Inscriptions of Yaxchilan, Part II. *Estudios de Cultura Maya* 4:177–201.
1973 The Hand-grasping-fish and Associated Glyphs on Classic Maya

Monuments. In *Mesoamerican Writing Systems*, edited by Elizabeth P. Benson, pp. 165–178. Washington, D.C.: Dumbarton Oaks.

Proyecto de evaluación forestal, FAO-FYDEP

1968 Mapa sobre las condiciones físico-mecánicas de los suelos de El Peten para construcción de caminos. Guatemala City: Instituto Geográfico Nacional.

Puleston, Dennis E., and Donald W. Callender, Jr.

1967 Defensive Earthworks at Tikal. *Expedition* 9(3):40–48.

Radcliffe-Brown, A. R

1970 Preface. In *African Political Systems*, edited by M. Fortes and E. E. Evans-Pritchard, pp. xi-xxiii. Oxford: Oxford University Press.

Rands, Robert L., and Ronald L. Bishop

1980 Resource Procurement Zones and Patterns of Ceramic Exchange in the Palenque Region, Mexico. In *Models and Methods in Regional Exchange*, edited by Robert E. Fry, pp. 19–46. Society for American Archaeology Papers 1. Washington, D.C.

Redfield, Robert

1941 *The Folk Culture of Yucatan*. Chicago: University of Chicago Press.

Reents, Dorie, and Ronald Bishop

1985 History and Ritual Events on a Petexbatun Classic Maya Polychrome Vessel. In *Fifth Palenque Round Table, 1983*, edited by Virginia M. Fields, pp. 57–63. San Francisco: Pre-Columbian Art Research Institute.

Renfrew, Colin

1982 Polity and Power: Interaction, Intensification, and Exploitation. In *An Island Polity: The Archaeology of Exploitation in Melos*, edited by Colin Renfrew and Malcolm Wagstaff, pp. 264–290. Cambridge: Cambridge University Press.

1984 Trade as Action at a Distance. In *Approaches to Social Archaeology*, edited by Colin Renfrew, pp. 86–134. Cambridge, Mass.: Harvard University Press.

1986 Introduction: Peer Polity Interaction and Socio-political Change. In *Peer Polity Interaction and Socio-political Change*, edited by Colin Renfrew and John F. Cherry, pp. 1–18. Cambridge: Cambridge University Press.

Rice, Don S., and Prudence M. Rice

1981 Muralla de Leon: A Lowland Maya Fortification. *Journal of Field Archaeology* 8:271–288.

Riese, Berthold

1971 Grundlagen zur Entzifferung der Mayahieroglyphen, dargestellt an den Inschriften von Copan. *Beiträge zur mittelamerikanischen Völkerkunde*, vol. 11. Hamburg: Museum für Völkerkunde und Vorgeschichte.

1975 *Leitfaden zur Mayaschrift*. 2 vols. Hamburg.

1980 Katun-Altersangaben in klassischen Maya-Inschriften. Baessler-Archive. *Beiträge zur Völkerkunde* 28:155–180.

1984a Hel Hieroglyphs. In *Phoneticism in Mayan Hieroglyphic Writing*, edited by John S. Justeson and Lyle Campbell, pp. 263–286. Institute for Mesoamerican Studies, State University of New York at Albany, Publication 9. Albany.

1984b Kriegsberichte der klassischen Maya. Baessler-Archive, *Beiträge zur Völkerkunde* 30(2):255–321.

Ringle, William M.

1988 *Of Mice and Monkeys: The Value and Meaning of T1016, the God C*

Hieroglyph. Research Report on Ancient Maya Writing 18. Washington, D.C.: Center for Maya Research.

Rock, Miles

1895 *Mapa de la frontera entre Guatemala y México*. Guatemala City.

Ross, Kurt

1978 *Codex Mendoza: Aztec Manuscript*. Fribourg: Miller Graphics.

Rounds, J.

1982 Dynastic Succession and the Centralization of Power in Tenochtitlan. In *The Inca and Aztec States, 1400–1800: Anthropology and History*, edited by George A. Collier, Renato I. Rosaldo, and John D. Wirth, pp. 63–89. New York: Academic Press.

Roys, Ralph L.

1957 *The Indian Background of Colonial Yucatán*. Carnegie Institution of Washington Publication 548. Washington, D.C.

Runciman, W. O.

1982 Origins of States: The Case of Archaic Greece. *Comparative Studies in Society and History* 24(3):351–377.

Ruppert, Karl, J. Eric Thompson, and Tatiana Proskouriakoff

1955 *Bonampak, Chiapas, Mexico*. Carnegie Institution of Washington Publication 602. Washington, D.C.

Sabloff, Jeremy A.

1973 Continuity and Disruption during the Terminal Classic Times at Seibal: Ceramic and Other Evidence. In *The Classic Maya Collapse*, edited by T. Patrick Culbert, pp. 107–131. School of American Research Advanced Seminar Series. Albuquerque: University of New Mexico Press.

1975 *Excavations at Seibal: Ceramics*. Memoirs of the Peabody Museum of Archaeology and Ethnology, Harvard University, 13(2). Cambridge, Mass.

Sabloff, Jeremy A., and E. Wyllys Andrews V

1985 (eds.) *Late Lowland Maya Civilization: Classic to Postclassic*. School of American Research Advanced Seminar Series. Albuquerque: University of New Mexico Press.

Sáenz, César

1972 Exploraciones y restauraciones en Uxmal (1970–1971). *Boletín del Instituto Nacional de Antropología e Historia*, ser. 2, 2:31–40.

Sahlins, Marshall D.

1972 *Stone Age Economics*. Chicago: Aldine-Atherton.

Sanders, William T.

1960 *Prehistoric Ceramics and Settlement Patterns in Quintana Roo, Mexico*. Contributions to American Anthropology and History 12 (60). Carnegie Institution of Washington Publication 606. Washington, D.C.

Sanders, William T., and David Webster

1988 The Mesoamerican Urban Tradition. *American Anthropologist* 90(3): 521–546.

Sapper, Karl

1897 *Das Nordliche Mittel-Amerika nebst einem Ausflug nach dem Hochland von Anahuac: Reisen und Studien aus den Jahren 1888–1895*. Braunsweig, Germany: Friedrich Viewey und Sohn.

Satterthwaite, Linton, Jr.

1943 *Piedras Negras Archaeology: Architecture; Part 1, No. 1: Introduction*. Philadelphia: University Museum, University of Pennsylvania.

1958 *The Problem of Stela Placements at Tikal and Elsewhere*. Tikal Reports 3. University Museum Monographs. Philadelphia: University Museum, University of Pennsylvania.

Schele, Linda

1978 Genealogical Documentation on the Tri-figure Panels at Palenque. In *Tercera Mesa Redonda de Palenque, Vol. IV*, edited by Merle Greene Robertson and Donnan Call Jeffers, pp. 41–70. Monterey, Calif.: Pre-Columbian Art Research Center.

1982 *Maya Glyphs: The Verbs*. Austin: University of Texas Press.

1984 Human Sacrifice among the Classic Maya. In *Ritual Human Sacrifice in Mesoamerica*, edited by Elizabeth H. Boone, pp. 7–48. Washington, D.C.: Dumbarton Oaks.

1991 The Demotion of Chac-Zutz': Lineage Compounds and Subsidiary Lords at Palenque. In *Sixth Palenque Round Table, 1986*, edited by Virginia M. Fields (Merle Greene Robertson, general editor), pp. 6–11. Norman: University of Oklahoma Press.

Schele, Linda, and David Freidel

1990 *A Forest of Kings: The Untold Story of the Ancient Maya*. New York: William Morrow.

Schele, Linda, and Peter Mathews

1991 Royal Visits and Other Intersite Relationships among the Classic Maya. In *Classic Maya Political History: Archaeological and Hieroglyphic Evidence*, edited by T. P. Culbert, pp. 226–252. A School of American Research Book. Cambridge: Cambridge University Press.

Schele, Linda, Peter Mathews, and Floyd G. Lounsbury

1977 Parentage Expressions in Classic Maya Inscriptions. MS on file, Department of Art History, University of Texas at Austin.

Schele, Linda, and Mary Ellen Miller

1986 *The Blood of Kings: Dynasty and Ritual in Maya Art*. Fort Worth, Texas: Kimbell Art Museum.

1988 Letter to the Editor. *Art Journal* 47(3):253.

Shook, Edwin M.

1952 The Great Wall of Mayapan. *Current Reports* 7:35. Washington, D.C.: Carnegie Institution of Washington, Division of Historical Research.

Smailus, Ortwin

1975 *El maya-chontal de Acalan: Análisis lingüístico de un documento de los años 1610–12*. Centro de Estudios Mayas, Cuaderno 9. Mexico City: Coordinación de Humanidades, Universidad Nacional Autónoma de México.

Smith, A. Ledyard

1962 Residential and Associated Structures at Mayapan. In *Mayapan, Yucatan, Mexico*, edited by H. E. D. Pollock, Ralph L. Roys, Tatiana Proskouriakoff, and A. Ledyard Smith, pp. 165–319. Carnegie Institution of Washington Publication 619. Washington, D.C.

1972 *Excavations at Altar de Sacrificios: Architecture, Settlement, Burials, and Caches*. Papers of the Peabody Museum of Archaeology and Ethnology, Harvard University, 62(2). Cambridge, Mass.

1982 *Major Architecture and Caches: Excavations at Seibal, Department of Peten, Guatemala*. Memoirs of the Peabody Museum of American Archaeology and Ethnology, Harvard University, 15(1). Cambridge, Mass.

Smith, Mary Elizabeth

1983 Regional Points of View in the Mixtec Codices. In *The Cloud People: Divergent Evolution of the Zapotec and Mixtec Civilizations*, edited by Kent V. Flannery and Joyce Marcus, pp. 260–266. A School of American Research Book. New York: Academic Press.

Smith, Michael E.

1986 The Role of Social Stratification in the Aztec Empire: A View from the Provinces. *American Anthropologist* 88(1):70–91.

Sosa, John R., and Dorie J. Reents

1980 Glyphic Evidence for Classic Maya Militarism. *Belizean Studies* 8(3):2–11. Belize City.

Southall, Aidan W.

1956 *Alur Society: A Study in Processes and Types of Domination*. Cambridge: Heffer.

1965 A Critique of the Typology of States and Political Systems. In *Political Systems and the Distribution of Power*, edited by Michael Banton, pp. 115–140. London: Tavistock.

1988 The Segmentary State in Africa and Asia. *Comparative Studies in Society and History* 30:52–82.

Southwold, Martin

1961 *Bureaucracy and Chiefship in Buganda: The Development of Appointive Office in the History of Buganda*. East African Studies 14. Kampala: East African Institute of Social Research.

Soza, J. M.

1957 *Pequeña Monografía del Departamento del Peten*. 2 vols. Guatemala City: Editorial del Ministerio de Educación Pública.

Spencer, Charles S.

1982 *The Cuicatlán Cañada and Monte Alban: A Study of Primary State Formation*. New York: Academic Press.

Spinden, Herbert J.

1913 *A Study of Maya Art: Its Subject Matter and Historical Development*. Memoirs of the Peabody Museum of Archaeology and Ethnology, Harvard University, 6. Cambridge, Mass.

Spores, Ronald

1974 Marital Alliance in the Political Integration of Mixtec Kingdoms. *American Anthropologist* 76(2):297–311.

1984 *The Mixtecs in Ancient and Colonial Times*. Norman: University of Oklahoma Press.

Stein, Burton

1977 The Segmentary State in South Indian History. In *Realm and Region in Traditional India*, edited by Richard G. Fox, pp. 3–51. Durham: Duke University Press.

Stevenson, Robert F.

1968 *Population and Political Systems in Tropical Africa*. New York: Columbia University Press.

Steward, Julian H.

1942 The Direct Historical Approach to Archaeology. *American Antiquity* 7(4):337–343.

Stone, Andrea, Dorie Reents, and Robert Coffman

1985 Genealogical Documentation of the Middle Classic Dynasty of Caracol, El Cayo, Belize. In *Fourth Palenque Round Table, 1980*, edited by Elizabeth P. Benson (Merle Greene Robertson, general editor), pp. 267–275. San Francisco: Pre-Columbian Art Research Institute.

Strömsvik, Gustav, and John M. Longyear III

1946 A Reconnaissance of El Rincon del Jicaque, Honduras. *Carnegie Notes* 68:44–53. Washington, D.C.: Carnegie Institution of Washington, Division of Historical Research.

Stuart, David
1984a Epigraphic Evidence of Political Organization in the Western Maya Lowlands. MS on file, Department of Anthropology, Vanderbilt University, Nashville.
1984b A Note on the "Hand-Scattering" Glyph. In *Phoneticism in Mayan Hieroglyphic Writing,* edited by John S. Justeson and Lyle Campbell, pp. 307–310. Institute for Mesoamerican Studies, State University of New York at Albany, Publication 9. Albany.
1985a The "Count-of-Captives" Epithet in Classic Maya Writing. In *Fifth Palenque Round Table, 1983,* edited by Virginia M. Fields, pp. 97–101. San Francisco: Pre-Columbian Art Research Institute.
1985b *A New Child-Father Relationship Glyph.* Research Reports on Ancient Maya Writing 2. Washington, D.C.: Center for Maya Research.
1985c *The Yaxha Emblem Glyph as Yaxha.* Research Reports on Ancient Maya Writing 1. Washington, D.C.: Center for Maya Research.
1986 The "Lu-Bat" Glyph and Its Bearing on the Primary Standard Sequence. Paper presented at the I World Symposium on Maya Epigraphy, Guatemala City.
1987 *Ten Phonetic Syllables.* Research Reports on Ancient Maya Writing 14. Washington, D.C.: Center for Maya Research.
1989 Kinship Terms in Mayan Inscriptions. Paper presented at the conference on "The Language of Mayan Hieroglyphs," University of California at Santa Barbara.
1990a The Decipherment of "Directional Count Glyphs" in Maya Inscriptions. *Ancient Mesoamerica* 1:215–226.
1990b Historical Inscriptions and the Maya Collapse. Revised version of paper presented at the 1989 Dumbarton Oaks Symposium, "On the Eve of the Collapse," Washington, D.C.
1990c *A New Carved Panel from the Palenque Area.* Research Reports on Ancient Maya Writing 32. Washington, D.C.: Center for Maya Research.

Stuart, David, and Stephen D. Houston
1990 Classic Maya Place Names. MS on file, Department of Anthropology, Vanderbilt University, Nashville.

Stuart, George E.
1981 Maya Art Treasures Discovered in Cave. *National Geographic* 160(2): 220–235.

Symonds, Stacey C.
1990 A Statistical Study of Classic Maya Stelae from the Pasión Region of Guatemala. MS on file, Department of Anthropology, Vanderbilt University, Nashville.

Tambiah, Stanley J.
1976 *World Conqueror and World Renouncer: A Study of Buddhism and Polity in Thailand against a Historical Background.* Cambridge Studies in Social Anthropology 15. Cambridge: Cambridge University Press.
1977 The Galactic Polity: The Structure of Traditional Kingdoms in Southeast Asia. *Annals of the New York Academy of Sciences* 293:69–97.

Thompson, J. Eric. S.
1950 *Maya Hieroglyphic Writing: An Introduction.* Carnegie Institution of Washington Publication 589. Washington, D.C.
1954 *The Rise and Fall of Maya Civilization.* Norman: University of Oklahoma Press.
1977 A Proposal for Constituting a Maya Subgroup, Cultural and Linguis-

tic, in the Petén and Adjacent Regions. In *Anthropology and History in Yucatán*, ed. Grant D. Jones, pp. 3–42. Austin: University of Texas Press.

Thompson, J. Eric S., Harry E. D. Pollock, and Jean Charlot
1932 *A Preliminary Study of the Ruins of Cobá, Quintana Roo, Mexico.* Carnegie Institution of Washington Publication 424. Washington, D.C.

Tourtellot, Gair, III
1970 The Peripheries of Seibal: An Interim Report. In *Monographs and Papers in Maya Archaeology*, edited by William R. Bullard, Jr., pp. 405–419. Papers of the Peabody Museum of Archaeology and Ethnology, Harvard University, 61. Cambridge, Mass.
1983a *Ancient Maya Settlements at Seibal, Peten, Guatemala: Peripheral Survey and Excavation.* Ph.D. dissertation, Department of Anthropology, Harvard University. Ann Arbor: University Microfilms.
1983b An Assessment of Classic Maya Household Composition. In *Prehistoric Settlement Patterns: Essays in Honor of Gordon R. Willey*, edited by Evon Z. Vogt and Richard M. Leventhal, pp. 35–54. Albuquerque: University of New Mexico Press.
1988 *Excavations at Seibal, Department of Petén, Guatemala: Peripheral Survey, Excavation, Settlement and Community Patterns.* Memoirs of the Peabody Museum of Archaeology and Ethnology, Harvard University, 16. Cambridge, Mass.

Tourtellot, Gair, III, Norman Hammond, and Richard Rose
1978 *Excavations at Seibal: A Brief Reconnaissance of Itzan.* Memoirs of the Peabody Museum of Archaeology and Ethnology, Harvard University, 14(3). Cambridge, Mass.

Tourtellot, Gair, III, Jeremy A. Sabloff, and Robert Sharick
1978 *Excavations at Seibal: A Reconnaissance of Cancuen.* Memoirs of the Peabody Museum of Archaeology and Ethnology, Harvard University, 14(2). Cambridge, Mass.

Tozzer, Alfred M.
1941 *Landa's Relación de las cosas de Yucatán: A Translation.* Papers of the Peabody Museum of American Archaeology and Ethnology, Harvard University, vol. 18. Cambridge, Mass.

Vansina, Jan
1968 *Kingdoms of the Savannah.* Madison: University of Wisconsin Press.
1985 *Oral Tradition as History.* Madison: University of Wisconsin Press.

van Zantwijk, Rudolph
1985 *The Aztec Arrangement: The Social History of Pre-Spanish Mexico.* Norman: University of Oklahoma Press.

Vinson, G. L.
1960 Las ruinas mayas de Petexbatun. *Antropología e Historia de Guatemala* 12(2): 3–9.
1962 Upper Cretaceous and Tertiary Stratigraphy of Guatemala. *Bulletin of the American Association of Petroleum Geologists* 46(4): 425–456.

Vlcek, David T., Silvia Garza de González, and Edward B. Kurjack
1978 Contemporary Farming and Ancient Maya Settlements: Some Disconcerting Evidence. In *Pre-Hispanic Maya Agriculture,* edited by Peter D. Harrison and B. L. Turner, pp. 211–223. Albuquerque: University of New Mexico Press.

Von Euw, Eric
1978 *Xultun.* Corpus of Maya Hieroglyphic Inscriptions 5(1). Cambridge, Mass.: Peabody Museum of Archaeology and Ethnology, Harvard University.

Von Euw, Eric, and Ian Graham
1984 *Xultun, La Honradez, Uaxactun*. Corpus of Maya Hieroglyphic Inscriptions 5(2). Cambridge, Mass.: Peabody Museum of Archaeology and Ethnology, Harvard University.

Webb, Malcolm C.
1975 The Flag Follows Trade: An Essay on the Necessary Interaction of Military and Commercial Factors in State Formation. In *Ancient Civilization and Trade*, edited by J. A. Sabloff and C. C. Lamberg-Karlovsky, pp. 155–209. School of American Research Advanced Seminar Series. Albuquerque: University of New Mexico Press.

Weber, Max
1968 *Economy and Society: An Outline of Interpretive Sociology*, vol. 1. Berkeley: University of California Press.

Webster, David L.
1976 *Defensive Earthworks at Becan, Campeche, Mexico: Implications for Maya Warfare*. Middle American Research Institute, Tulane University, Publication 41. New Orleans.
1977 Warfare and the Evolution of Maya Civilization. In *The Origins of Maya Civilization*, edited by R. E. W. Adams, pp. 335–372. School of American Research Advanced Seminar Series. Albuquerque: University of New Mexico Press.
1978 Three Walled Sites of the Northern Maya Lowlands. *Journal of Field Archaeology* 5(4):375–390.
1979 *Cuca, Chacchob, Dzonot Ake—Three Walled Northern Maya Centers*. Occasional Papers in Anthropology 11. University Park: Department of Anthropology, Pennsylvania State University.
1980 Spatial Bounding and Settlement History at Three Walled Northern Maya Centers. *American Antiquity* 45(4):834–844.
1989 (ed.) *The House of the Bacabs, Copan, Honduras*. Studies in Pre-Columbian Art and Archaeology, No. 29. Washington, D.C.: Dumbarton Oaks Research Library and Collection.

Webster, David, and Elliot Abrams
1983 An Elite Compound at Copan, Honduras. *Journal of Field Archaeology* 10(3):285–296.

Willey, Gordon R.
1986 The Classic Maya Sociopolitical Order: A Study in Coherence and Instability. In *Research and Reflections in Archaeology and History: Essays in Honor of Doris Stone*, edited by E. Wyllys Andrews V, pp. 189–198. Middle American Research Institute, Tulane University, Publication 57. New Orleans.

Willey, Gordon R., Richard M. Leventhal, and William L. Fash, Jr.
1978 Maya Settlement in the Copan Valley. *Archaeology* 31:32–43.

Willey, Gordon R., and A. Ledyard Smith
1969 *The Ruins of Altar de Sacrificios, Department of Peten, Guatemala: An Introduction*. Papers of the Peabody Museum of Archaeology and Ethnology, Harvard University, 62(1). Cambridge, Mass.

Willey, Gordon R., A. Ledyard Smith, Gair Tourtellot III, and Ian Graham
1975 *Excavations at Seibal: No. 1, Introduction: The Site and its Setting*. Memoirs of the Peabody Museum of Archaeology and Ethnology, Harvard University, 13(1). Cambridge, Mass.

Winter, Irene J.
1981 Royal Rhetoric and the Development of Historical Narrative in Neo-Assyrian Reliefs. *Visual Communication* 7:2–38.

Wood, W. Raymond
1990 Ethnohistory and Historical Method. In *Archaeological Method and*

Theory, Volume 2, edited by Michael B. Schiffer, pp. 81–110. Tucson: University of Arizona Press.

Wright, Arthur F.
1979 Chinese Civilization. In *Propaganda and Communication in World History*, vol. 1, edited by H. Lasswell, D. Lerner, and H. Speir, pp. 220–256. Honolulu: University Press of Hawaii and the East-West Center.

Wright, Henry T.
1986 The Evolution of Civilizations. In *American Archaeology: Past and Future, A Celebration of the Society for American Archaeology, 1935–1985*, edited by David J. Meltzer, Don D. Fowler, and Jeremy A. Sabloff, pp. 323–365. Washington, D.C.: Smithsonian Institution Press.

Wright, Henry T., and Gregory A. Johnson
1975 Population, Exchange, and Early State Formation in Southwestern Iran. *American Anthropologist* 77:267–289.

Index